Perilous Trails, Dangerous Men

Early California
Stagecoach Robbers
and their
Desperate Careers
1856 - 1900

By
William B. Secrest

Printed in the United States of America.

Published by
Quill Driver Books/Word Dancer Press, Inc.,
8386 N. Madsen, Clovis, CA 93611
559-322-5917 / 800-497-4909
QuillDriverBooks.com

Word Dancer Press books may be purchased for educational, fund-raising,
business or promotional use. Please contact Special Markets, Quill Driver Books/
Word Dancer Press, Inc. at the above address or phone numbers.

ISBN 1-884995-24-1

**To order a copy of this book, please call
1-800-497-4909.**

First Printing September 2001

Also by William B. Secrest
I Buried Hickok (College Station, Texas, 1980)
Lawmen & Desperadoes (Spokane, Washington, 1994)
Dangerous Trails (Stillwater, Oklahoma, 1995)
California Desperadoes (Word Dancer Press, California, 2000)

Quill Driver Books/Word Dancer Press Project Cadre:
Doris Hall, John David Marion, Stephen Blake Mettee
Cover and interior design by William B. Secrest

Library of Congress Cataloging-in-Publication Data

Secrest, William B., 1930-
    Perilous trails, dangerous men : early California stagecoach robbers and their desperate
careers, 1856-1900 / by William B. Secrest.
        p. cm.
    Includes bibliographical references and index.
    ISBN 1-884995-24-1 (trade paper)
    1. Brigands and robbers--California--Biography. 2. Outlaws--California--Biography. 3.
Coaching--California. I. Title.

HV6452.C29 S43 2001
364.15'52'09794--dc21

                                                                                2001045595

CONTENTS

ACKNOWLEDGMENTS

A lthough there are very few books on the early California stage robbers, a great deal of information is available in primary and institutional sources. I have been gathering material for this book for some forty years. It was an unconscious effort for the most part, but as I read the old newspapers, gleaned prison records and studied court documents on other subjects, the stage robbers always lurked in the recesses of my mind. By the time I began this present work, I had already assembled much material, but there was much more to be done.

Invariably, I owe much to my mentor and pal, John Boessenecker who has helped me so much in this and other projects. As author of such ground-breaking California history books as *Badge and Buckshot*, *The Grey Fox: The True Story of Bill Miner, Last of the Old Time Bandits* (with Mark Dugan), *Lawman, The Life and Times of Harry Morse, 1835 - 1912, Gold Dust & Gunsmoke* and *Against the Vigilantes,* John has set the standards for us all. He not only critically read this manuscript, but generously provided valuable illustrations from his collections. Every California history writer needs a friend like John Boessenecker, and I will always be in his debt.

Beginning with Irene Simpson in 1960, Wells, Fargo's History Department has always been most helpful. This relationship has continued to the present day, and I owe Dr. Robert J. Chandler a great debt for much insightful assistance over the years. Sibylle Zemitis (retired) and the wonderful staff at the California State Library were always generous in their help, also, both in person and through the mail. Joseph P. Samora's knowledgeable and prompt responses to my numerous requests for information and documents at the California State Archives are greatly appreciated. The Fresno City and County Historical Society deserves applause, and Diane Kathleen of the Shasta Historical Society was very helpful, as was Beverly Everest of the Trinity County Historical Society. My thanks also to Cheryl Cruse of the Shasta County Library for her assistance.

William A. Jones of the Meriam Library at California State University, Chico was also helpful, as was the staff at the Folsom History Museum.

Individuals who assisted me in a variety of ways are: Harold Edwards, who is always ready to drop his own current history project to aid others; Dick Nelson, Shirley Sargent and Hank Johnston; Joe Rosa, the skilled British historian of our Wild West; my collector pals, Joe Silva and Robert G. McCubbin; Fresno County Deputy Sheriff and historian Kevin Fitzgerald; Mariposa County Sheriff Pelk Richards and Bob Grycel; Roy P. O'Dell, of Cambridge, England, who generously shared his own work on the subject with me; and my brother, Dr. James Secrest, who found valuable material for the project in the Mariposa County Museum. I owe Ray Silvia, supervisor of the California Room, Fresno County Public Library, a great debt, not only for his steady encouragement, but for his beneficial suggestions and reading of the manuscript. And, a more enthusiastic and helpful publisher than Steve Mettee and his staff at Word Dancer Press would be difficult, if not impossible, to find.

As always, my wife Shirley and son Bill have assisted in great and small ways, mainly just by allowing me the time to pursue my interests. Of my two parrots I have nothing to say. Both impeded my progress at every turn, but they are still great pals. To you all and anyone I may have overlooked, my grateful thanks.

William B. Secrest

INTRODUCTION

"The coaches were of various kinds. Some were light spring wagons — mere oblong boxes, with four or five seats placed across them; others were of the same build, but better finished, and covered by an awning; and there were also numbers of regular American stagecoaches, huge high-hung things which carry nine inside upon three seats, the middle one of which is between the two doors."

Englishman J. D. Borthwick was describing the vehicles gathered in front of a Sacramento hotel for an early morning start to the mining country. It was the fall of 1851, and the scene was one of bedlam as passengers sought their particular stage, runners called out destinations and cursing drivers tried to avoid locking coach wheels or backing into one another. Borthwick was describing the very dawn of stagecoaching in California, but this dawn had been a long time in arriving.

■ A magnificent Concord Coach of 1850s California. *Trinity County Historical Society.*

The cart, wagon, and coach concept was made possible by 2000 B.C. with the domestication of the horse and the invention of spoked wheels. Harness was being developed by the fifth and sixth centuries, and a drawing of a fourteenth-century Swiss wagon shows a covered body suspended by straps above the axle. The stagecoach concept had germinated.

It was with the Berlin coach, built by the Italian Filippo di Chièse in the city of Berlin about 1660, that stagecoaching really took off. The vehicle had a curved body suspended on leather braces, and it moved up and down instead of swaying from side to side. With front wheels that were smaller than the rear ones to prevent abrasions to the body when it turned, the coach was fast and could hold more than one person. Originally utilized only by nobility and the well-born, coaches were now being adapted to carrying a few passengers, some baggage, and the mail.

The first coaches in the American colonies were imported from Mother England, but blacksmiths and carriage makers were soon making their own vehicles.

■ Original Downing logo, 1852.
Author's collection.

As in the rest of the world, roads in the colonies were an important aspect of stagecoach travel. Europe and England had centuries to establish a fairly good road system, which was essential to commerce, war, and travel between states and countries. The colonies were still a frontier, however. There were more established roads in the East, but the frontier was always being pushed westward with new trails and roads being established. There was a call for new types of vehicles, tough and durable, yet fast and light — coaches that could carry ten to fifteen passengers, with space for baggage, mail, and express boxes.

When Lewis Downing established his wheelwright shop in Concord, New Hampshire, in 1813, he had no idea that he was on the cutting edge of a legend. Downing was a superb craftsman, but up until 1826 his products were primarily heavy farm wagons constructed by some dozen journeymen and apprentices. Probably influenced by his father-in-law, who was an expert stage

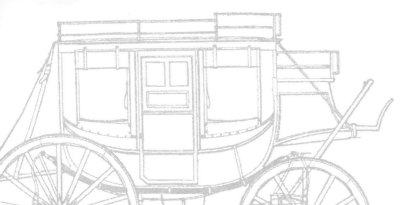

driver, in 1826 Downing took in a partner named J. Stephen Abbot, a twenty-two-year-old Salem chaise builder. Within a year, the two men were partners, and they began planning and constructing one of the most famous vehicles in American history: the Concord stagecoach.

The two men were not only highly skilled craftsmen, but they also insisted on the finest materials and the most precise methods of construction. Their new coach bodies had a framework of straight-grained white ash, each piece steamed until pliable and bent to the exact curve needed. The wood was then kiln dried until it was tough as iron. Into this frame was hand-fitted the poplar panels, shaped by steam, that gave the coach body its curved, egg-shaped bottom. The roof of the coach bulged slightly for drainage purposes and was surmounted at the back and sides with an iron railing to accommodate baggage. A tailgate, supported by straps from the top of the coach, was covered with black, oiled leather and lined with a waterproofed canvas to safeguard more luggage space. The driver's seat rested two feet down from the roof and was supported by another boot used as a footrest and baggage carrier. There was room for two passengers next to the driver, while three more could be seated on the roof behind.

The prime portions of fourteen ox hides were utilized for the thoroughbrace suspension, as well as for the straps and other leather items used on other parts of each coach.

Iron, used sparingly to save weight, was the finest hand-forged Norway stock. The all-important wheels were made of choice, straight-grained ash or white oak, seasoned for at least three years and sun-warped until no tendency to warp remained. Each spoke was shaped by hand to the exact measurement and weight of the other spokes in the same wheel. The individual spokes were mortised into the hub so tightly that they could not be removed by hand. The wheel rim segments (fellies) were cut to an exact arc and weight and then fitted to the spokes. The outer iron tire was made slightly smaller in circumference, then expanded by heat to fit onto the completed wheel. When the tire cooled, everything was locked into place, and there are Concord coach wheels today that are nearly as snug as the day they were made.

The Concord bodies were given several coats of bright red paint, varnished, then trimmed in yellow and gold. The sides and doors were decorated in colorful scrollwork and miniature pastoral scenes, then the coach body was polished till it glowed. Lanterns were added to the front, and rolled-up leather curtains to the windows for protection of passengers and upholstery from the weather. All this precision craftsmanship resulted in the most durable and popular coach of its kind ever built. At a cost of $1,500, the finished result was magnificent, and these beautiful vehicles were shipped all over the world during the nineteenth-century heyday of the stagecoach.

Abbot and Downing also built other coaches. Their mud wagon model had a simple, square body and was lighter, although it had much the same thoroughbrace system. It was made for mountain travel, sold for about $500, and was used extensively throughout the West. During the 1850s most coaches were imported to California, but soon such cities as San Francisco, Sacramento, and Stockton were boasting wagon shops that were turning out every kind of wheeled vehicle, from hotel coaches to passenger hacks and fast little celerity wagons. By the 1880s stageline operators, such as the Washburn brothers of the Yosemite route, could order custom-constructed tourist coaches made in California. But there has never been a coach as fine as the Concord.

Highwaymen have been with us almost as long as the wheeled vehicles they stopped and robbed. By the seventeenth century, robbers were plaguing the European highways, knowing that only the wealthy and privileged class could afford coach travel. In England, Dick Turpin, Jonathan Wild, and countless others were romantic and sympathetic figures to the lower classes, who admired their nerve at a time when there were few career choices available to the poor. The concept of stage robbery easily made its way to the colonies, and although coaches were held up in the East, it was in the West, in the second half of the nineteenth century, that stagecoach robbery took root and flowered. And it was California that spawned the most colorful, desperate and dangerous stage robbers in United States history.

In 1885 *The Report of Jas. B. Hume and Jno. N. Thacker, Special Officers, Wells, Fargo & Co's Express*, otherwise referred to as the "Robbers' Record," was published. Compiled by the company's two special officers, James B. Hume and John N. Thacker, it was an accounting of company burglaries, train and stagecoach robberies between November 1870 and November 1884. Appended to this was the amount of money stolen and recovered; a list of guards and drivers wounded or killed; passengers killed and wounded; and robbers killed by stage guards, lawmen, or lynch mobs. It was a valuable record at that time and for future historians.

The primary purpose of this "Record," however, was to list the 208 burglars and bandits who had robbed or attempted to rob Wells, Fargo. Listed roughly in alphabetical order, the name and aliases of the outlaws were given, along with a brief description and chronology of their crimes and prison records. It was a veritable who's who of Western bandits and desperadoes who had preyed on Wells, Fargo & Company over a fourteen-year period.

For the time, it was a handy reference allowing various officials to keep an eye out for criminals likely to be considering an unlawful withdrawal from their own institutions. For scholars one hundred years later, the value of this "Record" as an historical document is more limited. The list included only those who robbed Wells, Fargo treasure boxes and, of course, this eliminated many road agents who stopped coaches carrying other companies' express boxes. Also, the time span — between 1870 and 1884 — excluded many outlaws of the 1850s and '60s and those practicing their trade after 1884. And, there were no mug shots of these criminals during this time when photographic halftones were much too expensive to publish. It seemed clear that an updating of some sort might prove useful to scholars and laymen, alike.

In compiling this new record of California highwaymen, I expanded upon the more interesting bandits, while eliminating most one-time amateurs who were caught, served their time and then disappeared. Burglars were discarded, except where they also operated as stage robbers. Exceptions were made for some of the more colorful and tragic characters. As it has evolved, these are the stories of only the most daring and interesting of California's early highwaymen.

In the hundred and more years since Hume and Thacker put together their "Robbers' Record," much new information on these desperadoes has come to light. Many, from good families, fell into bad company and sought a fast buck among dangerous characters far from home. Some, bad apples to begin with, evolved into dangerous gunmen and didn't hesitate to shoot it out with pursuing lawmen when their freedom was threatened.

Stage robbers came from all walks of life. Among them were engineers, farmers, lawyers, photographers, druggists, lawmen who went bad, and menial laborers who yearned for more than just enough money to eke out an existence.

Most American penitentiaries of the time were notorious "schools for crime" where mere children were thrown among vicious career criminals. California prisons were no different. Even when prisons began segregating these youngsters, they were put among other teenagers who were as vicious as their adult counterparts. Needless to say, many stage robbers were "schooled" in prison.

Most convicts did their prison time quietly, anxious to acquire those "coppers" that allowed them time off for good behavior. Some continually planned daring escapes that were frequently successful. Others plotted crimes to commit after their release. Various desperadoes spent their lives in and out of prison, and many died there. Some dropped from sight to plague other territories, while a few settled down to a law-abiding existence. The latter usually did so only when old age forced it upon them.

The Hume and Thacker "Record" also indicated the cost in money and lives to protect the public's treasure. The cost had been great, but the two detectives also were able to show the results of that cost: a great many captures and convictions of the bad guys. And along the way, Hume and Thacker showed that they had more than earned their paychecks.

The reader might bear in mind that these brief descriptions of outlaw careers necessarily list only the crimes of which they are known to be guilty. Criminals seldom summed up the crimes they had committed for their captors. On the contrary, they were anxious to make the list as short as possible to prevent a large number of holdups or convictions from being held against them at their trial. Aliases were a part of this mentality, and many criminals entered prison under different names over the years, making identification more difficult. Periodic political changes in prison administration often accommodated these shenanigans.

The one trait shared by most stage robbers was the propensity to promptly identify their associates in crime upon capture. With the exception of Tom Bell, who refused to identify his gang members before he was lynched, stage robbers invariably sang like a canary to lighten their sentence in state prison, or obtain clemency of any sort.

A brief word concerning the many mug shots of the old stage robbers in this book might be interesting. Both John Boessenecker and I have collected them over the past forty years. Many were obtained from Wells, Fargo in the 1960s, while others have been gleaned from old police and sheriffs' mug books in various official, private, museum, and library collections. Although the San Francisco vigilantes of both the 1851 and 1856 committees photographed their prisoners, none has survived so far as is known. The San Francisco police also began photographing criminals in the mid-1850s and some of these have survived. Beginning in 1860, San Francisco criminal portraits were placed in leather-bound mug books and this is believed to be the beginning of the system in California.

To sum things up, if some of these early highwaymen were dangerous killers, others can only be likened to Don Quixote's sidekick, Sancho Panza, as comic characters. What can you say about a ruthless bunch of Mexican bandidos, led by Ysidro Padilla, who stopped a stagecoach in Butte County and demanded the treasure box? The cool driver had been held up previously, and calmly assured the bandits that the box they were seeking was on the next coach behind him. The coach was waved on, and the bandits might still be waiting for that next stage.

Likewise, a suspected stage robber in the Madera jail once told of stopping a stage only to find the coach empty of passengers and treasure. Sympathizing with the frustrated highwayman, the driver offered him a lift down the road. "You have ruined the business on this road," admonished the driver. "Nobody travels here anymore. You have scared them all off. Now, you might as well git too. There's no money here and won't be till you restore confidence. You can't work a stage line without confidence any more than you can a banking institution. You must clear out and stay out and when the arteries of trade open up again you can come back, but you musn't be too enthusiastic. You must hold up a stage and then take a rest. Go over to San Francisco for a few weeks and enjoy yourself. Mingle in society and seek diversion. Then you can come back and take another crack."

If there was any psychology to road agentry, this driver's suggestions come as close to the mark as any.

Finally, I would be remiss if I did not comment on the lack of California settings in western writing and films, both fiction and non fiction. This has been true since the inception of the genre, since *The Virginian* and *The Great Train Robbery*. The fine western novelist Wallace Stegner once noted that "California is west of the West," and this seems to have been the prevailing thought in the past. But this is not the way it was. Despite its location, California was, and is, the very heart of the West. Anyone reading this book will, hopefully, come to the same conclusion.

But let's get on with it. Here are the stage robbing desperadoes who livened up the pages of California history for over fifty years. They were not a moral crowd, but they were colorful, bold and frequently surprising. It was a time of hard-riding lawmen who relied on their wits in the days before forensic science, fingerprinting and DNA — a time when desperate outlaws took almost any risk to avoid a term in a primitive state prison. Read on now about stagecoaches rattling down perilous trails haunted by dangerous men eager to steal that Wells, Fargo treasure box. So hang on! It just might be a ride you will never forget.

The Stage Robber's
EARLY
CALIFORNIA

Locations are approximate.
Many towns and cities were not
in existence at the same time.

Yreka

Shasta

SIERRA

Chico

Downieville
Camptonville
Foster's Bar

Nevada City

Marysville

Auburn

Coloma
Sutter's Mill

Placerville

Sacramento
Sutter's Fort

Folsom

Mokelumne Hill

Benecia

San Andreas

San Quentin

Martinez

Stockton

Angel's Camp

Sonora
Chinese Camp

Yosemite

San Francisco

SAN

Mayfield

San Jose • *Pacheco Pass*

NEVADA

Hornitos
Mariposa

Santa Cruz

San Juan
Bautisa

• *Firebaugh's*
Ferry

Monterey

Soledad

JOAQUIN

Fresno

Young's Cabin

Visalia • *Stone Corral*

Coast

Range

VALLEY

San Miguel

San Luis Obispo

Bakersfield

MOJAVE DESERT

Santa Barbara
Ventura

• *Castaic Creek*

San Gabriel

San Bernardino
El Monte
Los Angeles

0	50	100

Scale of Miles

San Diego

The
Famous Concord Stagecoach

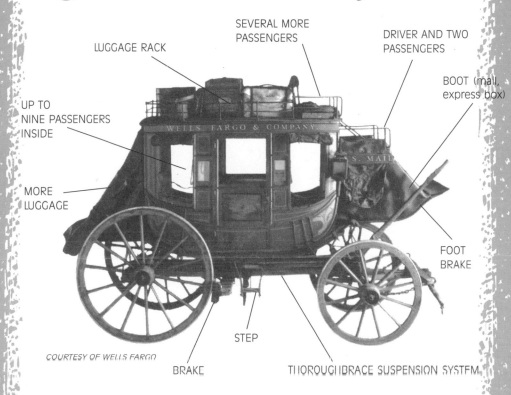

SEVERAL MORE
PASSENGERS

DRIVER AND TWO
PASSENGERS

LUGGAGE RACK

BOOT (mail,
express box)

UP TO
NINE PASSENGERS
INSIDE

WELLS, FARGO & COMPANY

S. MAIL

MORE
LUGGAGE

FOOT
BRAKE

COURTESY OF WELLS FARGO

STEP

BRAKE

THOROUGHBRACE SUSPENSION SYSTEM

The Concord coach of the 1840s weighed some twenty-five hundred pounds and sold FOB at the factory for about $1,200. It was primarily a passenger vehicle used on better roads and the foothills. For mountain travel on rough, muddy trails, Abbot and Downing built their "celerity" and "mud" wagons. These had canvas tops, were heavier duty and less comfortable than the Concords, but lighter and very popular and more widely used. A mud wagon was priced at about $500 FOB.

John Allen

alias "Sheet-Iron Jack"
(Real name John D. Gundlack)

■ Hero, liar, thief, or just plain
scoundrel, perhaps Jack Allen was all
of that, and more. He was certainly a
character, in any case.
Author's collection.

The Civil War honed and positively developed the characters of many who participated in this most terrible of American conflicts. But there were those who were adversely affected, also. For some the war was an excuse for their later failings. Others merely needed the push into crime provided by a rough, male society in a gold-mad and hectic period of history.

Born in New York State about 1849, John Gundlack enlisted in the 32nd Maine Volunteer Infantry Regiment in March 1864 at the age of fifteen. He lost a finger and suffered other injuries while participating in the siege of Petersburg in early 1864. His unit suffered severe battle casualties and he was mustered out in Virginia on July 15, 1865. His war wounds are fully described in army medical records and match his physical description in San Quentin prison records. An older brother had been killed at Antietam.

Perhaps ex-soldier Gundlack had gotten into trouble of some kind, for he apparently headed west immediately after his discharge. One account states he met a frontiersman named Hoag in San Francisco, and together they were hired as scouts or packers at Fort Crook in Shasta County. Somewhere along the way, Gundlack changed his name to John Allen. He was in southern Oregon in late September of 1866, where he claimed to have joined a party of civilians accompanying Captain Samuel Munson, 9th Infantry, and thirty troopers chasing Indian horse thieves. When one of the party, rancher John Townsend, was killed in an ambush, the party retreated. Although this is a documented incident, there is no documentation of Allen's participation.

Years later, Allen also claimed to have joined General George Crook's command as a scout and guide, but verification, again, is lacking. In September of 1867, Allen was ordered to climb a bluff near Steen's Mountain to scout and give signals for an attack. To protect himself, he strapped a large camp frying pan to his chest and was afterwards called "Sheet-Iron Jack." He also asserted that he had been in the party that rescued a "Miss Hattie Henderson" who had been carried off by the Indian war party that had captured a stagecoach and murdered her father and cousin. This seems to be another fantasy, based on an incident in which a family named Pierson was murdered by Indians in early 1868. There was a stagecoach captured by the Indians in November, 1866, in the same northeastern part of California. But no one was killed or captured, and again, Jack seems to

■ Jack Allen spent an uncomfortable amount of time in the Tehama County jail, pictured above. *Author's collection.*

have inserted himself into a real incident in order to utilize his hero status for his own purposes at a later date.

In 1873, Allen claimed to have carried the mail between Klamath, Oregon, and the lava beds during the Modoc War, but a search of records in the National Archives failed to turn up his name. It is perhaps significant to recognize that all these heroic claims were made at the time Allen was trying to secure a pardon from prison.

Reportedly a barber in Tehama County during the mid-1870s, Allen also was a laborer who sheared sheep and did other odd jobs.

He was frequently drunk and in trouble, and when his purse got too light, horse theft and other types of thievery were not beneath him, either. In early 1875, he was sentenced to San Quentin for two years when he tried to rob a blind old farmer named Dersche and his wife. In the custody of Deputy Sheriff Harold, Jack boarded the Shasta stage on the evening of February 18 for his one-way trip to state prison. The coach had gone some two miles from town when it was unceremoniously stopped, as reported by District Attorney Clay W. Taylor, who had convicted Jack:

> The stage left town about 7 o'clock, Jerry Culverhouse driving, with old man Harold, and a prisoner, John Allen, alias "Sheet-Iron Jack," and two or more passengers on board. When they arrived at the foot of the hill, just below Lower Springs, and while the team were in a trot, some men (They say there were three) stepped out, and one cried halt or stop, being nearly opposite the driver when he spoke. He spoke low, and Jerry gave his horses a cut with the whip, and they made several jumps, when one of the men fired with a shotgun, hitting Jerry in the head and shoulders.

The driver was badly wounded, but he held on to the horses until they stopped down the road. A passenger took the lines and the coach then returned to Shasta. All the way back to town, "Sheet-Iron Jack cussed the robbers," noted a local newspaper, "until the air smelled like brimstone…He said that it was an unmitigated outrage that a man could not be permitted to travel over Shasta County territory, especially when he was on his way

■ The stage preparing to leave Weaverville for Shasta and Redding. *Trinity County Historical Society.*

7

■ John Toney was a horse thief and a bank and stage robber. *Author's collection.*

to work for the interest of the state, without having his life endangered by shots fired by murderous highwaymen."

As a posse was being organized in town, a new driver was secured, and the stage again headed for Redding and other points south. When passing through Red Bluff on the stage, Jack seemed quite unconcerned about the incident as reported in the *People's Cause*, February 20, 1875:

DID NOT AGREE WITH HIM. - "Sheet-Iron Jack," while passing through this town on his way from Shasta to San Quentin, where he will work for the benefit of the state, or the prison contractors, for the next two years, when asked by one of our citizens where he was going, replied, "I am going

■ Instead of being able to roam free, Jack now found himself locked in a small San Quentin cell with three, and sometimes more, fellow convicts. *California State Library.*

where I can get some sea breeze; this Northern climate does not agree with my health and I must make a change."

Allen was issued No. 6395 in the San Quentin Inmate Register. His record makes note of the many scars on his body resulting from his Civil War wounds. On appeal, he was re-tried in July and released on an assault charge after serving some time and paying a fine.

In September of 1876, Allen was shearing sheep for a man named Berry at Cottonwood Station, between Redding and Red Bluff. He had met a notorious character named John Toney in prison, and the two met again after their release. Toney and a young Englishman named Frank Chapman were working for a local farmer nearby, and together the three men discussed making a little easy money. Allen later claimed to have planned the ensuing holdups, the first of which took place on November 6, 1876. In the evening, Toney and Chapman hunkered down in a clump of willows lining the road and stopped the approaching coach as reported in the *Yreka Union*, on November 11, 1876:

> On Monday evening, the Weaverville and Redding stage was stopped by two highwaymen, who, leveling shotguns at the driver requested him to hand over Wells, Fargo & Co's Express box. The driver, of course, complied with their request and was ordered to drive on. As the treasure was not in the box, the robbers got nothing but a few letters. ...This makes the second stage robbery in Shasta county within a week.

■ Letter to California's governor from the U.S. Consul in Ottawa seeking clemency for Jack Allen in behalf of his father.
California State Archives.

When his two partners held up two other stages, the second one containing $1,100 in the treasure box, Allen got drunk and turned them in. His motives are not clear, but perhaps there was a dispute over dividing the loot and Jack decided to try for the Wells, Fargo reward. When he admitted to planning the robberies with Chapman and Toney, Sheet-Iron Jack was also jailed as an accessory. The *Marysville Daily Appeal* reported that the outlaws were upset with their lodgings in the Shasta jail and voiced their displeasure by trying to break out on the night of December 12, 1876:

■ Frank Chapman.
California State Archives.

> Five noted State Prison birds nearly succeeded in escaping from the Shasta jail last Tuesday night. The list embraces Toney, Sheet-Iron Jack, Chapman, Leonard and Edwards. When Sheriff Hull and his deputies discovered their operations they had nearly dug a hole through the wall of the prison, and in a short time longer would have been free. Sheet-Iron Jack's trial has probably concluded, and Toney and Chapman pleaded guilty at the opening of the court. These beauties will probably get twenty years in the State Prison....

The prisoners had obtained tools, and when caught, they had already filed through their shackles and had tunneled nearly through the jail wall. "Since then," noted the *Appeal*, "they have worn jewelry that is more useful than ornamental." Ex-convict Toney received a twenty-one-year sentence, while Jack Allen received twenty-four years. Chapman got only four. They arrived at San Quentin on December 25, 1876. Chapman was pardoned in May 1877, on condition he return to England, which he did. Toney kept his nose clean and was released in 1889.

A newspaper reported Allen had married a girl named Parliee Parsons before he left for prison, and Jack later referred to his "little home" and "family" when appealing for a pardon. Again, documentation is lacking. As early as June 1877, Allen began churning out whining letters to witnesses, to the governor, Wells, Fargo executives and to lawyers to build a case for a pardon. In the blizzard of paperwork that followed, Allen and his lawyer played up his Civil War record and wounds, which were true, and his record as an Indian fighter, which was highly exaggerated, if any of it was true. In October 1882, when he didn't seem to be making any headway, Allen wrote his father, John G. Gundlack, a respectable retired businessman in Canada. Horrified at the news, the father immediately wrote Governor George Perkins through the United States Consul at Ottawa, Canada. Governor Perkins responded by commuting Allen's sentence to only ten years. He was released in June of 1883. Characteristically, he never left the state or visited his parents as he had promised the governor.

■ Sheet-Iron Jack Allen, a mug shot from his 1884 conviction. *Author's collection.*

We can assume Jack Allen stole horses and worked at odd jobs for the next six months or so. He rode into Red Bluff in Tehama County in late March 1884, and was ordered out of town as an undesirable character. A few days later, he was back in town, drunk and making a nuisance of himself. When Tehama County Sheriff Martin received a telegram from San Francisco asking that he arrest and hold Sheet-Iron Jack, he promptly sought out the badman, as

■ Folsom State Prison when it was home to Sheet-Iron Jack Allen. *California State Library.*

reported in the *Red Bluff Weekly Democrat*, April 5, 1884:

> Sheriff Martin at once went in search of his man, accompanied by Undersheriff Lennon, and found him in front of Cone & Kimball's store, near the California Beer Hall. Being well acquainted with him, the sheriff reached out his hand as if to shake hands, saying, "How are you Jack"; but Jack, instead of taking Martin's hand, pulled his pistol and thrust it into the sheriff's face. Sheriff Martin was too quick for him and caught his arm and turned the pistol toward Jack's breast, coolly saying, "Pull 'er off now if you want to." Undersheriff Lennon seized Jack from behind, and Policemen Gilson and Kennedy came to their assistance and it took all of them and one or two citizens to get him to the jail…fighting all the way.

It seems Jack had stolen a five hundred dollar horse in San Francisco and sold it for considerably less. Detective Dan Coffee arrived on April 4 and returned the prisoner to the Bay City. "If he was arrested because he sold a $500 horse for $75," commented a local newspaper, "we think the arrest was perfectly justifiable."

■ San Francisco Police Detective Dan Coffee. *Author's collection.*

Convicted and sentenced to a six-year term, Jack found himself in Folsom State Prison this time. A new governor, Robert Waterman, was now bombarded by Allen who unloaded his same tired war stories (this time claiming to have been only fourteen when he enlisted during the Civil War). Despite the shameless boasting in his letters and the fact that he was serving his third term in prison, Jack was pardoned again in 1888. Warden John McComb wasn't fooled, however. In a note among Allen's pardon papers, he scribbled: "Jack Allen represents himself to be a soldier of the Union Army, and has received a pension given to John Gundlack. I think Allen is an imposter, and that he has never been anything else but a thief."

Did John Gundlack, alias Sheet-Iron Jack Allen, see the error of his ways and finally stick to the straight and narrow? Of course not. In December of 1888, he was caught stealing a handkerchief in a San

Francisco saloon and hauled before a judge who knew of his prison record. He was sentenced to six months in the San Francisco House of Correction, together with a fine of five hundred dollars. Again came the flood of petitions, and Jack was released in May of 1889. After being picked up in Sacramento for petit larceny in 1893, he receded into history's pages.

Hume and Thacker's "Robbers' Record"; San Quentin State Prison Register; Governor's Pardon Files, California State Archives, Sacramento; Asa Merrill Fairfield, *Fairfield's History of Lassen County California,* San Francisco, H.S. Crocker Co., 1916; Military Reference Branch, National Archives, Medical and Pension Records of John D. Gundlack, Michael E. Pilgrim to the author, December 8, 1993; Marysville *Daily Appeal,* November 21, December 13, 15, 19, 1876; *Yreka Union,* November 11, 1876; Redding *Republican Free Press,* April 5, 1884; *Shasta Courier,* December 30, 1876; San Francisco *Examiner,* September 17, 27, 1882; *San Francisco Chronicle,* April 1, 1884.

STAGECOACH ETIQUETTE

1. The best stagecoach seat is the one next to the driver…you will get less than half the bumps and jars than on any other seat. When any old "sly Eph," who travelled thousands of miles of coaches, offers through sympathy to exchange his back or middle seat with you, don't do it.

2. When the driver asks you to get off and walk, do it without grumbling. He will not request it unless absolutely necessary. If a team runs away, sit still and take your chances; if you jump, nine times out of ten you will be hurt.

3. Don't growl at food stations; stage companies generally provide the best they can get. Don't keep the stage waiting; many a virtuous man has lost his character by so doing.

4. Don't smoke a strong pipe inside, especially early in the morning. Spit on the leeward side of the coach. If you have anything to take in a bottle, pass it around; a man who drinks by himself in such a case is lost to all human feeling. Provide stimulants before starting; ranch whiskey is not always nectar.

5. Don't swear, nor lop over on your neighbor when sleeping. Don't ask how far it is to the next station until you get there.

6. Never attempt to fire a gun or pistol while on the road, it may frighten the team; and the careless handling and cocking of the weapon makes nervous people nervous. Don't discuss politics or religion, nor point out places on the road where horrible murders have been committed.

7. Don't linger too long at the pewter wash basin at the station. Don't grease your hair before starting or dust will stick there in sufficient quantities to make a respectable "tater" patch. Tie a silk handkerchief around your neck to keep out dust and prevent sunburns. A little glycerin is good in case of chapped hands.

8. Don't imagine for a moment you are going on a picnic; expect annoyance, discomfort and some hardships. If you are disappointed, thank heaven.

Omaha Herald, 1877

S. A. Allen

alias Ned Allen or
Sol White

■ Entrance to San Quentin State Prison where Allen spent an uncomfortable amount of well-deserved time.
California State Library.

Born in Ohio about 1833, Allen was reportedly a farmer and probably came to California in the late 1850s during the waning days of the Gold Rush. As No. 4443, he was admitted to San Quentin on April 27, 1870, from Yolo County for the crime of grand larceny. His term was two years, but he was pardoned in early 1871.

While in prison, Allen may have met twenty-four-year-old George Robertson, who was doing one year for a Sacramento robbery. Robertson was discharged on October 20, 1870, and joined up with two other convicts, Bill Miner and Alkali Jim Harrington. Robertson was using the name Cooper now and, collaborating with his two pals, they held up the San Andreas and Stockton stage on January 23, 1871. The take was some thirty-six hundred dollars, but Cooper was picked up in San Francisco less than a week later. Miner and Harrington escaped after a shoot-out with an officer in San Jose, but both men were in custody by February 5. Feeling his pals had skipped out on him with the money, Cooper promptly "peached" on them, earning his own

■ George Cooper, from an early San Francisco Police mug book.
Author's collection.

freedom, while Miner and Harrington each received ten-year prison terms.

On January 15, 1875, Allen and Cooper held up the stage between Lone Pine and Bakersfield in Kern County. The *Bakersfield Southern Californian* reported:

> The Panamint stage was stopped on Saturday afternoon last, about twenty miles east of this place, by two men who presented a draft upon Wells, Fargo & Co.'s treasure box, in the shape of a shotgun....They took only coin, amounting to about five hundred dollars....

The two road agents were quickly caught by Kern County Sheriff W. R. Bower and Deputy Harry Bludworth. Cooper "rejected with scorn" an offer of turning state's evidence on Allen and was sent up for a ten-year term after learning his partner had already "peached" on him. Allen was released while Cooper was left to ponder this poetic justice for his earlier betrayal of Miner and Harrington.

■ Goshen railroad depot, in Tulare County. *Author's collection.*

On March 30, 1875, Allen stole a Wells, Fargo treasure box from the depot at Goshen, near Visalia, securing about one thousand dollars. Fleeing to the coast, on the morning of May 29, 1875, he robbed the Salinas stage near the Monterey/San Luis Obispo County border. He secured the Wells, Fargo box, but was captured within a few weeks under the name of Sol White. As he was awaiting the action of the grand jury while in the San Luis Obispo jail, White whiled away his time planning an escape.

■ Coast Line stages had to drive through the surf on part of their route as shown in this early print. *Author's collection.*

White and a "Spaniard" had access to a room during the day in which they met with their attorneys. Dismantling one of the chairs in the room, White kept a leg handy to use as a club in his scheme. When Jailor Ross let the two prisoners into their cells at eight o'clock on July 19, he closed the Spaniard's door first. White quickly stepped behind Ross and knocked him down with a heavy blow from the chair leg. Locking the jailor into his cell, White grabbed the keys and dashed for the door, clubbing a trusty named Campbell before disappearing into the night. The *San Luis Obispo Tribune* commented:

■ A scene in San Luis Obispo as it appeared in 1880. *John Boessenecker collection.*

A reward of two hundred dollars has been offered for his arrest and confinement in any jail in the State, and other steps taken to secure him if living. White is a man about thirty-five years of age, 5 feet, 10 inches high, weighs about 160 pounds, sandy whiskers, light hair, blue eyes, high forehead, little bald on top of the head, nose slightly turned up, downcast look, had on dark corded cloth pants, coat and vest, high crown light brown hat and is gentlemanly in address. In addition to the above reward, the jailor offers one hundred dollars for his return.

Allen promptly left the area and later teamed up with James "Texas" Jones, another ex-convict. Their first known venture together was to hold up the stage between Oroville and Laporte on June 27, 1876. "The treasure box was demanded," reported the *Butte Record*, "and when broken open was found to contain only twenty dollars." Whether it was twenty dollars or twenty-five hundred dollars made no difference to Wells, Fargo detectives, and the two highwaymen fled over the Sierra.

They stopped the stage traveling between Aurora and Carson City, Nevada, on October 3, 1876, and made off with another Wells,

Fargo treasure box. But Wells, Fargo was on their trail. Allen and Jones were arrested by a detective at Jackson, California, then taken to the Douglas County jail at Genoa, Nevada. Allen escaped on December 17, 1876, but was recaptured the same day. Tried and convicted in Douglas County, Allen and Jones were received at the Nevada State Prison on December 19, 1876, Allen to serve an eight-year sentence and Jones, five years.

Jones escaped in December, 1880, while Allen served out his term. He was discharged at the expiration of his sentence on December 5, 1883, and either went straight, which isn't likely, or moved to another state. If Allen served any other terms in California prisons, he probably did so under another name in an effort to hide his previous career.

Hume and Thacker's "Robbers' Record"; San Quentin State Prison Register; Governor's Pardon Files, California State Archives, Sacramento; San Francisco *Morning Call*, March 4, 1876; Visalia *Weekly Delta*, April 8, 1875. Bakersfield *Southern Californian*, January 21, 1875; Kern County *Weekly Courier*, February 27, March 13, 1875; Boessenecker, *Badge and Buckshot*.

Charles Baker

alias Charles Hanlon

■ Stage robber Charles Baker was always contrite while in custody, but when he got out it was another story. *California State Archives.*

The home of Charles Baker was Ohio, where he was born about 1853. Reportedly a stove moulder by trade, it is not known when Baker came to California, but he was convicted of embezzlement in Mono County in the summer of 1877. Received at San Quentin September 29, 1877, to serve a one-year term, he was released July 29, 1878. He returned to Mono County and apparently worked for a time, but on December 11, 1880, he stopped the Benton to Darwin coach, alone, and took the Wells, Fargo express box. Captured, he was again sent to San Quentin, where he took up residence on April 5, 1881, as No. 9843, to serve a ten-year stretch.

Pardoned in early February 1885, Baker adopted the name Hanlon and moved to San Francisco, where he may have worked as a moulder for a time. In the Bay City, he met a kindred felonious spirit named Charles Manning and the two planned to hold up a Mendocino County stagecoach for some easy money. After a trip to the area between Cloverdale and Mendocino City, they discovered that two stages made the trip between the two cities on certain nights, one going south and the other north. They decided to hold up both coaches in Anderson Valley, stopping the stages at two points, just before they crossed paths. It was a daring plan.

On the night of January 5, 1889, the two highwaymen positioned themselves a short distance apart and began their wait. The Mendocino coach, heading south, arrived about 10:30 P.M. and was stopped by the first robber. Demanding the Wells, Fargo box, the man asked a few questions, then told the driver to move on. "It was the most business-like bit of work I ever saw in my life," recalled one of the passengers.

The coach proceeded south and in a few moments pulled up alongside the northbound stage. "Well," said the one driver, "I've been robbed."

"He's got my box, too," said the south-bound driver. After the drivers had concluded that both had been robbed by the same man, the stages moved on.

Mendocino County Sheriff Jeremiah "Doc" Standley did not go along with the one bandit

■ One of California's top lawmen, "Doc" Standle[y] once chased an outlaw band for a thousand mil[es] killing one and capturing the other three. *A contemporary sketch by Grace Hudson.*

theory. Piecing together descriptions of recent strangers in the area and what the stage passengers could tell him, the sheriff sent out notices in the hope that the two highwaymen had hidden their loot

near the robbery scene and would return for it. In late February, Standley received word that two men fitting the descriptions had purchased provisions in Cloverdale and were taking the stage for Anderson Valley. He was promptly on their trail. The two highwaymen had just recovered their loot when they were met on the road by the sheriff who provided lodging for them in the Ukiah jail. After their trial, the *Mendocino Beacon* commented:

■ Stage robber Charles Manning. *Author's collection.*

The conviction of Charles Manning and Charles Hanlon for robbing the

■ The ominous walls and guard towers of California's San Quentin State Prison were a formidable barrier to escape, but Charles Hanlon had the will and he found a way. *California State Library.*

stages in Anderson Valley on January 5, and their sentence of seventeen years in San Quentin, was received with satisfaction on the coast. We hope that the manner in which these rascals have been treated will have a salutary effect upon those who are inclined to engage in this daring, but disgraceful, business.

This was Baker's (Hanlon's) third commitment at San Quentin, and he was determined to escape, if at all possible. But for now, he was simply No. 13523.

Manning, his partner, contacted a cousin who promised to secrete some weapons at a certain site near where the two convicts were working outside the walls on windmill tanks. The day after receiving news that the guns had been deposited, Hanlon, Manning and a convict named Abe Turcott suddenly began moving unobtrusively away from their work site. As they seized the hidden Winchester rifles and two pistols, the convicts were hailed from a guard post and sent several bullets in response. They then fled

■ A group of San Quentin guards, armed and ready for business. An undated photograph, but taken some years after Hanlon's break. *Author's collection.*

to a nearby thicket in a hail of Gatling gun lead.

A large posse of prison guards, uninformed the convicts were armed, promptly rode after the escaping men. A guard named Bowen was in the lead and was startled when he was shot in the arm. Hanlon, reportedly an expert with a rifle, next shot the horse out from under a guard named Porter, who had tried to cut off their escape route. As the rattled guards now attempted to regroup, the convicts disappeared in the brush and forests and ran some three miles to the small village of Larkspur in Marin County. Climbing a ridge, the tired convicts quickly positioned some

■ Charles Baker, alias Hanlon, the jail-breaking stage robber. *A contemporary newspaper sketch in author's collection.*

fallen pine logs into a makeshift fort and began firing at the approaching guards. That night, as the convicts tried to slip past the guards, they were driven back by rifle fire. At daybreak, Hanlon yelled out, "You think you've got us, don't you?…We'll never surrender. We'll make this spot our grave first!"

Sheriff Standley had arrived that night from Mendocino County. After more exchanges of rifle fire, the convicts asked to parley with him, as noted in the *San Francisco Chronicle*:

One of the convicts met Standley, the two being only twenty feet apart. The fugitive wanted to know if they had killed anyone, and when answered in the negative, would not believe it. They had fired at a young officer, the convict said, and he had dropped to the ground at the shot. After holding two or three consultations with his comrades, the convict was convinced that they had not killed any one and surrendered the weapons they held to Sheriff Standley….

■ "Doc" Standley would rather talk to an outlaw, than shoot him. *California State Library.*

Back in his cell, Hanlon told a reporter that he was sorry he hadn't taken Standley's advice "when he had originally arrested us and told Manning and myself to act square."

Despite his pious pronouncement, Hanlon was quick to sign on to another escape plot that was hatched in the summer of 1891.

Convict C. C. Sullivan had a brother in Santa Cruz who, over a period of time, brought five Smith & Wesson pistols to the prison. They were smuggled inside the walls in a bucket of milk by a trusty. Abe Turcott then hid the guns in a tunnel under the prison carpentry shop. Besides Sullivan and Turcott, the other plotters included Hanlon and Manning, Charles Dorsey, George Ross, and Mickey Delaney. All were long-term convicts and desperadoes. When Warden William Hale heard rumors of an impending escape, he put a stool pigeon into the yard and soon identified the plot leaders. The suspects were put into solitary, on bread and water, and soon Turcott had had enough of the punishment. Sullivan's brother was then arrested in Santa Cruz, along with the trusty who had smuggled the weapons behind the walls.

Hanlon (Baker) did his time, was released on November 11, 1899, and perhaps left the state. In any case he disappeared and was not heard from again.

Hume and Thacker's "Robbers' Record"; San Quentin State Prison Register; California State Archives, Sacramento; Boessenecker, *Badge and Buckshot; Mendocino Beacon,* January 12, March 2, April 13, 1889; *Mendocino Dispatch Democrat,* August 15, 1890; *San Francisco Examiner,* September 6, 7, 10, 26, 27, 1891; *San Francisco Chronicle,* August 12, 13, 1890, 26, 28, 1891.

FRONTIER CALIFORNIA PRICES

Boarding house room and board .... **$1.25** per day
Santa Cruz House, 1874

Hotel board with lodging .... **$8.00** per week
U. S. Hotel, Marysville, 1857

Toll road fee **$1.50**
Stagecoach w/six horses, 1867

Ferry crossing fee **$2.00**
Stagecoach w/six horses, Millerton, 1871

Steamboat fare **$2.50**
San Francisco to San Jose, 1861

Stagecoach fares **$16.00**
Yreka to Reading, 1876
$25.00 San Francisco to Visalia, 1869

Bottle of whiskey **75**c
Academy Store, 1875

Cigars .... **5**c ea./homemade
*four for **25**c, Stockton, 1874*

Bath, haircut .... **25**c ea.
Santa Cruz, 1874

Calfskin pair of boots **$3.50**
Sears catalog, 1897

J.B. Stetson hat **$3.90**
Sears catalog, 1897

1873 Winchester rifle **$11.85**
Sears catalog, 1897

.45 caliber, double action revolver **$20**
Spirit of the Times, 1877

Single action Colt, Frontier model **$12.95**
Sears catalog, 1897

Tom Bell

Real name Thomas J. Hodges

■ Tom Bell's pillaging operations in Gold Rush California included the first attempt to stop and rob a stagecoach. *Trinity County Historical Society.*

Thomas Hodges came from a respectable family in Rome, Tennessee, where he was born about 1826. Well educated, young Hodges served during the Mexican War as a medical orderly in Colonel Frank Cheatham's Tennessee Volunteers. He came to California in 1850 and although reportedly successful in a Mariposa County mining claim, he quickly lost his money gambling. Caught after a horse stealing raid, he was sentenced to state prison, where he arrived in the fall of 1851 as prisoner No. 24.

The state prison at this time consisted of an old ship named the *Waban*, a bark of 268 tons. In December of 1851, it was anchored at Angel Island, in San Francisco Bay, where the convicts, including Tom Hodges, were put to work quarrying stone. Feigning illness, Hodges was placed in the San Francisco county jail, where he was given privileges and soon managed to escape. He was recaptured and returned the following year, however.

Most of the state convicts at this time worked at preparing the site in Marin County where the state had purchased land for a prison. There were some 250

■ A convict work party at San Quentin in the 1850s. *Author's collection.*

prisoners in late 1854 when the first stone and brick cell-block and various prison buildings were constructed. On May 12 of the following year, Hodges and a small group of friends escaped while on a

■ The road station at Strawberry, a typical stage stop where Bell gang members could pick up information on travelers and gold shipments. *Author's collection.*

wood chopping detail. Prison officials had actually arranged the break to rid themselves of troublesome inmates.

Jim Smith, Bill White (alias Gristy), and Edward "Ned" Connor were among the escaped convicts who now formed a robber gang, with Hodges as leader. Hodges now adopted the name Tom Bell and the group began preying upon mountain travelers and isolated mining camps. The gang headquartered at Jack Phillips' Mountaineer House, a stage stop and hotel near Auburn. Phillips would point out wealthy travelers at his place, and the gang would later stalk and rob them.

The gang was carefully organized, even to the extent that each carried a bullet marked with an "X" as identification. Juan Fernandez, the Skinner brothers, Adolph Newton, Monte Jack Lyon, "English Bob" Carr, and others were gang members. One early lawman totaled over thirty men who at one time or another belonged to the gang.

■ Jim Smith was a Bell gang member, but left after the Camptonville stage fiasco. *Author's collection.*

In one instance, after robbing a peddler on the road, Bell tied him to a tree and murdered him. Another time, when a victim was shot in the leg, the inconsistent highwayman bandaged the man's leg, then placed him in a passing wagon to seek aid.

Bell's gang soon became a plague in the Gold Rush country. At one point, there was talk in the state legislature of a statewide police force to combat the burgeoning crime wave in Central California.

After many robberies of travelers, stores, teamsters, Chinese mining camps, and after committing at least the one murder, Bell and his men decided to rob a stagecoach. Although California stages had been pilfered and had satchels and treasure boxes stolen before, no stage-

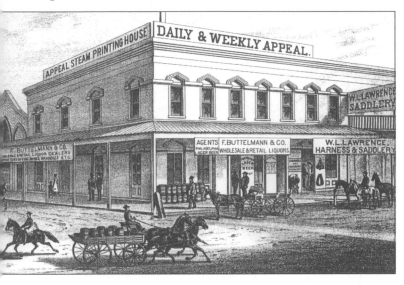

■ Street scene in old Marysville, the destination of the Camptonville stage when it was attacked.
Author's collection.

coaches had reportedly been stopped and robbed on the road. However, Bell and his band plotted what was to be the state's first attempted stage robbery by armed bandits. The planning of the operation was later described by ex-convict Bill White, one of the outlaws:

> We were about three weeks on the lookout for this; all of this time we were staying at the California House, 25 miles from Marysville, on the road to Camptonville. This house is kept by Madam Cole,…[who] was in with us. It was one of our stopping places. Our party at this time consisted of Thomas J. Hodges, alias Tom Bell; Ned Convery, alias Ned Connor; Montague Lyon, alias Monte Jack; Jim Smith; Bob Carr, alias English Bob; Juan Rocher, alias Juan Fernandez and myself — seven in all. Our plan was to send Smith Sutton, a miner living near the California House, to Camptonville, to spot the treasure as it came down. He was faithful to his promise. He came down as far as the California House on the stage on the day of the attack and reported everything all right. I went to John Gardner and borrowed his rifle, and we then all started for the place of attack….

Bell and five of his men waited alongside the Marysville road on August 12, 1856. Despite their plans, the holdup was a fiasco. Instead of surrendering meekly, the coach driver whipped up his horses as the guard and passengers opened fire on the bandits. One of Bell's men received a minor injury, while several passengers were badly wounded. "The stage is riddled with bullet holes," commented the *Marysville Herald* after the coach arrived in town.

Posses immediately fanned out over the countryside. When Juan Fernandez and Bill White were captured after a series of robberies, a bullet with the secret "X" mark on it was obtained, allowing Calaveras County Deputy Sheriff Robert Paul to trick Jack Phillips into revealing his participation. It was the beginning of the end. Others who had provided information for the stage robbery were picked up, also. In late September, Bell and several of the gang engaged in a desperate gun battle with officers, and Ned Connor was killed. One of the group, Perry Owens, alias "Texas," was later picked up aboard a coastal steamer while attempting to flee to Mexico. Quoting the *Calaveras Chronicle*, on October 6, 1856, the *San Francisco Bulletin* reported:

> Our county jail now contains five of Tom Bell's freebooters. On Tuesday last Deputy Sheriff Shuler arrived in the Sacramento stage, having in charge Jack Phillips, a Sydney Duck, who was arrested at the Mountaineer House, near Auburn.... Day before yesterday, the Sacramento and Stockton stages brought each two more of the highwaymen....

After the gun battle, Bell fled south to a ranch he was setting up on the San Joaquin River. Others were captured as lawmen closed in on the ranch. Bell was discovered nearby, as noted in the *Stockton Argus* that

■ Pierre Ridge claimed to have been Bell gang member and his prison rec indicates he might well have been. *Author's collection.*

reported "from good and reliable authority, that on Saturday morning last, 4th October, about 11 o'clock, Tom Bell was captured by a party who were in search of him, and at 5 o'clock in the evening of the same day, he was hung." Other reports verified the news that after being allowed to write a letter to his mother, the outlaw leader was indeed lynched by a posse near Firebaugh's Ferry and was probably buried in the area. He had refused to identify any of his men.

An examination of the San Quentin Prison Register indicates few of the Bell gang members served time for their crimes. Jack Phillips was sentenced to two years and his wife was at the gate waiting for him when he was discharged.

■ Tom Bell was lynched just a few miles downstream from Firebaugh's Ferry, shown here in an old lithograph. *Author's collection.*

Bill White was returned to San Quentin to serve out his old term, but he was pardoned out in November 1858, for turning state's evidence on his fellow gang members. Jim Smith was later captured for another crime and spent the remainder of his life in and out of prison. Perry Owens seems to have been let off for lack of evidence, while English Bob and various others were not heard from again.

But that was all anticlimactic. The first stage had been stopped and robbed in the aftermath of the great Gold Rush. Now, it was open season on the treasure-carrying stagecoaches in California.

San Quentin State Prison Register; Governor's Pardon Files, California State Archives, Sacramento; Secrest, William B., *Lawmen & Desperadoes*; Boessenecker, John, *Gold Dust and Gunsmoke*; Lamott, Kenneth, *Chronicles of San Quentin*; *San Francisco Herald*, October 6, 1856; San Francisco *Daily Evening Bulletin*, October 8, 1856; Marysville *Daily Herald*, August 13, October 25, 1856; the *Placer Herald*, February 28, 1857; Wells, Fargo Bank History Room, San Francisco.

CHILD BORN IN A STAGE COACH

A fine boy first saw the light of this wicked world in a stage coach yesterday, while his mother was journeying from San Antonio to San Jose. We learn that some four ladies and two Frenchmen were passengers in the stage and that during the trip a lady requested the driver to stop. He instantly complied, and was informed that one of the ladies was in a very delicate condition, at the same time the gentlemen were requested to leave the stage. The two Frenchmen declined, saying they had paid for their passages, and would not move. The driver, however, compelled them to get out and walk. In the meantime, the ladies present did all they could for the assistance of their suffering companion, who shortly became the mother of a fine boy. The driver was again appealed to and requested to go on, which he did, and soon landed the lady and her babe at a comfortable hotel, where, at last accounts, they were getting on as prosperously as could be wished.

San Francisco Herald, May 8, 1859

A BRAVE ACT

One day last week the driver of one of the California Stages was thrown from his box, a short distance this side of Cottonwood. The team at once commenced going at a frightful pace. The outside passengers jumped off, and the chances for a beautiful smash-up were quite flattering. This would doubtless have been the consequences, but for the conduct of Mr. Lusk, messenger of the Pacific Express, who, with a daring seldom equalled, climbed from the inside of the stage upon the driver's foot board, thence upon the tongue of the stage, and finally upon the back of the near wheel horse, from which position he gathered up the lines, and brought the frightened team, and still more frightened passengers, safely up to the Cottonwood station. The roads in the country are represented to be in a worse condition than at any time during last winter.

Shasta Courier, December 22, 1855

Charles Bowles

alias Charles Boles / Bolton and Black Bart

■ As a husband and father,
he wasn't much, but as a stage
robbing legend, Black Bart
topped them all. *Author's collection.*

The first seven children of John and Maria Bowles were born in England, with Charles, the youngest of these, arriving in 1829. Migrating to the United States in 1830, the family took up residence on a 100-acre farm in New York State, where two more children were born.

Young Charles had a good education and, in his teens, was known as a skilled wrestler. He and a cousin went to California during the 1849 Gold Rush, but Charles returned east in 1854. He married Mary Elisabeth Johnson about 1856 and the following year moved to Iowa, where their first child was born. The family was living in Illinois when the Civil War erupted and Charles enlisted as a private in Company B of the 116th Illinois Volunteer Infantry in 1861. He served honorably in the Union army, fought in seventeen battles, was badly wounded, and rose to the rank of first sergeant.

He rejoined his wife in Iowa in June 1865, and the family soon after moved to Minnesota. There were four children now, and by 1870 the family was again living in Iowa, although Charles had left for the gold fields of Montana in May 1867. The family would never see him again.

Charles probably changed his name to Boles because it was misspelled that way so often. His military papers indicate this, and when he turned up in California in the early 1870s, he was using both this name and the name Charles E. Bolton.

He was living in San Francisco when he robbed his first stagecoach on the Sonora to Milton route. Near Reynolds Ferry at 6:30 in the morning on July 26, 1875, a bandit, later to be known as Black Bart, suddenly appeared and called for the coach to halt.

"Please throw down the box," the highwayman shouted. When driver John Shine tried to hold his horses steady as he wrestled with the express box, the masked robber called out: "If he makes a move, give him a volley, boys!" It was then that Shine noticed several rifle barrels protruding from around some brush and boulders. Later, after the robber made a safe getaway, the supposed accomplices' "rifle barrels" were discovered to be merely sticks of wood.

REWARD!

WELLS, FARGO & CO.'S EXPRESS BOX, CON-
taining $160 in Gold Notes, was robbed this morning, by one man, on the route from Sonora
to Milton, near top of the Hill, between the river and Copperopolis.

$250

And one-fourth of any money recovered, will be paid
for arrest and conviction of the robber.

San Francisco, July 27, 1875.

JOHN J. VALENTINE,
General Supt.

■ Black Bart reward poster. *Author's collection.*

Over the next eight years, Boles robbed twenty-eight stages in locales stretching from the Gold Rush country to the coast and southern Oregon. After robbing the stage between Point Arena and Duncan's Mills on August 3, 1877, Charley Boles left a bit of doggrerel on a stump nearby, which would resound forever on the pages of California history:

Here I lay me down to sleep
to wait the coming morrow.
perhaps success, perhaps defeat
And everlasting Sorrow.

I've labored long and hard for bread
for honor and for riches
But on my corns to long you've tred
You fine haried sons of Bitches

Let come what will I'll try it on
My condition can't be worse,
and if there's money in that Box
Tis munny in my purse

It was signed, "Black Bart, the Po8." This was the mysterious bandit's fourth robbery and now he had a name. It was quickly to become the most famous name in stage robbing history.

Operating out of San Francisco, Bart walked to most of his robbery sites. Although nearly fifty years old, he had prodigious stamina and could walk for days without tiring. He rightly assumed that renting horses or riding in trains or stagecoaches would just leave a trail that would eventually lead to his capture.

A typical robbery of Bart's was later described by stage driver Horace Williams, driving north out of Redding on the evening of October 8, 1881:

> I had three passengers riding inside and, with fresh horses, was making fine time. We had reached almost the top of Bass Hill, which is 14 miles from Redding, when one of the passengers asked me the time. I told him just 12 P.M.

> About three minutes after we had reached the top of the hill, I saw what I thought was an animal running down the hill towards me, but when he straightened up and raised his gun, I knew what was up and halted at his command.

> "Throw that box out," he said, but when I explained to him that the express box was locked to the stage, he asked me how many passengers I had. I told him three inside and he gave me orders for them to get out and walk away down the road...As they came down past the team he came toward the stage and when they had gone about three hundred feet away he told me to get down and hold my leaders. I did so and he stood on the front wheel and broke the box open with a small ax he carried under his belt, putting everything into a white

■ Bart robbed the Oroville to LaPorte stage three times. The coach, shown here on the street at Oroville, has two women posing on the driver's seat. *California State Library.*

sack he carried and also threw out the mail sacks to be opened after I had driven on.

I remarked that it was a beautiful night and he answered, "It is." After he had ordered me back on the stage, I said: "How did you make it?"

■ George Hackett nearly cut short Bart's stage robbing career. *John Boessenecker collection.*

He answered: "Not very well for the chances I have to take."

Between holdups Bart lived a life of retirement in San Francisco, posing as a mining man named Charles E. Bolton. He gambled some, enjoyed shows and saloon life, and occasionally would take a trip out of town to "look after his mining interests."

His closest call was in attempting the robbery of the stage between Oroville and LaPorte on July 13, 1882. He had just jumped out in front of the stage horses when the express messenger, George Hackett, cut loose with a shotgun. Bart scampered for cover, his scalp furrowed by the deadly buckshot.

Bart's last attempted holdup took place on the same road and spot as his first robbery. Early on the morning of November 3, 1883, he again stopped the Sonora to Milton stage. With a levelled shotgun, he had driver Reason McConnell unhitch the team and take them to the top of the next hill. Unknown to Bart, young Jimmy Rolleri carrying a .44 Henry rifle, had gotten off the coach a short distance back and had walked around the hill, hoping for a shot at some deer. After Bart had begun trying to break open the coach strong box, McConnell waved his hat at Rolleri, and the two began walking toward the coach and the bandit. Bart emerged from the coach suddenly, saw the two figures approaching, and bolted for the brush. McConnell, who was carrying the rifle, got off two quick shots, but missed. Young Rolleri grabbed his weapon back, fired, and saw the outlaw stagger, then disappear into the trees and brush.

■ Stage driver Reason McConnell. *Author's collection.*

■ Reported to be the last stage held up by Black Bart, now restored and in a private collection. *Meade Simpson collection.*

A civilian posse and Calaveras Sheriff Benjamin K. Thorn were quickly on the scene. Some blood-splattered letters indicated the bandit had been wounded, and when Thorn found a valise Bart had left at his camp, the noted bandit's days were numbered. In the valise was a handkerchief and an all important laundry mark.

Wells, Fargo Special Officer James B. Hume employed private detective Harry Morse to find where that laundry mark— F.X.O.7 —had originated. Morse thought San Francisco would be a good place to start and he began a canvas of the ninety-one laundries in the city. Within a week, the detective had discovered the California Laundry on Stephenson Street to be the source of the mark. Charles E. Bolton, alias Black Bart, was quickly in the toils of the law.

Black Bart's capture and the revelation of his identity made for sensational copy in the California press. To the public he seemed a dapper rogue, even a Robin Hood, who robbed only the treasure boxes of wealthy corporations and never the passengers of the coaches he stopped. Jim Hume, the Wells, Fargo detective, had other ideas on the matter, however:

This is a delusion. He is, in fact, the meanest and most pusil-

■ Black Bart's captors: *Left to right,* Sheriffs Tom Cunningham, Ben Thorne, and Harry Morse. *Standing,* Appleton Stone and John Thacker.
John Boessenecker collection.

lanimous thief in the entire catalogue, for by his own statement he made all his large hauls from the mail, which he always rifled, and from which, excepting his last robbery, he always obtained more than from the express, and by so doing he robbed the most needy, those who, to save a small express charge, used the mails as a means of transmitting their money. From these hard earnings Black Bart, with his boasted magnanimity, realized his largest revenue.

And, Hume was always quick to add details of Boles' desertion of his wife and children while he revelled in the theaters and dance halls of San Francisco.

Taken back to Calaveras County, Bart pleaded guilty to the last attempted robbery and was sentenced to six years at San Quentin. Under the name C. E. Bolton, he was received on November 21, 1883, as No. 11046, and he was released on good behavior four years later, on January 21,

■ This and several other photographs were taken of the famous bandit after his capture. *Courtesy Wells, Fargo.*

1888. Reported later that year at Visalia, Black Bart then disappeared. Although there were reported sightings in New York, Saint Louis, Hawaii, and California over the years, the old man was, so far as is known, never seen again.

Hoeper, George, *Black Bart, Boulevardier Bandit*; Dajani, Laika, *Black Bart, Elusive Highwayman-Poet*; Hume and Thacker's "Robbers' Record"; Dillon, Richard, *Wells Fargo Detective*; Calaveras *Weekly Citizen*, November 17, 1883; *Redding Searchlight*, April 1, 1930; San Francisco *Daily Alta California*, November 14, 1883; *San Francisco Chronicle*, January 6, 1884; Fresno *Daily Evening Expositor,* August 6, 1889; San Francisco *Examiner*, April 3, 1887; Stockton *Evening Mail,* November 20, 1883; Robert Chandler, Wells, Fargo Bank Historical Services, San Francisco.

HANK MONK

Legend of the Sierra

Of all the stage drivers who handled the ribbons in California, Henry James Monk was probably the most famous. Coupled with being an excellent driver, he could also tell a good story and so helped create his own place in California stagecoach history. It was "Hank" Monk who carried Horace Greeley, the famous editor of the *New York Tribune*, over the Sierra to keep an 1859 lecture date in Placerville. When Greeley complained they were going too fast, Hank had replied, "Keep your seat, Horace. I'll get you there on time."

The story may very well be apocryphal, but the fact remains that it made a name for Monk, and many other tales emphasize his story-telling propensities. The following anecdote, reported by a stage passenger in the San Francisco *Daily Alta California* on November 13, 1864, took place just a few years after the Greeley incident:

Who that has ever traveled over the Sierra Nevada on the Pioneer Line of stages, but has encountered Hank Monk, who has achieved a celebrity on the stage almost rivalling that of Charles Kean. Hank, besides being a dashing driver, always up to schedule time, is like the most of his class — a bit of a wag.

On one trip a nervous old gentleman in spectacles, unused to mountain travel, crossing the Sierras on his way to Washoe, by some means happening to be placed alongside our hero, and everything being new to him, for it was his first appearance on any stage in California, was curious to know the why and wherefore of everything, wanting detailed explanations, and distracting the attention of the "Governor" of the vehicle from his fiery team.

Looking over his gold-rimmed specs, and casting his eyes down among the mail bags in the "boot," at their feet, he spied a hatchet; A horrid suspicion flashed across the nervous man's mind, and he tremblingly enquired the use of this indispensable accompaniment — which his imagination distorted into the tomahawk of the "ruthless savage," of whose murderous deeds he had read in the "Yaller kivored"; raw head and bloody bones stories familiar in his youthful days. Knowing his man, and wishing to put a stop to his inquisitorial leading and cross-questioning, Monk gravely replied: "Well, sir, I don't often tell the use I make of that hatchet; but as you seem to be a sensible man, and one whom I can trust with the secret, I'll tell you. The fact is, there have a good many accidents occurred on this line; limbs been broken, and other injuries from the overturning of coaches, for which the Company have had to pay heavy damages; now, in order to avoid any such after-claps, when an upset occurs, and passengers have legs or arms broken, or are otherwise seriously injured, we end the matter by knocking them in the head with a hatchet and putting them out of their misery at once."

When he passed on, the Virginia City *Enterprise* of March 6, 1883, began his obituary in a manner Hank would have truly appreciated. "Hank Monk," it began, "the famous stage driver is dead. He has been on the down grade for some time. On Wednesday his foot lost its final hold on the brake and his coach could not be stopped until, battered and broken on a sharp turn, it went over into the canyon, black and deep, which we call death…"

Thomas Brown

alias Tom Foster

■ Glaring at the camera in this mug shot, Tommy Brown was one of early California's most dangerous desperadoes.
John Boessenecker collection.

Born in Missouri about 1854, Tommy Brown was living in Yuba County with his brother, John, and half brother, Joe, in the early 1870s. There seems to have been at least two sisters in the family, also. The boys were all laborers who longed to make a fast buck. John, who gloried in the cognomen of "Rattling Jack," went off to become a gambler, while Joe and Tommy thought they could do better as rustlers. Joe was first to run afoul of the law. He was reported to have done time for horse theft, entering San Quentin in October 1865. All three brothers were on a slippery slope headed for death and disaster.

Tom and Joe joined a gang of horse thieves operating in the central part of the state. Other members of the group included David Tye and Volney Cleveland. Things were running smoothly until late summer of 1874, when lawmen began to close in. Tom fled to Modoc County in the north, where he was arrested and returned to Stockton. Joe was in the same jail on a charge of burglary and horse theft. Returned to Sutter County for trial, Tom received a two-year prison sentence for grand larceny. He took up residence at San Quentin as No. 6204 on October 16, 1874. A few

■ David Tye. *Author's collection.*

■ The Brown brothers were very familiar with the San Joaquin County Courthouse, shown here. *Author's collection.*

days later, brother Joe arrived, fresh from his conviction in Stockton.

When another of the gang, Volney Cleveland, was convicted also, he appealed his case but was promptly indicted on another horse theft charge in which the Brown brothers were involved. Tom and Joe were brought back to Stockton by the sheriff to testify, as reported in the Stockton *Daily Evening Herald*, November 28, 1874:

> Witnesses Foster and Brown the two young men who were brought to this city last night in charge of Sheriff Cunningham, are once again reclining in our County Jail. They are half brothers, and have had quite a history in the line of horse stealing, having been in the business for some years. They both blame themselves for being caught....

■ Sheriff Tom Cunningham. *John Boessenecker collection.*

Both brothers refused to testify, however, stating they might be incriminating themselves. Later Sheriff Cunningham jumped up in court, claiming that the prisoner Cleveland was giving signals to the witnesses. As it turned out, Cleveland was convicted without the Brown brothers' testimony, and he was received at San Quentin on December 19, 1874.

When Tommy was released on July 5, 1876, he went straight to Stockton to look up Dave Tye, his old horse thief buddy. He found Tye living with his parents at their Twenty-one Mile House, a wayside hotel south of Stockton. Tom helped Tye with some odd jobs around the place, probably for room and board. As work fell off in the fall, the two began talking of stopping a stage. Traveling to Chico to visit an ex-convict friend named Charles Frazier, Tom learned that his brother had broken out of prison and was anxious to see him. The two brothers met and together with Tye decided to rob the Shasta stagecoach running between Yreka and Redding. They missed the stage the first two days, but on November 3, 1876, they stopped the coach and made a good haul: $1,230 in currency, a gold bar worth $275, $130 in gold notes from the U.S. Mail bags, $1,060 in gold dust and $45 in gold notes from the Wells, Fargo box.

The job went smoothly, but Tye had performed poorly and was dismissed. The brothers planned to tackle the next coach just ten days later. Visiting Charles Frazier, their ranch foreman friend, the

■ Stage at the Redding railroad depot during the period of the Brown brothers' robbery.
California State Library.

Brown boys spent several days helping him dig post holes, while coaxing him into participating in the next robbery. After Frazier agreed to provide horses for the expedition, the two brothers hid along the road on the trail from Downieville to Marysville, stopping the coach as reported in the *Marysville Daily Appeal*, November 14, 1876:

> While the driver was trying to rein up his team, Mr. Scammon, a Downieville banker, fired from the stage, without effect. The fire was immediately returned by the robbers and Mr. Scammon seriously wounded…. When the box and mail bag was thrown out one of the robbers stopped and brought out an axe with which he broke it open…. They then demanded all the money and jewelry from the passengers and

got from one $60 in gold and a $300 watch, and from another $70 and about $20 in jewelry, and a small sum from another. They then went through the male passengers regularly; even the pockets of Mr. Scammon who was on the back seat wounded....

Fleeing the scene, the brothers stole fresh horses from the ranch of Charles L. Wilson at Norco, then fled to Nevada, trailed by Charley Wilson, the rancher's son; a Mexican tracker; and Butte County Deputy Constable Alonzo Dolliver. At Susanville an eight-man posse was acquired, and the group pressed their pursuit. On November 21, young Wilson's posse came within sight of the two Brown boys at a corral near Deep Holes Springs in Nevada. When the fugitive brothers began to run, Wilson and others opened fire, seriously wounding Joe in the thigh and capturing Tom. According to the *Butte Record*, up to this point Dolliver and Charley Wilson had believed they were just trailing two horse thieves:

■ The pain in the eyes of the dying Joe Brown is evident as he is propped up for his mug shot.
John Boessenecker collection.

On searching the suspects, a little over fourteen ounces of gold dust was found, together with $52.50 in coin. They begged hard and earnestly for the constable to throw away the gold dust and begged for their release, offering to give their captors $1,000 if allowed to go free. At this juncture Mr. Dolliver immediately commenced to "smell a mice."

Realizing they had a pair of stage robbers in tow, Dolliver and his posse returned to Chico. As Joe Brown lay in the Chico jail groaning in agony from his wound, other lawmen were gathering evidence against the outlaws. Joe died on December 5, after "expressing a wish to die," reported the *Butte Record*, "and begged the attendants would give him poison and end his misery."

When Jim Hume and Marysville officer Henry McCoy told Tom of the evidence collected against him, the outlaw promptly implicated David Tye and Charles Frazier, who were apprehended and sentenced to seven and seventeen years, respectively. Tye's mother and sister were also arrested for having some of the stolen money, but they were apparently dismissed for lack of evidence.

Wells, Fargo's standing reward of $300 for each of the robbers had been matched by the state, the wounded passenger adding another $500. Of the $1,100 in rewards, only Wells, Fargo paid its share—but it was many years later in September 1892!

Tommy Brown was given a prompt trial, convicted and received on January 13, 1877, as No. 7336 to serve a ten-year sentence in San Quentin. Promising to testify against Charley Frazier, Tommy was taken from prison on April 13, 1877, and placed in the Marysville jail to await the trial. After Frazier's conviction, Brown was kept in jail pending his own appeal. It was just the break he was looking for.

In the cell across from Brown was one Wee Lee, a notorious Chinese thief and jailbreaker who had escaped from this same jail five times in the last fourteen months. At every opportunity, the two jailbirds plotted to escape, first securing the confidence of another Chinese prisoner, Ah King. Late on the night of April 25, Ah King, a petty thief who was not locked

■ The Yuba County jail had little chance against the ingenuity of Tommy Brown and his Chinese allies. *Author's collection.*

up at night, removed a bar from a window and used it to pry open the doors on Brown's and Wee Lee's cells. The three prisoners were now loose in the hallway and escaped to the yard through the window where the bar had been removed. The yard was surrounded by a two-story brick wall, which the men tunneled through, and they were free.

Tommy ditched his two Chinese pals, took a horse from the sheriff's stable, then rode quickly out of town on the Colusa road.

■ Martin Myers, when he was sent up for another stage robbery in 1885.
San Quentin Museum Association.

Riding north along the Sacramento River, Brown met an old pal named Tom Connors (alias Durant) and Martin Myers. They both needed money and agreed to rob the Shasta stage running between Roseburg and Redding. The robbery came off without a hitch on the evening of May 27, 1877, but only fifty dollars and a few watches were realized. The bandits split up, Brown heading north again, stopping for several days at Little Shasta. Here he accidentally met Lon Dolliver, who was in town to serve a warrant. Dolliver was angry at the Marysville officers who had spirited Brown from Chico to Marysville after he had been captured originally. He did not arrest Brown at this time, but spent some time with him and even promised not to give him away. Tommy had no sooner headed north again, however, than Dolliver contacted Deputy Sheriff John Hendricks and Wells, Fargo shotgun messenger John Reynolds, who obtained horses and took up the chase.

Crossing the Oregon line, the fugitive was shoeing his horse at Ashland when pursuing officers got the drop on him. The outlaw found himself promptly secured in the Yreka jail. Brown first gave the name Foster and insisted they had the wrong man, but he soon saw the game was up when stolen articles in his possession were identified. While in the Yreka jail, Tommy was observed taking off his boot, then slipping off his ankle shackles. He was quickly adorned with heavier and tighter irons for the trip south to attend his Redding trial.

■ Charles "Red" Frazier.
Author's collection.

Telling various stories of the officers who had captured him, Brown managed to get the Butte and Yuba county officers into a newspaper squabble, into which even Jim Hume became involved. The outlaw must have had a good laugh over the trouble he had caused.

Realizing he had too much going against him, Brown pleaded guilty to his latest stage robbery and was sentenced to seventeen years at San Quentin. Deputy Sheriff Robert Kennedy escorted Brown back to prison and later reported "…the slippery fellow tried numerous tricks to escape on the way down, and close watching was required to checkmate him." He again took up residence at the prison as No. 7336 on September 22, 1877.

But Tommy never gave up. Brought to Marysville to testify in the Frazier trial, he managed to secrete an old coal shovel in his cell and at night began tunneling out. His cell had a brick floor, and after removing a number of the bricks, he began digging. He had struck the concrete foundation of a hotel next door when he was caught backing out of the tunnel into his cell.

When a local character called at the jail to see his old pal Tommy, the *Marysville Daily Appeal* reported:

> The man calling claimed to be a particular friend of Brown's, and here comes in another part of the joke. While the man was hugging Brown, the noted thief took a breastpin from his friend's bosom worth $8 or $10. When the owner discovered his pin was gone friendship ceased between Tommy and the countryman, and hard words ensued. Finally, officer Colford, who was on duty, told Tommy he must tell where the pin was, and Tommy responded saying "It would

■ The Folsom State Prison guard post where Tommy Brown entered in 1880. The guard could see approaching visitors, as well as the prison yard. Housing for the fourteen guards and their families is in the background. *Folsom History Museum.*

be found in the back yard, as he had thrown it through the window."

At San Quentin in April 1878, Tom was stripped and searched before being taken to Shasta to testify in the Connor trial. He was holding a package of cigarettes while searchers found two ribbon

■ The mess hall at Folsom, as it appeared when Tommy Brown made his last escape.
California State Library.

saws sewn into his clothes. On the way, he was guarded again by Deputy Bob Kennedy, who never took his eyes from the bad man. Arriving at the Shasta jail, Kennedy took Tommy's cigarette package and emptied it on a table. The *Shasta Courier* commented:

> The mysterious little package of cigarettes was…found to contain numerous skillfully made keys and wires for unlocking handcuffs and shackles.

Because of his shenanigans Brown was moved to the new maximum security Folsom State Prison in early September 1880. Working in the prison quarry, he quickly learned that if he behaved himself, he could obtain an easier job. In time, he was put to work in the prison kitchen and allowed various liberties. Before daylight on the morning of June 15, 1886, he saw an opportunity for a break. There were no walls at Folsom, but cell blocks and other buildings partially surrounded a yard. Strategically placed around the area were guard towers with Gatling guns, manned by eagle-eyed, sharpshooting guards.

Notice of Tommy Brown's Folsom escape. *Author's collection.*

That morning, as breakfast was being prepared, Tom innocently asked a guard if he could step out back for a smoke. Given permission, he stepped through the door and "severed his connection with that reformatory institution," as one newspaper put it.

Hiding in a large group of boulders above the quarry, Tom watched as searching parties looked for him all day. That night, he slipped away, sprinkling his trail with cayenne pepper to foil the dogs that would be tracking him. He made a three-mile trek to a nearby farm and hid in a barn that night. Dozing in a pile of hay, he left the next day after sundown, making his way toward Ione, where he spotted a farmer working in his hay field. Tommy later recalled for a newspaperman how he:

"...went down to a nearby creek, took off his striped pants and buried them. Fortunately he left the prison with a citizen's overcoat, so that his striped shirt was hidden from view. He told the farmer that he had been bathing in the creek and that the wind had blown his pants into the water and they had been carried away. The farmer gave him a pair of overalls and Tommy continued on his journey."

Wanted posters with photographs of the convict were sent

Brown was captured in the saloon of the hotel at Mammoth Grove, shown here as it looked at the time. *Author's collection.*

all over the area, and Calaveras County Sheriff Ben Thorn was quickly on the alert. Tommy made his way through the foothills, then crossed into Calaveras County and headed for the Big Trees area. Thorn was already on his trail and tracked him for some fifty miles. Brown was in a wayside saloon near the Big Trees when the sheriff came up behind him and grabbed his shoulder. "Brown refused to submit to arrest," noted a newspaper account, "assuring the sheriff that he had made a mistake and threatened to assault the officer if the arrest was insisted upon. In the struggle that followed, Brown was overpowered and stunned by a blow on the head and the handcuffs were at once put on his wrists." Two Folsom guards picked him up in Thorn's custody at San Andreas. The *Folsom Weekly Telegraph*, July 17, 1886, reported:

Tommy Brown is now enjoying solitary confinement for awhile.

The *Telegraph* noted that Tommy had but twenty-two months left to serve, but would now have to remain about nine years more. However, it did not matter. Brown had been worn down. He could not win. He gave up any idea of escape, and after four years of good behavior, on February 7, 1890, he petitioned the prison directors for restoration of the credits he had lost during his final 1886 escape attempt.

His petition was finally granted and he was discharged on April 3, 1891. It was thought he might have returned to Missouri, but his further history is not known.

Hume and Thacker's "Robbers' Record"; Boessenecker, *Badge and Buckshot*; San Quentin Prison Register; Folsom Prison Register; California State Archives, Sacramento; *Stockton Daily Evening Herald*, November 17, 27, 28, 30, 1874; *Marysville Daily Appeal*, November 5, 14, 15, 23, 28, December 3, 21, 23, 24, 25, 1876; *Shasta Courier*, October 6, 1877, February 16, April 27, 1878; *Yreka Journal*, December 6, 1876, July 11, 1877; *Yreka Union*, July 14, September 22, 1877; *Folsom Weekly Telegraph*, July 3, 17, 1886: *Calaveras Chronicle*, March 6, 1880; *Calaveras Prospect*, June 2, 1886; *Sacramento Daily Record-Union*, June 16, 30, 1886, November 18, 1905.

Clodoveo Chavez

■ Thought to be the head of Chavez, this old, retouched photograph was obtained from Vincent Mercaldo many years ago. *Author's collection.*

Raised in the village surrounding Mission San Juan Bautista, Clodoveo was born in 1849 to Francisco and Dolores Chavez. With seven children in the family, Clodoveo and the older boys all probably worked to help put food on the table. The town was known simply as San Juan in those days, and Luis Raggio, Isaac Mylar, and their friend Clodoveo played childhood games in the dusty streets during the late 1850s. Mylar described his Californio pal as "rough, thick-necked, dark and heavy set," and "hard-looking," but not a bad boy. Raggio, however, later commented that Chavez was a bully, even as a boy.

As he grew older, Clodoveo worked at various laboring jobs, tended sheep, and also became a skilled vaquero. He was working for Estanislaus Hernandez in early 1873, when the notorious Tiburcio Vasquez rode into the ranch one day. Everyone knew Vasquez. He had done several terms at San Quentin and was suspected of many crimes, including murder. Vasquez was re-

■ The old mission town of San Juan was the home of Clodoveo Chavez in the days just after the great Gold Rush. *Author's collection.*

cruiting. He told Chavez of the carefree life of a bandido, and the poor vaquero liked what he heard. Despite the entreaties of Hernandez, Chavez rode off that day with the bandit leader.

On the evening of February 26, 1873, Vasquez, Chavez, and several others rode up to the store at Firebaugh's Ferry on the San Joaquin River. The *Fresno Weekly Expositor* reported:

> They made their appearance in the store about dark, all masked, save one, and commanded those in the store to lie down on the floor and keep quiet. Enforcing their demands by presenting cocked revolvers, they proceeded to tie the captors hands.... The robbers then began to make a general search for coin and valuables. About this time the stage drove up, which startled the outlaws somewhat, but a deputation went out and took charge of what money the driver had, and also Wells, Fargo & Co.'s box....

The bandits had hoped the stage would be carrying a large payroll from wealthy cattleman Henry Miller, but were disappointed. Instead, they continued to pillage the store, took what they could from the coach and driver, then fled into the night. That spring and summer they robbed various travelers in the Coast Range and San Joaquin Valley, then prepared for another major raid on a small village southeast of San Juan, in the Coast Range.

Riding into Tres Pinos in late August, they tied up many of their victims, shooting and killing three who resisted. Andrew Snyder, a store owner, later said Chavez wanted to kill him but Vasquez intervened. "He told Vasquez that I knew them and would be the cause of their arrest some time," wrote Snyder later. "Vasquez told him no, that I had submitted and had been a friend to their people and the first man that undertook to harm me he would shoot the top of his head off."

They fled with half a dozen stolen horses loaded with loot but also with

■ A small supply village for the ranchers and farmers in the Kings River area, Kingston proved to be too much for the bloody Vasquez gang. *Author's collection.*

posses on their trail. After several close brushes with lawmen, the gang struck again, holding up Jones' store three miles below Millerton on November 10. Again, they tied up all their victims, then fled, avoiding posses while hiding out in the Coast Range.

The day after Christmas 1873, the gang suddenly appeared again, this time at Kingston, a small village on the Kings River. Tying up over thirty residents, the bandits pillaged the town, but were chased out by sharpshooting rancher John Sutherland and some of his men. Several of the bandits were captured, and writing to Governor Newton Booth, Alameda lawman Harry Morse reported:

> Sir:—I rode 40 miles through the mountains today to get to the outside world and a post office. Three of the Vasquez party were wounded at the Kingston robbery, one of them, Refugio Montejos, has since died. Another named Manuel Lopez was shot through the neck and the worst man of the gang, to wit Chavez, was shot through the leg....

The gang split up after Kingston, but Chavez could ride again by February 25, 1874, when he and Vasquez robbed the stage at Coyote Holes in the Mojave Desert. Vasquez then fled to Southern California, where he was captured the following May and later hanged in San Jose on March 19, 1875. Chavez fled to Mexico, but

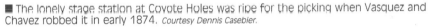
■ The lonely stage station at Coyote Holes was ripe for the picking when Vasquez and Chavez robbed it in early 1874. *Courtesy Dennis Casebier.*

returned to assemble a new gang in early 1875. He lost no time getting into action as reported in a Bakersfield newspaper:

> On Sunday night last he, with his band of outlaws, appeared at the store of Mr. Scoby on the South Fork of Kern River. They captured five horses, a large amount of store goods and $800 in money. Sheriff Bowers heard of them again afterward and on Monday telegraphed to the sheriff of Los Angeles County, as Chavez was evidently shaping his course in that direction.

■ When Vasquez paid for his crimes on the gallows, Chavez continued the gang's raids in Southern California.
Author's collection.

Chavez moved swiftly through the Mojave Desert country, pillaging travelers, mining camps, and isolated stores. Raiding stage stops at Little Lake and Granite Springs in late March, the outlaws also stopped and ransacked the goods of a party of teamsters near Borax Lake.

A squad of soldiers had pursued the bandits after a stage holdup in Indian Valley, forcing them to bury a Wells, Fargo box containing nearly $50,000. This loot was found by several treasure hunters many years later, in 1961.

There was a $2,000 state reward on the head of Chavez now. Several other stations and stages were plundered, however, before pursuing lawmen once again compelled Chavez to visit Old Mexico. He took a herd of stolen horses south, but when his animals were rustled in Mexico, he went to work on an Arizona ranch while again waiting for a favorable time to return to California.

Strangely enough, Clodoveo's boyhood acquaintance, Luis Raggio, was in the area at the time, working on the ranch of King Woolsey. One day in late October 1875, Raggio delivered some Woolsey cattle to the ranch of a man named Baker. To his surprise, he discovered Chavez was working for Baker under an assumed name. Raggio's younger brother, Vincent, was also at Baker's. When Luis learned that Vincent had stolen some Baker property at the direction of Chavez, he was furious. After giving the boy a stern lecture, Raggio went over to visit the outlaw. It was obvious after

■ Yuma was just a hot and isolated desert village when Raggio and his posse brought in the Chavez's body. *Author's collection.*

■ The ferry at Yuma where Raggio and his men crossed after the killing of Chavez. *Author's collection.*

the meeting that the boy was under the influence of the outlaw and Raggio determined to either capture Chavez, or kill him.

After confirming that the rewards were still in place, Raggio talked two friends, Clark Colvig and Harry Roberts, into assisting in the capture. Later, Raggio succinctly commented on the events that followed in a letter to his father:

> Next morning we rode over and I told my men to ride ahead and go to the house and wait for me. But as soon as they saw Chavez they told him to surrender and he ran and my partner shot him in the back and he fell dead.

The three men loaded the body into a wagon and took it to Yuma, where excited crowds of Mexicans surrounded the wagon. Chavez was known by an alias in the area, and at first it was assumed the wrong man had been killed. The local Mexican residents were considering lynching Raggio and his posse until Chavez's identity was verified and a coroner's jury found the killing justified. A Fort Yuma physician removed the bandit's head and it was transported back to California by Harry Roberts. Eventually, a reward of $2,199.42 was paid. In a *San Diego Union* interview in December 1875, Dolores Chavez, the brokenhearted mother of the dead desperado, could only be pragmatic about her loss:

> The mother of Chavez resides in Hollister, and when informed of the death of her son at the hands of the Raggio brothers, said she had no doubt it was true, as the Raggio boys were brought up in San Juan with Chavez and knew him well, and that there had been an enmity between them from boyhood. The old lady wept over the death of her mis-

guided son, but said she would rather he should die in this way than be dragged over the state and then hanged as Vasquez was.

Secrest, William B., "The Return of Chavez," *True West*; 1860 Federal Census, Monterey County, California; Mylar, Isaac, *Early Days at the Mission San Juan Bautista*; Latta, Frank F., "The Death of Chavez"; *Fresno Weekly Expositor*, March 5, November 25, December 31, 1873; *San Francisco Chronicle,* March 20, 21, 24, 27, April 11, 1875; *Yuma Sentinel*, December 4, 1875; San Francisco *Daily Morning Call*, January 11, 1876; documents and reward files in California State Archives, Sacramento.

Louis J. Dreibelbis

alias Walker, alias Dribblesbee

■ Stage robberies seemed simple enough to Louis Dreibelbis, but he never took "Murphy's Law" into account.
John Boessenecker collection.

T he coach rumbled out of Downieville at three in the morning on June 23, 1873, heading for the regularly scheduled trip to Marysville. Besides three passengers, the stage was carrying some $2,600 in gold coin, dust, and a gold bar for Marysville banks. About twenty-one miles east of Marysville, driver Johnny Sharp saw three men scrambling down an embankment in front of the coach. As he hauled up on his reins, he saw the men were masked and pointing shotguns at him. One man stood at the head of the horses, while the others came alongside and called out, "Hand down the box." Daniel Kime was riding on the driver's seat and he promptly hauled out the box and threw it to the ground. Pulling the treasure box to the side of the road, one of the bandits said, "Don't be frightened. We won't disturb you."

As the outlaw began a spirited pounding on the box with a rock, the driver proposed to move on, as his horses were becoming difficult to manage.

"Hold where you are!" commanded a bandit.

When the box gave in, the robber took what he wanted and returned the box to the stage, telling Sharp to "drive on."

Both Kime and Sharp had paid close attention to the robbers. The leader, who had handled the box, was a tall man wearing a calico shirt that was not tucked into his trousers. While opening the box, he had badly gashed the back of his hand, which had bled profusely. Although the three road agents were masked with

sacks over their heads, Sharp thought they were local characters whose clothes he had recognized. His suspicions were confirmed by the *Downieville Messenger* of June 28:

> It is thought that one of the parties, at least, is known. He is supposed to be a man who has just served out a term in San Quentin... The chief actor in the robbery was a large man, and the description given of him tallies pretty clearly with that of Louis J. Dribblesbey (sic), sent from this county to the State Prison in 1855 (sic), for a term of twelve years....

■ Sacramento police officer Sam Deal, who helped round up the LaPorte stage robbers.

Wells, Fargo had promptly offered $500 each for the robbers, plus one fourth of any amount recovered of the treasure. With this incentive, lawmen were quickly on the highwaymen's trail. The robbers had been wearing sacks on their feet to disguise their tracks, and the lawmen found a discarded mask on their route of travel. Just outside Grass Valley, evidence of a campfire was found where the men probably camped. and, while the search proved unsuccessful, it was neither the beginning nor the end of the story.

Louis Dreibelbis had been a respectable citizen of Galena, Illinois, where he had served as county sheriff. He traveled to California during the Gold Rush in 1849 and apparently engaged in mining until the mid-1860s, when he drifted into bad company.

With two mining partners named Dutch Fred Carpenter and Jack Wolfington, Dreibelbis held up the LaPorte stage in August 1865. The robbers obtained a gold bar worth $2,199 and some $800 in gold dust. The gold bar was sawed into three pieces and the gold dust was split up, but when Wolfington stole Dreibelbis' share, a fight took place and the loot was returned at the muzzle of a pistol. Officers quickly found one of the pawned sections of the gold bar, and Dreibelbis and his two cohorts were soon in irons. Dreibelbis and Carpenter both pled guilty, while Wolfington was apparently released for lack of evidence. The demeanor of Dreibelbis in court was hardly conducive to leniency from the judge, as reported in the San Francisco *Police Gazette*, October 14, 1865:

> Dreibelbis is a man between forty and fifty years of age, and hardened to the last degree. He told his story of the robbery as though it was a good joke; too good, in fact, to keep. He implicated Dutch Fred Carpenter, Wolfington and himself. He said they all entered into the scheme voluntarily, etc. He gave what he apparently calculated to be a very humorous account of his treatment in the Sacramento Station House; what they had to eat, and their accommodations generally….

Sentenced to a twelve-year term, Dreibelbis entered San Quentin as No. 3106 on October 6, 1865. He kept his nose clean, and when his sentence was commuted, he was released on September 30, 1871. He apparently returned to mining but, unfortunately, was soon mixed up with questionable characters again, but not for an entirely selfish motive. This time, it would seem, a woman was a factor.

Dreibelbis had been courting a young Gilroy, California, school teacher through the mail for some time. Advertising himself in a San Francisco literary journal as a "lonesome miner" who wanted a

■ Stagecoaches meeting the train at Colfax a few years before the Dreibelbis holdup.
Southern Pacific Railroad collection.

■ A contemporary newspaper sketch of a stagecoach robbery in progress. *Author's collection.*

wife with whom to share his life, Dreibelbis convinced twenty-two-year-old Eleanor Berry that he was wealthy and lacked only a companion to make his life perfect. A mutually communicated attraction blossomed to the extent that when Dreibelbis proposed marriage, Eleanor readily accepted. The date was set for July 27, 1873, when she would join him at the Grass Valley cottage of his landlady in Nevada County. Meanwhile, Dreibelbis and two pals had stopped and robbed the Downieville stage as previously related.

Eleanor put together her trousseau and in late July boarded a train for the first leg of her journey. At Colfax, she disembarked with other passengers and boarded a stagecoach traveling to Grass Valley, Nevada City, and other mountain mining camps. The weather was hot, but the thirteen passengers enjoyed the scenery and were entertained by an attorney named Ryan who sang some lusty Irish ballads to help pass the time.

Five miles from Grass Valley, driver Bob Scott suddenly pulled up the six-horse coach. Looking out the stage windows, the passengers saw four masked men blocking the road. "We want that treasure box," one of the highwaymen yelled, "so climb down and unhitch your team." The driver did as he was told while two of the bandits herded the passengers down the road where they were lined up next to a fence.

61

The rear seat of the coach was a padded iron safe on which the passengers could sit. On this particular evening, the safe was carrying $7,000 in gold coin for Wells, Fargo.

As the outlaws prepared to blow open the safe, Eleanor Berry screeched that they would destroy her trousseau, which was in her trunk on top of the coach. When they agreed to remove it to a place of safety, she pointed it out and it was passed down to one of the bandits who had a noticeably

■ Stage robber Ormstead Thurman. *Author's collection.*

fresh scar on the back of his hand. The safe was then blown, the loot

■ Wells, Fargo's Special Officer James B. Hume was one of the best of the early California detectives. *Author's collection.*

obtained, and the robbers disappeared into the brush and tree-covered hills. Although three hundred dollars worth of damage had been done to the stage, it was able to limp into Grass Valley that evening.

Scott quickly informed the Grass Valley officers of the robbery, then dropped Miss Berry off at a cottage on the outskirts of town where she was to be married. When Dreibelbis showed up, the bride and groom assumed their places, and the minister proceeded with the ceremony. Afterwards, the couple were signing their marriage documents when Eleanor was startled to notice a scar on her new husband's hand. She realized with hor-

ror that she had just married one of the bandits who had robbed her stagecoach. She ran screaming from the room and caught the next stage leaving for Sacramento and San Jose. Dreibelbis quietly disappeared, his new bride failing to notify the authorities of her husband's dual identity.

Nevada County Sheriff Joseph Perrin was quickly at the robbery scene, tracking the outlaws. He picked up several men who were able to prove alibis, but Ormstead Thurman, an ex-convict, was another matter. His alibi was provided by a local saloon owner and known "fence" and associate of outlaws. Thurman, who had a long criminal record, was also identified by his sunken eyes, as noticed by several victims on the stage.

Meanwhile, Wells, Fargo's new special investigator, James B. Hume, had picked up a man named Walker in Coloma. Walker had in his possession a small bar of gold bullion and some gold coins that were powder-burned as if in an explosion. The bullion bar was from an earlier robbery of the Downieville stage on June 23. In jail, Walker finally broke down and admitted being Louis Dreibelbis. After trying to wheedle complete immunity out of the lawman, the outlaw finally "peached" on his pals, identifying Thurman, Nat Stover, and George Lane as the balance of the gang. He also admitted to the Downieville stage robbery in June. Eventually, the outlaws all received long terms in San Quentin, with the exception of Dreibelbis. By turning in his pals, he had earned his immunity and returned to Illinois.

And Eleanor Berry? She returned home to Gilroy and never did reveal the secret of her terrible experience. The *Grass Valley Union* revealed the marriage on August 3, but did not identify the groom as one of the robbers. On the contrary, he was noted as being "a most excellent man." It was left to Hume to tell the whole story some years later. Eleanor only admitted that her bridegroom had not turned out to be what she expected. A month after the holdup she reportedly attempted suicide by chloroform but was resuscitated in time to save her life. After that, she dropped from sight and one of early California's most bizarre stage holdup stories was relegated to history.

Hume and Thacker, "Robbers' Record"; San Quentin State Prison Register; Boessenecker, John, "The Bride and the Brigand," *The Californians*; Dillon, Richard, *Wells, Fargo Detective*; *Sacramento Daily Record-Union*, April 6, 1889; *Grass Valley Daily Union*, June 25, 26, 27, July 3, August 2, 3, 8, 14, 15, 17, 19, 27, 1873; *Downieville Messenger*, June 28, 1873; *Marysville Daily Appeal*, September 12, 16, 23, 1865; *San Francisco Police Gazette*, August 19, October 14, September 16, 1865.

BOB SCOTT, THE STAGE DRIVER

The stage robbed by the Dreibelbis gang was driven by Bob Scott, a popular driver of the area. While researching an article on mining, a San Francisco newspaper reporter toured Nevada County on Scott's coach and devoted much space to the idiosyncracies of the reinsman:

From Colfax to Grass Valley, as the crow flies, might be eight or nine miles; as the stages go, wind around and up and down, it is about fourteen. When the Chronicle *representative landed at Colfax he found an inviting (!) mud wagon awaiting to convey him to the bustling town of Grass Valley.*

And so the Chronicle *representative soon found himself sitting beside the Jehu of the establishment, one Bob Scott, who has made the round trip twice a day for fifteen years past. As a general rule stage drivers are companionable fellows. They are full of experience; know every man who has ever traveled the road; understand human nature, and can spin more yarns than any ordinary man could remember in a year.*

The weather was not pleasant; the air chilly, and the clouds lowering. Lighting a cigar, we asked Bob's opinion, "Will it rain before we get in?" and gathering up the reins as he cracked his whip, Bob made answer: "Well, I rather guess it will. You see I bet two bottles of wine last night that it would rain before 12 o'clock tonight, and it must come. I haven't been driving this stage these fifteen years without becoming a weather sharp. Last night the moon was belly down, and that means full of water. The old Indian tradition that when you can hang your powder horn on one horn of the moon, it won't rain, don't apply here. She's got to lay on her back for fair weather." And with this oracular weather prognostication, we climbed up the mountain side overlooking Colfax.

Bob's barometrical prediction was verified, for long before we rolled into Grass Valley the heavens opened and rolled down torrents of rain and bushels of hail. "When it rains up here," remarked Bob, "it rains; and when it blows, it blows. No discount on either. Been down to the Bay in Winter — don't rain there worth carrying a parasol."

The roads from Colfax to Grass Valley are horrible in Winter. As the upper ridge road was considered better than the lower, Bob took the former. As the mud wagon would mercilessly jump up and down, and thump and labor, it wasn't the pleasantest kind of riding. An inside passenger stopped the stage, saying, "I want a rope." "What for?" asked Bob. "To lash myself to the seat."

"Oh, you be damned!" ejaculated Bob, as he whipped up his team. "If I had known you were so hard to please, I'd have come the lower road. Why, this road's as smooth as a barn floor compared to that. Get along, boys!" And so we rolled into Grass Valley.

Grass Valley Union, March 22, 1873

Lawrence B. "Buck" English

■ "Buck" English found it difficult to decide between decency or being a desperado, and he paid a high price for making the wrong choice. *California State Archives.*

"Twenty-five years ago I was a farmer's boy in Lake County. Now I am a convict, sentenced to spend the rest of my life within these walls."

It was Buck English speaking—a desperado of wide repute in old California. The story of Buck and his family is a tale of violence, crime and redemption, little-known to a modern generation.

Benjamin F. English and his wife, Pauline, were among a party of Missouri immigrants arriving in the Oregon country in 1846. Members of Pauline's family, the Durbins, had traveled in the same caravan, as had others of the English clan. They apparently settled north of Corvallis on 640 acres where Benjamin farmed and carved a home out of the wilderness. Five children had come west with Ben and Pauline, and a son, Lane Buchanan, was born at their farm on November 10, 1853. When young Lane was ten years old, in 1863, the family moved to California. The move may, or may not, have had something to do with a tragedy of the previous year. In late 1862, David, the eldest of the English children, was lynched, with two other men, in the Idaho mines after operating briefly as high-waymen. An 1881 county history stated that the family had lost five children, the six remaining being Charles H., Benjamin F., Harmon H., Eugene, Lane B. (Buck), and Lucretia.

The family and various other relatives settled in Green Valley, in Solano County. The English family lived near Perry Durbin, Pauline English's brother, a hulking Kentuckian. A quarrel, originating over some property, together with Durbin's rejoicing over Lincoln's assassination, ignited a bloody fight between the two families at the Bridgeport polls on September 6, 1865. In a political argument, Ben English called Perry Durbin a liar and began shooting when Durbin appeared to be drawing a weapon. Although wounded, Durbin pulled out a large dirk and began slashing his nephew, Charles English. Charlie had been stabbed three or four times when he finally put a bullet into his attacker. His father now jumped in and began carving on the infuriated Durbin. When young Perry English, named for his uncle, jumped into the fight, he was shot dead by Frank Grady, a cousin, who quickly disappeared. Fortunately, young Lane was not around.

"I postponed the inquest on the boy Perry English three hours," recalled the coroner at the time, "thinking that I would have to hold an inquest on the father and brother, too, but they recovered. The Coroner's jury found Frank Grady guilty of the murder and I issued a warrant for his arrest, but he eluded the pursuers...." Grady was later captured, tried twice, and acquitted. Charles, although terribly cut up, was convicted of assault with a deadly weapon and sentenced to two years in San Quentin.

■ John "Blackjack" Bowen, burglar, highwayman and ex-convict. *Author's collection.*

As he grew older, young Lane changed his name to Lawrence, but he was always "Buck" to the family. He and his brothers worked with their father on the farm, but the boys seemed to always be in trouble, primarily because they associated with ex-convicts, loafers, and robbers such as Bulger Raines and John "Blackjack" Bowen. A favored form of recreation was carousing in the dives of Spanishtown, near Napa, then refusing to pay for their entertainment. When pistols were brandished and threats—instead of payment—offered, the Mexican owners would back off. Since the area was considered "a nuisance to respectable people," the English brothers and their thug friends had things pretty much their own way.

One night in March 1868, the boys again marched over to Spanishtown for some entertainment at the expense of others. They had pulled their routine once too often, however. About 9:30 in the evening, there was a volley of pistol shots, and several of the roisterers fled back to town. When a crowd returned with them to a

■ Scene in old Middletown, in the days of the English boys. *Author's collection.*

Spanishtown dance hall, a horrible scene was discovered according to a report in the *Napa Register*:

Upon the floor in the center of the room lay the body of Daniel English in a pool of blood.... To add to the awful tableau, his brother Charley lay within a foot of him, groaning, and weltering in his own blood, which was flowing from a ghastly wound in the right breast....

It was thought Charley's wound was mortal, but an operation saved him. Dan English was dead, however. Four Mexicans were arrested, but it was quickly determined they had only acted in self-defense. Two of the group, Dolores and Guadalupe Coronado, rode over to Merced County the following month. Near Snelling, in a saloon dispute over drinks, the brothers were shot and killed by the owner, Joe Griffith. "Many persons," noted the *Napa Register,* "are of the opinion that they were followed up by friends of English with revengeful intent..."

In 1872, the English family moved to southern Lake County, where they purchased property near Middletown. Buck should have settled down to life as a farmer, but like his brothers, he continued to court trouble. In August 1875, Buck and a pal robbed several Chinese miners, following this up in October with a stage holdup. On the ninth they robbed the Calistoga Lower Lake stagecoach four miles south of Middletown. They obtained little loot, but Wells, Fargo offered a $500 reward for the two bandits.

Buck, along with a friend named William Turner, was arrested for stock theft in the summer of 1876. Buck's story was that he was gambling some and was a pretty wild character at the time, but had broken no laws.

A church group was determined to convert everyone and when a Captain John Good warned young English he must mend his ways or be run out of town, Buck pulled his pistol and ran Good off.

"Half an hour later someone told me he was coming up the street with a big navy pistol in his hand," Buck later recalled. "I stepped to the door...just as he was raising his hand to fire and cut loose myself and the first bullet struck his pistol hand and broke his fire-arm...."

Buck was not prosecuted for this, but later claimed he was framed on a rustling charge while working in his brother's butcher shop. Tried and convicted of grand larceny in September, Buck entered San Quentin, as No. 7235, in October 1876. He was exonerated after obtaining a new trial, but was no sooner released than he was back in trouble. Convicted on a robbery charge after he and several others had taken to holding up travelers on back country roads, Buck entered San Quentin, as No. 7984, on January 20, 1878, to serve a seven-year term.

Released in late October 1882, Buck apparently sought to make a new start and for two years drove a stage in Lake County. He was suspected of a stage robbery at the time of his father's death in 1883, and this may have been the reason he joined brother Ben, Jr., at his British Columbia ranch, working as a cowboy. Returning to California in 1886 to escort his mother north, Buck then continued his work herding cattle and breaking horses. He led an adventurous life, reportedly being badly wounded while scouting for the Canadian army during the Riel Rebellion. Later he smuggled whiskey over the border near Fort McLeod.

■ The stagecoach stopped by Buck English and Breckenridge in 1895. *Contemporary newspaper sketch in author's collection.*

In 1892, Buck was arrested in Oregon for robbing a Chinese miner near Baker City. He was convicted and sentenced to five years in prison, but in a personal interview, Buck was able to convince the governor he had been wrongfully accused. He was pardoned after serving two years of his sentence. In Portland, he worked for an electric light company, then as a bartender. In early 1895, Buck met R. N. Breckenridge, an ex-con he had known in prison. Broke from gambling and bitter over his prison experiences, English talked his pal into returning to California with him and the two boarded a San Francisco-bound steamer at Portland in mid-April 1895.

On May 7, 1895, the Calistoga and Clear Lake stage was proceeding along a stretch of level ground near the Napa-Lake County line. It was a beautiful afternoon and the coach was carrying six San Franciscans, heading for the resorts at Clear Lake. Suddenly, two masked men jumped from the bushes lining the road. "Throw up your hands," the bandit with a shotgun shouted, as his partner grabbed the lead horses. The passengers were quickly lined up and the express box broken open. When nothing was found in the box, the highway-

■ Two of the posse involved in the fight with English and Breckenridge were Theodore Bell (left) and Undersheriff R. A. Brownlee. *Contemporary newspaper sketches in author's*

men began robbing the passengers, taking some valuable watches and whatever money they had. "I noticed that the driver seemed to be very cool," recalled a passenger. "He chewed his tobacco naturally and expectorated in the usual way. I have since been told he had been held up once or twice before in about the same place."

When two freight wagons pulled up behind the coach, one of the bandits forced the two drivers to line up with the other victims, although they were not robbed. The passengers were then ordered back into the coach and the drive was told to drive on. The two freight teams followed.

Officers from both Lake and Napa counties were promptly on the robbers' trail. John Thacker, the Wells, Fargo detective, was also at the scene. The morning after the holdup, a phone call to Napa established that the robbers had camped in Berryessa Valley and had breakfast at Moore's ranch, near Monticello. The two suspects had told their host they were catching the stage for Napa. The Napa sheriff was absent, but Undersheriff R. A. Brownlee quickly organized a posse made up of himself, District Attorney Theodore A. Bell, John Williams, and John True.

Leaving town in a two-seat surrey, the posse hurried to meet the down stage, hoping the two outlaws would stay aboard the coach until they could set up an ambush. Before they could do so, however, the Napa stage, driven by Johnnie Gardiner, loomed up before them from around a bend in the road. Buck English sat beside Gardiner with a shotgun across his knees. His partner, Breckenridge, sat on a seat behind him. English realized the surrey was filled with officers at about the same time the posse spotted him as the highwayman they were seeking.

English got off the first shot, blasting a hole in Brownlee's shotgun stock and peppering the undersheriff's face with birdshot. The two vehicles were passing each other now as Williams fired and saw English lurch in his seat. "Drive on fast," shouted English as he poked his pistol in the driver's face and Breckenridge scrambled from the coach.

Bell jumped from the surrey and dropping to one knee fired a shotgun blast that also hit English, who fell into the driver, who had also been wounded. Bell was picked up as the surrey turned around and pursued the coach which had stopped in the road. True and Brownlee had hit the ground running and now pursued Breckenridge. After one shotgun blast from True, the outlaw surrendered with some minor wounds.

■ The wounded English as he lay on a jailhouse cot. *Contemporary newspaper sketch in author's collection.*

The stage, driven by Williams and carrying Bell and the badly wounded Gardiner and English, headed back to Napa. The surrey followed with the balance of the group. In Napa, physicians operated on English, who was thought to be mortally wounded as reported in a dispatch to the *San Francisco Chronicle:*

The surgeon says the probabilities are that the wounded man will not recover, but that owing to his hardy constitution he may pull through. English was greatly pleased with the operation and for the first time talked of his affairs. He said that he had a brother who was shot through the lungs in Napa some years ago and that the same operation was performed upon him with beneficial results.

This statement is considered important, as it is known that one of the English boys [Charley] was shot some years ago and this operation was performed....

During the operation the doctor removed three rifle bullets lodged near Buck's spine during a previous gunfight. To nearly

everyone's surprise, the outlaw managed to survive his wounds and was tried as soon as he was on his feet again. After an unsuccessful escape attempt, he was easily convicted, and his past record almost guaranteed he would be sentenced to life imprisonment. He entered San Quentin on July 9, 1895 as No. 16426. Breckenridge received a twenty-five year sentence.

■ Buck was back in stripes, but this time sentenced for life. *California State Archives.*

Buck knew the ropes and adapted once again to the prison routine. In time, he made himself useful and gained various privileges. He looked after the electric lights in the administration building and roomed with one of the clerks, Donald Lowrie. They were not locked up, had an adjoining bathroom, and accumulated a serviceable library of their own. He became a good friend of the notorious Charles Dorsey and helped furnish a farewell dinner, stolen from the prison kitchen, when Dorsey was paroled in 1911.

After his release, Dorsey worked at newspaper editor Fremont Older's ranch in Santa Clara County. Buck English sought a parole in 1909, securing a promise of employment from Luke Fay, a prominent San Franciscan. Although this effort was turned down, he later obtained a parole in 1912 through Fremont

■ The convicts called this space between the end of the cellblocks and the wall "Easy Street," but it was not what they had in mind when they initiated a life of crime. *Contemporary newspaper sketch in author's collection.*

■ Buck English. *A contemporary newspaper sketch in the author's collection.*

Older and joined Dorsey in working at the ranch. His pal Donald Lowrie remembered how Buck had always counseled the younger prisoners to go straight when they got out.

But Buck's life was nearly over. He was taken ill sometime later and Older sent him to the San Francisco City and County Hospital, where Dorsey frequently visited him. When the old outlaw died on January 15, 1915, he was given a good funeral at Saint Mary's Church and buried at Colma. The *San Francisco Chronicle* reported:

"Crime doesn't pay. I only wish that I might have seen things forty years ago in the light that I can see them today."

That was one of the last things uttered by Lawrence B. English, better known as "Buck," one of California's noted stage robbers, before he died Friday at the City and County Hospital. He was buried yesterday.

A totally reformed man at the end, Buck had gone full circle from ruthless desperado to a useful citizen who could only look back sadly at his wasted life. His funeral ushered him out of this world with an interesting mixture of genuine pioneer settlers and a sprinkling of ex-convicts representing his former lawless ways.

San Quentin State Prison Register and Pardon Files in California State Archives; *History of Solano County*; *History of Napa and Lake Counties, California*; *California Police Gazette*, September 9, 1865, March 28, 1868; Chegwyn, Michael, "Showdown with Shotguns: The Capture of Buck English," *True West*; *San Francisco Examiner,* May 8, 9 10, 11, 1895; *San Francisco Chronicle*, May 10, 15, 30, 1895, January 20, 1915; *Yreka Journal*, May 15, 1895; Oregon State Archives; Older, Fremont, *My Story*; Lowrie, Donald, *My Life in Prison*.

STAGE DRIVERS

Stage driver Dan Burch, dressed for a Sierra winter.
Author's collection.

Speaking of old time stage drivers, and he was one of them, E. W. Church once commented:

There was a time in my life when, I believe, I knew every stone and rut between Truckee and Tahoe blindfolded, and my horses knew as much as I did. Staging in the Sierras is a great art; and the reason there is seldom or no accidents is because the drivers have been well-trained elsewhere, and are men of experience, skill, caution and sobriety. Every particle of harness and running gear has been examined before starting and the drivers had absolute control of their teams and vehicles, and a perfect knowledge of the laws of stage motion that govern all their acts.

Few in a modern age can appreciate the skill and consummate artistry of a nineteenth-century Western stagecoach driver. He has been compared to a concert pianist—a concept not at all as farfetched as it might seem. The stage driver's fingers and brake foot were all that stood between his passengers and injury or death. A passenger sitting next to the driver on the box might never notice the subtle finger-shifting of the reins that dictated the actions of the horses and coach as they turned a sharp corner. But the timing of a turn was split-second and the result of many years of experience.

Stage passengers assumed the horses simply knew the road well and the driver had little to do. They couldn't have been more wrong. A driver knew his animals, and they knew him. They had respect for each other. A driver was always considerate to his teams and his whip cracked above their heads only as a warning or to keep them alert. The animals were seldom overloaded or overworked and came to know the slightest pressures of the reins handled by their master. This was very important, since a constant changing of pressure could result in a "cold" or insensitive mouth on a horse. A cold-mouthed animal is difficult to control and requires much more of the driver's energy because the animal is unsure of what he should do. Yes, by almost any standard, there was much more to stage driving than met the eye.

LEFT HAND, ALL NEAR-SIDE REINS

RIGHT HAND, ALL OFFSIDE REINS

LEADERS
SWING HORSES
WHEEL HORSES
LEADERS
SWING HORSES
WHEEL HORSES

Dick Fellows

alias Richard Perkins
(Real name George B. Lyttle)

■ A man with everything to live
for, Dick Fellows chose a path that
might very well have led to his
early death. *Author's collection.*

"I left Kentucky in 1866," wrote Dick Fellows from prison in 1893. "Just prior to starting out in the world in that same year, I took out a license to practice law…. I had become addicted to drink, however, and to not distress my relatives and friends, thought it best to leave them, at least until I could free myself from that inordinate appetite." And so a bright, idealistic young man veered from a promising career to a road that so often led to crime and a felon's cell.

Born in Clay County, Kentucky, in 1846, George Lyttle served in the Confederate army and spent the closing years of the war in a Union prison. Returning home, Lyttle was expected to follow in the footsteps of his prominent attorney father, but it was not to be. In the course of his legal studies, he had acquired a drinking problem, and he made the fateful decision to leave town and all the associations that might have been his salvation.

Drifting west, he settled in Southern California in the late 1860s. As might be suspected, being far from home, his problem became worse. Hanging out in saloons with loafers and drunks eroded any character he had left, and he soon found himself holding up stages and stealing horses to support his habit.

According to his own story, he went into the hog business with one Ed Clark in the mountains between Bakersfield and Los Angeles. Running short of supplies due to a fire, Lyttle assumed the name of "Dick Fellows" and again took up stage robbery. He stopped a Los Angeles-bound coach south of San Fernando, but when a passenger took a shot at him, Dick gave him all his attention and the stage galloped off. "I told him to put up his hands," Dick later recalled. "He had $350 which I took…with the advice that hereafter he keep out of difficulties which did not concern him."

Dick bought and shipped a load of supplies to Clark, then set out to stop another stage. After careful preparations, this holdup also blew up in his face when a passenger shot at him and the stage raced off on its way. Despite a wound in his cheek, Dick rode furiously and set up an ambush ahead of the same coach. Using some old clothes, Dick rigged up several fake accomplices and had no trouble this time getting the driver to throw out the Wells, Fargo box. Telling the driver to move on, the highwayman broke into the box with a stone and was rewarded with a $485 prize. On October 20, 1869, the *Los Angeles Daily News* reported:

> On the last down trip, near Santa Barbara, an adventurous knight of the road attempted to stop and rob one of the coaches of the Coast Line Company. His modest request to halt was answered by a volley of pistol bullets. A shot which laid open his cheek caused the highwayman to beat a hasty retreat. The next night he stole a cream colored horse from a citizen, and, it is supposed, started in the direction of Los Angeles.

LOS ANGELES TO SAN FRANCISCO.

COAST LINE STAGE CO.

80 Miles Railroad Travel.

THROUGH TO SAN FRANCISCO IN THREE DAYS.

THE Stages of the Coast Line, San Juan and Los Angeles Stage Co., *via* San Buenaventura, Santa Barbara, San Luis Obispo and Paso de Robles' Hot Springs

On and after Thursday, January 21st, the stages of the Coast Line Stage Company for San Francisco, will leave this city at 4 o'clock, A. M., instead of 1 o'clock, P. M., as they are now doing.

Wells, Fargo & Co.'s Express for packages, will close at 9 o'clock, every evening. Letter Express closes on departure of stage.

This will give passengers the benefit of a day light ride to Santa Barbara. They will also get one night's sleep in San Luis Obispo.

WM. BUCKLEY, Gen'l Sup't.

OFFICE—Bella Union Hotel, Los Angeles.
Jan. 20, 1869. tf

Captured at a road house after taking a bullet in the foot, Fel-

lows found himself in the Los Angeles jail subjected to further complaints, as noted in the *Daily News*, December 24, 1869:

> Yesterday a Mr. Olmstead appeared before Justice Gray, filed a complaint against Dick Fellows, the highwayman now in jail, charging him with horse stealing in Santa Barbara. It seems that Fellows has been a somewhat notorious character in that section. Mr. Olmstead has recovered his horse, and obtained what he deems conclusive proof of the stealing. Another horse stolen, as is supposed, by the same party, from a citizen of Santa Barbara, has not been recovered.

Tried and convicted in January 1870, Dick was received at San Quentin on January 31 as prisoner No. 4378 and began serving an eight-year term.

When he was pardoned in April 1874, the ex-convict began calling himself Richard Perkins. He may have worked for a time, but in late November 1875, he robbed the Los Angeles stage as it was nearing Caliente, reportedly obtaining some $1,800.

■ Dick's escape reward poster. *Author's collection.*

The outlaw's horse ran off, and Dick broke his ankle in falling off a precipice in the dark. Stealing a freshly-shod horse, Perkins was easily tracked and soon found himself in the Bakersfield jail.

Tried and convicted in January 1876, Perkins escaped from jail the night after being sentenced to another eight years in state prison. Despite his broken ankle, the fugitive was at large for a week, but was recaptured while eating breakfast at a nearby ranch. "The prisoner is a man of fine personal appearance," noted the *Kern County Courier*, "with an intelligent countenance, and there is an air of cool and superior audacity about him...."

Back in San Quentin, Perkins did his time quietly and was released on May 16, 1881, as a result of his good behavior. He worked briefly for a Santa Cruz newspaper, but when things did not go his way, he again drifted into crime. Reverting to his Dick Fellows moniker again, he stopped the San Luis Obispo stage in late August and in December held up two more coaches. On January 2, 1882, the San Luis coach was stopped again. The string of robberies quickly captured the attention of Wells, Fargo's ace detective, James B. Hume, who sent operative Charles Aull to investigate.

Even as Aull was pinpointing Fellows as the lone highwayman, the bandit robbed the San Luis Obispo coach on January 8, then again on the 13th. Locating his quarry in the Santa Clara Valley, Aull blanketed the area with descriptive circulars and posses of lawmen. The wiley outlaw was in their midst most of the time and was finally recognized by a farmer as he walked across his property. A former constable named Van Buren was nearby and, with several others, approached and recognized the fugitive, as stated in the *San Jose Mercury:*

■ Charles Aull led the hunt ending in Dick's capture, and later was warden at Folsom when Fellows was incarcerated there. *Courtesy Folsom State Prison.*

> Taking hold of him, (Van Buren) said, "You are my prisoner." A desperate struggle ensued, during which Fellows was felled to the ground. When he was disarmed and secured, it required the united efforts of all three men, who were unarmed, to overpower him. A gold watch of considerable value was found on him. He carried a bull-dog pistol, of American make. Fellows was put in a buggy and started for Mayfield, his captors acting as guard. When in the center of town he attempted to jump from the buggy, when Van Buren, who had armed himself with Fellows' weapon, assured him that it would not be safe for him to repeat his act....

At Mayfield, Dick was turned over to a Santa Clara constable named Burke, who escorted the outlaw to San Jose. They had no sooner reached town when Burke agreed to take the famous highwayman into a local saloon for a last drink. It was less of a humanitarian act than an opportunity for some industrial-strength boasting on the constable's part. It was a bad mistake, as noted in the *San Jose Mercury*, January 28, 1882:

Fellows called for brandy and managed to pour out an extra large horn in spite of his handcuffs. After drinking, both left the saloon. Upon reaching the sidewalk, Fellows darted around the corner and down St. John street....

■ San Jose as it appeared during Fellows' exciting time there. *California State Library.*

After a spirited chase by both Burke and the bartender, Dick managed to disappear and was at large for a brief time. He spent the night in a barn, but was captured the next day and finally lodged in the city jail. When a reporter asked him if he had, in fact, held up those seven coastal stages, Dick replied, "No, one of those jobs was done by some one else." The reporter then ticked off the robberies in question, but when he described the holdup near San Luis Obispo on July 19, 1881, Dick looked up.

"I don't have the honor of doing that last named job," interrupted Fellows. "I own up to the rest."

Some seven hundred people visited the jail to see the captured desperado before he was sent to Santa Barbara for his trial.

Dick saw fit to defend himself at his March trial, but, being out of practice, was easily convicted and sentenced to life imprisonment at the new Folsom State Prison. On April 2, 1882, he managed to assault his jailer, who was bringing him breakfast. With the

deputy's pistol, Dick bolted from the jail, but when he attempted to escape on a staked-out horse, he was thrown to the ground. The outlaw was quickly back in his cell. In a letter to the local press, Dick concluded that "My unfortunate experience has thrown me into the society of thousands of law breakers from every clime and all walks of life and in every instance the result is the same. It is the same sad story; 'It don't pay,' in any sense."

■ Old and tired of prison life, Dick cultivated friends on the outside and reconciled with his family to finally secure a pardon. *Author's collection.*

At Folsom, Dick kept his nose clean, reestablished relations with his family in Kentucky and began applying for a pardon. He managed to secure recommendations for clemency from Jim Hume and other Wells, Fargo officials, and on March 8, 1908, he was pardoned by the governor.

Although he had stated he was returning to Kentucky to see his family, there is no indication of just where Fellows went after his release. Like many another convict before him, Dick would say anything to obtain his freedom. As had Black Bart, Dick managed to effectively disappear from the pages of western history, and to this day his fate is unknown.

Secrest, William B., *Lawmen & Desperadoes*; Correspondence with Harold L. Edwards, Bakersfield, California; San Quentin State Prison Register; Governor's Pardon Files, California State Archives; *Los Angeles Daily News*, December 10, 24, 1869; *Los Angeles Star*, December 11, 1869, January 22, 1870; *Kern County Weekly Courier*, December 4, 11, 1875, January 15, 22, 1876; *San Jose Herald, San Jose Mercury*, January 28, 29, February 3, 4,5, April 2, 22, 1882; *San Francisco Examiner*, June 24, 1894.

A. P. Hamilton

alias Albert Tarlton

■ Hamilton, still in bandages from his shootout in the Santa Cruz Mountains, glares defiantly into the Rogues Gallery camera.
Author's collection.

riginally from Ohio, "Al" Hamilton was born about 1849. He joined the army when just a teenager and served in the West, but soon tired of military life. Deserting his post one night, he made his way to Tulare County, where he adapted the name "Henry Tarlton." In late August 1867, he forged orders upon a Visalia store, stole a horse, and then fled the county. Deputy Sheriff W. W. Bowen was promptly on his trail, but Tarlton managed to give him the slip at McFarlane's Toll Road and headed east, over the Sierra. Bowen dogged his trail, however, and arrested him at the army post of Camp Independence, in Inyo County. The *Visalia Delta* reported:

> It appears [Tarlton] was not only a thief, but a deserter. Finding himself closely pressed by Bowen, he gave himself up to the authorities as a deserter, hoping, doubtless, to escape the effects of his crime thereby. But the military had no use for him and were glad to give him up....

On September 10, 1867, he was indicted, pled guilty and found himself on the way north to San Quentin to serve a six-year term. As No. 3619, and now known as "Albert" Tarlton, he began his sentence on September 16. In prison, he no doubt refined his criminal craft by swapping stories with his cellmates. When he was released on September 28, 1872, he was anything but a reformed man.

Tarlton probably worked off and on for the next year or so while he shopped around for an illicit way to make a buck. He had not worked for some time when he met a kindred spirit named Peter Carr, a West Virginia stable hostler who was a year his junior. The two men made their way to San Jose, then over the mountain stage road to Santa Cruz in late March 1874. A picturesque town on the edge of the Pacific, Santa Cruz was just across the bay from old Monterey. Both Tarlton and Carr were broke and looked for work in the coastal village. Finding a job as a cook, Tarlton only worked long enough for a payday, then disappeared along with his employer's shotgun.

Although they apparently had only the one weapon, Tarlton and Carr plotted to stop and rob the Pioneer stage traveling between San Jose and the coast. Throwing some supplies in a bag, they walked north on the stage road, stopping just over the summit that led down into the Santa Clara Valley. At a spot where the coaches usually stopped to let passengers walk over the grade, the two highwaymen stretched a rope across the road, then concealed themselves in one of the large clumps of brush that lined the trail. Tarlton had a flannel mask that covered his face, with holes for his eyes and mouth. A knife dangled from his wrist. Carr was to remain hidden. The date was April 1, "April Fools' Day."

MOUNTAIN STAGES

Pioneer Stage Line,
WARD & COLGROVE, Proprietors and Drivers.

Run Daily,

LEAVING Santa Cruz at 7½ A. M., for Santa Clara and San Jose, connecting with the cars for San Francisco and Stockton.

In Schedule Time.

Returning, leaves Santa Clara on arrival of the morning train from San Francisco, 11 o'clock A. M., arriving in Santa Cruz at 5 o'clock P. M.   Fare, $3.00.
Buy R. R. Tickets to Santa Clara only. Stage Offices New York Exchange, San Jose, W. O. Barker, Agent, Santa Rruz House, Santa Cruz, P. V. Wilkins, Agent.

It was a quarter-to-three in the afternoon when a four-horse mud wagon came toiling up the grade with J. P. Smith at the reins. A woman and her young son sat beside him, while seven other passengers were inside the coach. Just prior to the horses reaching the rope, Tarlton stood up, pointing his shotgun, and called for the coach to stop, as reported in the *Santa Cruz Sentinel*:

> As soon as the stage stopped, he demanded in nervous tones that Wells, Fargo & Co.'s treasure box be passed down to him. The driver informed him that he had no express box with him. The road agent said he knew better and told him to hurry and pass down the box. The driver protested, and Mrs. J. M. Smith also told the robber there was no box on board. The driver threw out to the robber two of Uncle Sam's mail bags…. The robber kicked the bags aside and said he guessed there was nothing in them that he wanted. He came for money and if he couldn't get any out of the box, the passengers would have to shell out their loose change.

While Mrs. Smith's little boy screamed in fright at the appearance of the bandit, Tarlton watched as the passengers began flinging their coins out the window onto the road. Several women passengers gave him dirty looks, as well, a Mrs. Canney refusing to give him anything. When the driver asked if he could move on, the embarrassed bandit handed back the mail sacks and waved for the

■ A light stage at a way station in the Santa Cruz Mountains.
California State Library.

coach to move on. As the coach moved up the grade, the passengers could look back and see the highwayman on his knees in the road collecting bills and change totaling some forty-five dollars.

Nearly a month later, on April 28, the San Jose stage was stopped again. This time, it was several miles east of the previous site, closer to San Jose, but still in rough, mountain country. Just before two o'clock in the afternoon, a Concord coach driven by W. E. McFarland was toiling slowly up the grade, when the two masked men stepped from behind a long pile of cordwood stacked alongside the road. Both men carried shotguns and had knives dangling from their wrists. Both wore dark hats and tightly knit masks with holes for the eyes and mouth. Tarlton stood in the middle of the road and called for the coach to stop.

As Tarlton walked toward the coach, Carr took his place in front of the horses. The bandits promptly got down to business, as reported in the May 2, 1874 *Sentinel*:

■ *Santa Cruz Sentinel*, May 2, 1874. *Author's collection.*

The stouter-built companion in crime proceeded to the rear and passing 'round the stage, stopped at one of the windows.

"Now hand out your wallets damned quick," he exclaimed, tipping the muzzle of his shotgun on the edge of the coach window, at the same time thrusting through the window a soft, white hand with the gleaming knife oscillating from the wrist. There was no delay on the part of the terrified passengers. The gentlemen fumbled in their pockets and began to deposit half-dollars, quarter-dollars and dimes in the palm of the white hand.

Realizing he was only getting change again, Tarlton now demanded everyone's wallets. When he still only realized about nine dollars, he asked for watches, but received only one. As this was going on, a Mr. Brothers, sitting next to the driver, managed to hide his wallet containing sixty dollars under his seat cushion. When Tarlton turned and asked for Brothers' coin, the highwayman was disgusted when he was handed only seventy-five cents.

"Oh, you've got more money than this. Get down from there so that I can go through you," demanded Tarlton.

Mr. Brothers then handed down his watch, but Tarlton told him again to get down. At that point the horses were becoming restless and the driver asked if he could leave so he could stay on schedule. Tarlton told him to move on and the coach started slowly up the grade.

When the pilfered coach reached Santa Cruz, driver McFarland immediately contacted Santa Cruz County Sheriff Robert Orton. Telegraphing Sheriff John H. Adams of Santa Clara County, Orton gave him what information he had and asked that he meet him on the summit of the Santa Cruz Mountains that night. He next sent Deputy Jackson Sylva and Frank Curtis north to Felton and Zayante Creek to look for the outlaws, then directed two other men to head up the Soquel Road to the top of the mountain. The sheriff and stage driver George Colgrove then proceeded up the main stage road towards the first robbery site. Several suspects were picked up, but all had alibis. It was near midnight when Orton met Sheriff Adams and a posse, and after more searching they decided to spend the night there and resume searching in the morning.

Meanwhile, Deputy Sylva and Curtis had been searching the Felton area and picked up another posse member named George Newell. They learned that two men had stopped to spend the night at a local vineyard, but had been turned down. The two men had then moved off towards Dougherty's Mill. Sylva caught up with the men at the mill, but they were able to provide an alibi.

Keeping on the move, Sylva's party next headed for Mountain Charley McKiernan's place. Charley was one of the earliest settlers in the Santa Cruz Mountains. A pioneer rancher and road builder, he still farmed and operated his toll road over the mountains. He had been terribly disfigured in a fight with a grizzly bear and always wore a hat to minimize his facial scars and the metal plate covering a hole in his forehead.

It was three o'clock in the morning when they reached Mountain Charley's rude cabin and roused him. McKiernan told them he had seen two strangers shooting at a squirrel late the previous day. From his description of the pair, Sylva was sure they were on the right track of the outlaws. After eating and getting a few hours rest, the posse, including Mountain Charley with his Henry rifle, left at daybreak and headed for the site where the suspects had been seen. Tracks at the scene were measured, carved on a stick, and followed some four miles to Jones Creek. Here the tracks were lost. One of the party was sent down to the toll road gate to see if anyone had passed through that morning. When he learned that no one had been seen, Sylva knew he was close to his quarry.

Spreading out, the posse discovered an old barn in a clearing. A close watch disclosed two crouching figures inside, and the posse fanned out to prevent any escape. Sylva called out for the men to surrender, but a posseman shouted that he had seen them cocking

■ The Santa Clara County Court House where Hamilton and his partner were tried and convicted. *California State Library.*

their weapons. Tarlton stood up and fired his revolver, but missed. A moment later, after Newell fired and missed, Mountain Charley wounded Tarlton in the arm with his first shot. The fugitives surrendered, and the fight was over.

After a fifteen-mile hike, Sylva's party met Orton and Adams at Mountain Charley's place and the posses and outlaws all had a good meal. The stolen property had been recovered and Adams and his prisoners returned to San Jose.

The following month, Tarlton and Carr were convicted in the Santa Clara County court and given ten-year terms. On May 26, 1874, the two men found themselves behind San Quentin bars, Tarlton acquiring his new number, 6020, under the name A. P. Hamilton.

■ Reward notice sent out around the state after Tarlton's escape from San Quentin.
John Boessenecker collection.

A convict again, Tarlton immediately began looking for a means to escape. Plotting with his three cell mates, the convicts made an exact paper duplicate of the brass lock that secured the door of their cell. On the night of November 15, the men pried off their padlock with an iron bar, left their cell, and replaced the broken lock with their paper duplicate. The convicts then scaled the wall and were gone. The *Mariposa Gazette* reported:

Four of the worst criminals confined at San Quentin made their escape on the 15th inst., by scaling the wall while one of the guards was asleep. Their names were, John Acker, John Clark, Thomas Barnwell and A. P. Hamilton.

Tarlton lay low for a time, but in the spring of the following year, he was ready to go on the road again. On April 16, 1875, he robbed the Wells, Fargo express box on the Grass Valley-Colfax stage. He stopped the Ione-Galt coach on May 3, again robbing the Wells, Fargo box, then fleeing to San Francisco. Sixteen days later, he was picked up by detectives, ever alert for the reward on the head of escaped convicts and stage robbers.

■ Stagecoach in front of the Metropolitan Hotel in San Andreas. *Calaveras County Historical Society.*

Back in San Quentin, Tarlton began angling for other means of escape. He and his lawyer initiated a letter-writing campaign, hoping to instigate some sort of reprieve. On May 8, 1876, Governor William Irwin commuted his sentence to eight years. Finally, on December 3, 1879, Tarlton was released on a writ of habeas corpus, and he was free once again.

In prison, Tarlton had a thirty-year old cell mate named Roger O'Meara, a Napa cow thief doing time for grand larceny. O'Meara, a clerk in the prison turnkey's

■ R. W. King, alias O'Mera, alias Roger O'Meara. *Author's collection.*

office, was probably intrigued by Tarlton's stage-robbing exploits, and the two planned to meet outside after gaining their freedom. Released on November 3, 1879, O'Meara met Tarlton the following month at the time of his discharge. The two men promptly began planning a stage robbery in Calaveras County.

Stopping the stage running between San Andreas and Milton (probably the most robbed route in the country!) on April 29, 1880, the two bandits broke open the Wells, Fargo box, then disappeared into the countryside. A week later, they attempted to stop the Jackson to Ione coach, but after exchanging shots with the guard, Tarlton and O'Meara fled.

On May 26, the two robbed the Wells, Fargo box on the Georgetown to Placerville stage, but Tarlton was wounded in the arm. The two men escaped capture, but were either scared or realized that a change of scene might be beneficial to their health. Together, they fled the state, O'Meara reappearing when he was picked up on a burglary charge in Saint Louis.

Tarlton, or Hamilton, was never heard from again.

Hume and Thacker's "Robbers Record"; Secrest, William B., *Lawmen & Desperadoes*; San Quentin State Prison Register; Governor's Pardon Files, California State Archives, Sacramento; *Visalia Delta*, September 11, 1867; *Santa Cruz Sentinel*, April 4, May 2, 1874; *Mariposa Gazette*, November 28, 1874.

William M. Harrall

■ A quiet, peaceful man, Bill Harrall made a bad decision and destroyed everything he held dear. *A contemporary newspaper sketch in author's collection.*

The man was baking bread in his small, mountain cabin. His wife had recently given birth and was in bed with the new baby and chatting with a neighbor girl as her husband prepared for his trip. He had baked extra bread for his family and now took the last loaf from the oven, wrapped it in a cloth, and placed it in a sack. Putting some jerky and a tin of butter in the sack also, he turned and smiled at his two-year-old daughter playing in the corner.

Times had been hard. William Harrall had been out of work for some time. The local general store, in the tiny hamlet of Delta, had even refused him any more credit. Today he was leaving on a trip to look for work, but work or not he was going to bring home some money. A man had to feed his family, no matter what....

Born in Wayne County, New York, in 1863, William M. Harrall learned farm work at an early age and came west about 1880 when he was seventeen years old. When Thomas Harrall, his father, lost most of his remaining family in an epidemic, he too went west to seek out his remaining son. It was five years before he traced his boy to Chico, in Butte County, where he was working on the Glenn Ranch. Parent and son separated again when William moved to the small village of Delta, in northern Shasta County.

About 1894, William Harrall was married to the pretty young daughter of a man named Lloyd, and a baby girl was soon added to the family. The new father worked at any job he could get. At various times, he was reportedly a logger, miner, rancher, railroad section hand, and liner in a sawmill. He had a good reputation locally, was quiet and did not drink or gamble. Although the struggle to support his family would at times upset him, his wife insisted he was a kind and loving father and husband.

On September 17, 1897, Harrall packed his small sack of supplies, kissed his wife good-bye and began walking north over the hill behind his home. He had told his wife he was going to look for work at the Altoona Quicksilver Mine at Cinnebar. Soon he had disappeared into the chapparal and trees.

A week later, on the afternoon of September 25, the Yreka to Fort Jones stage was stopped. The same stage had been robbed on April 3 and June 27, at the same spot. The *San Francisco Chronicle* reported:

> Yreka, September 25—The Scott Valley stage was held up nine miles from here this afternoon by a lone highwayman, who got the express box. The amount it contained is unknown. The robber was effectually disguised, even his feet being muffled in sacks. Four passengers, including a lady and Father Quinn, the Catholic priest from here, were aboard, none of whom were molested.

The highwayman stepped from behind a rock and demanded the express box, which was handed out, and the stage proceeded

■ The sparsely settled mountain areas were perfect for quick stage robberies, while the forests made ideal hideouts for the highwaymen. Clever lawmen and Wells, Fargo detectives paid no attention to all this and usually caught the bad guys anyway. *Trinity County Historical Society.*

on its way. Officers were quickly in the field, but could find no trace of the robber. An Indian woman on the stage had given a good description of the man's height, weight, and blue or grey eyes, while Wells, Fargo employees were alerted to watch for a twenty-dollar United States Gold Certificate that had been taken in the robbery. Such certificates were quite rare in Northern California and shotgun messenger Daniel N. Haskell began a search of banks and business firms in the Redding area. When he found such a certificate in the Bank of Northern California, Haskell purchased it and forwarded it to John Thacker at Wells, Fargo headquarters in San Francisco.

Now, there was something tangible with which to work. Haskell had a bank clerk locate the source of the note and found that it came from the grocery firm of McCormick Saltsen Company. Fred Irwin, who clerked at the store, started checking records and finally determined the certificate had been given in payment for a load of supplies purchased on September 29. A medium-sized man had bought $22.90 worth of goods and had shipped them to a F. W. Lloyd, in Delta. The buyer fit the Indian girl's description. His name was William M. Harrall.

Thacker sent a Wells, Fargo detective named Charles Jennings north to see what he could find out about the suspect. Deputy Sheriff George Stewart lived in Delta and pointed out Harrall's rough, one-room house where he lived next to his in-laws, the Lloyds. Certain that the stage robber had been found, Jennings sent for Thacker, who later discussed the investigation:

As to the robber, I am convinced that we had the right man spotted. I had him traced from the time he left home, ostensibly to go to the mines, until the day he appeared at

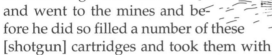

home after his trip to the stores at Redding, and not a link in the chain is missing. When his baby was born, he had a servant girl who tells me that he got his outfit and went to the mines and before he did so filled a number of these [shotgun] cartridges and took them with him. He got $50 in the robbery and was traced by the gold note which he spent in Redding, but in addition to that I was able to trace almost every cent of the cash. I also had him tracked from the point of the robbery to his home and there is no doubt of his identity.

Jennings met Thacker at the Redding station on the morning of October 14, 1897. It was decided to make the arrest as soon as possible, and since the robbery occurred in Siskiyou County, Thacker wired the sheriff at Yreka, who sent down his undersheriff, William A. Radford, to make the arrest. Radford met Thacker, Jennings and Deputy Stewart at the small Delta depot. Stewart had been watching the Harrall home and knew that the suspect was there. Thacker later told a reporter of the battle plan:

Radford insisted that as he had the warrant he would go to the house and take his man. He had an idea that Harrall did not know him and so thought he could make the capture without a fight. I had an idea that Harrall would not fight in the house myself, and so sent Jennings to the back door that there might not be a break for the brush....

I was known and so did not go to the house, instead waiting on the station platform for the party. I did not approve of the course and that is another reason why I did not go. I saw Jennings reach the rear door. Just a few moments before he got there Harrall appeared on the porch and stretched his arms in the air. Then he disappeared inside and drew down the blinds and locked the door....

While Thacker stood watching from the depot platform, Jennings guarded the back door, and Stewart and Radford walked toward the front. Stepping onto the porch, Radford knocked on the door, which was opened by Mrs. Harrall. When asked if her husband was in, the woman said yes, then closed the door. In another moment the door flew open, and Harrall stood framed in the doorway. Stewart knew Harrall and, standing just behind the Siskiyou officer, said, "This is Mr. Radford." The officer said, "I want to see you," then held out his hand which was grabbed by Harrall. Thacker could see what was happening up to this point, as he later recalled:

> Instantly grasping the hand of the deputy sheriff, Harrall stepped back just a trifle. Radford seemed to make a step as if to go into the room and then stumbled, it appeared, but in reality he was pulled off his balance by Harrall....

Holding Radford's hand with his own right hand, Harrall had pulled him off balance, drawn his pistol with his left hand and fired with the weapon pressed against the officer's body. Radford groaned and tried to draw his own weapon, but his eyes were already glazing. Grabbing Harrall around the neck, the wounded lawman was dragging the outlaw down when Stewart saw an opening and clubbed the outlaw several times with his pistol. Meanwhile, Harrall's two-year-old daughter was screeching and clinging to her father's

■ Deputy Sheriff William A. Radford lost his life in the shootout at the Harrall cabin. *Contemporary newspaper sketch in author's collection.*

pant leg, while Mrs. Harrall screamed and held onto one of her husband's arms. Prior to this, Stewart could not shoot, afraid of hitting Radford, but he now fired five times with deadly effect, even as the struggling outlaw shot him in the leg. Harrall now slumped to the floor, Radford collapsing, also. Thick gunsmoke filled the small room as wife and daughter screamed over the body of the fallen stage robber.

"By the time I got there," Thacker recalled, "Jennings was coming around the house on the run, and the people were collecting from all around. Stewart stumbled out of the door and fell to the ground just as I came up. I asked him if he was hard hit, and he said only a ball in his leg, and I went on into the house. The two men were lying on the floor, and I knelt beside the deputy sheriff, putting out the fire in his clothing."

The dead undersheriff's body was placed in the depot and tended by the Delta coroner. Thacker was surprised when no money was found on the corpse. He had given him twenty dollars the night before, and Radford had only paid for one meal. Someone had robbed the corpse. It was Thacker's unpleasant task to accompany the body to Yreka on the train where it was met by his grieving widow and three daughters.

There was ample evidence to tie Harrall to the recent stage robbery, and Thacker laid several other holdups at his door as well. Clearly, there seemed to be no other reason an innocent man would react as Harrall had to officers knocking on his door. The fact that he would engage in such a desperate contest in the presence of his family can only be a gauge of his desperation. Thacker noted that although Harrall was said to be a worker in mines and saw mills, his "hands were as white as those of one who works in an office. I believe he worked on the stages more than he did on anything else."

At the request of his wife, the dead outlaw was buried in the potter's field at Redding.

San Francisco Chronicle, September 26, October 15, 16, 1897; San Francisco *Examiner*, October 15, 16, 1897.

WHAT WAS IT LIKE TO RIDE IN A STAGECOACH?

As you might suspect, it depends on the rider and the route. Riding between Santa Barbara and Ventura on a Coast Line stage, a woman stagecoach passenger wrote in the *Ventura Signal*, September 27, 1873:

Thirty miles of stage riding over the roughest (in some places) road imaginable, when only by hanging on to the sides of the coach, literally "tooth and nail," could we avoid the involuntary game of base ball which the combined efforts of the six prancing steeds, aided and abetted by the implacable driver, caused us to play with our fellow passengers, they alternately acting as bats and we as balls, and vice versa.... Moreover we are a woman, and wasn't our back hair all tumbled down? Wasn't our hat knocked into as many angles as there are pieces in a bologna sausage? And as for our bruises and mangled flesh — ough! Don't mention it.

Across the state, in the foothills of the Sierra, another stage passenger traveling from Sonora to Stockton, gave a lyrical account of his journey in the *San Francisco Daily Alta California*, June 28, 1853:

This is the most delightful road to travel which I know of in the State. There is no dust upon it and it winds around the hills and through the most beautiful and picturesque country to be seen anywhere in the Southern mines. This road leaves the old one at a place called the New York Tent, and after riding over a fine undulating country for about four miles, we reach the summit of the hill that overhangs the Stanislaus River. From this point is the finest view of wild and picturesque scenery that can be imagined. Directly opposite, the Table Mountain boldly juts forth at a point many hundred feet above the river, and the bluff stands out in bold relief, and to the traveler as he passes along it presents one of the finest views that the country boasts.

This account, penned twenty years earlier, perhaps delineates the difference between the perceptions of a male and a female traveler. The woman, reacting to every bump in the road and very naturally concerned with her appearance, finds it impossible to describe much more than her inconvenience. The man, however, perhaps more accustomed to such travel, can relax and enjoy the trip while obviously enjoying a ride that must have been just as bumpy, or more so, in 1853.

John Hays

alias "Shorty." Real name was perhaps James F. Costello.

■ Shorty was a rowdy scamp, but who knows what his future might have been if his restaurant dream had come true?
Author's collection.

I reland was the reported birthplace of John Hays, where he first saw the light of day about 1843. His parents were probably immigrants to America during the tragic potato famine era. John's diminutive height (five feet, one inch) caused him to be tagged early in life with the nickname "Shorty."

He worked for a time as a laborer in Placer County, then operated a saloon on San Francisco's Barbary Coast until various petty larcenies put him into the local hoosegow. Upon release, he left town, but was convicted in July 1868, of horse stealing and the theft of a watch in Yuba County. As No. 3869, he took up residence for the first time in California's state prison at San Quentin. On expiration of his five-year term, he was released on October 31, 1872.

Like so many of the San Quentin inmates, Shorty Hays probably learned many tricks of the criminal trade from his cell mates. Nothing is known of his movements immediately after release, but the following year he joined up with two ex-cons he had met in prison and plotted a stage robbery. On September 12, 1873, Hays, Eddie Lee and Jake Clark stopped the Forest Hill-Auburn stage, robbing the Wells, Fargo express box. Indications are the trio then engaged in a number of robberies in Sacramento and San Francisco, before moving up the Sacramento Valley. Along the way, the three men added a fourth to the group when they met up with another recently paroled prison bird calling himself Charlie Thompson. They quickly planned another stage robbery.

On October 10, 1873, the four masked highwaymen stopped the Yreka to Redding stage near Buckeye, just north of Redding. A *Sacramento Record* reporter was a passenger and promptly wrote up his experience for his newspaper:

We were ranged on the side of the road, while the "agents" went through us. Here I want to enter a protest against green men undertaking such close work. Their hands trembled so I was fearful they would shoot accidentally and hurt someone…. Well, they went through us, hitting one Chinaman on the head because he did not yield readily enough to their demands. From Ah Yain they got $200, from Ah Hing, $200, from Ah Hie, $600, from Ah Jim, $265, from Ah Jim No. 2, $195; from Cochran, $35, from —— $165; and from another $260, making $2,015 [sic], besides Wells, Fargo & Co.'s box which contained $2,000 and valuable letters and papers, total $4,015….

■ A well-loaded Concord stage pulling up through the foothills into the mountains. Shorty and his men probably stopped their coaches on an up-grade such as this—a standard holdup procedure of the time. *California State Library.*

After cleaning out the Wells, Fargo box, the bandits fled south and rusticated in the capital for a few days. Eddie Lee and Thompson remained in Sacramento. The two had separated when Thompson was picked up and promptly sought to better his position by "peaching" on his pals. Hays and Clark went on to San Francisco where Shorty had plans. Hays had no way of knowing Captain Isaiah Lee's San Francisco detectives were already looking for him. The *San Francisco Daily Alta California* told what happened next:

SUMMER ARRANGEMENTS

Change of Route.

CALIFORNIA & OREGON COAST LINE STAGE CO.

Barlow, Sanderson. & Co. Proprietors

DEPARTURE OF STAGES

Stages leave Reading going North, on and after Dec. 1st, 1874, at 6 o'clock A M. for Pit River, Dog Creek, Portuguese Flat, Soda Springs, Strawberry Valley, Butteville, and: Yreka, ' al., and Jacksonville, Canyonville and Roseburg—there connecting with the Oregon & Cal. R. R. for Portland, Oregon.

All fares 15 cts. a mile.

W. S. STONE. Gen. Supt.

John Hayes, or better recognized in police circles as "Shorty" Hayes, was arrested on Wednesday afternoon, in this city, by detectives Jones and Coffey. This prisoner is wanted by the authorities of Shasta County to answer a charge of robbery…. Two of the robbers were arrested some days ago in Sacramento City, but no clue could be had to the others, until Wednesday, when Hayes was arrested in a small

restaurant, on the wharf, at the foot of Jackson street. Some time since he purchased an interest in the establishment for $800—more money than his kind usually command….

Only Eddie Lee had made a successful getaway, although he was captured the following year. The three prisoners were delivered to Sheriff Hull at Redding, and in due time Hays, Thompson and Clark found themselves behind bars in the Shasta County jail. Shorty just grinned and bided his time.

■ Detective John Coffey.
Author's collection.

Indicted by the Shasta County grand jury, the three highwaymen were awaiting their trial, when they seized an opportunity to escape on the evening of December 14, 1873. The three bandits were in the exercise room when it was noticed that no officers were present. With a piece of firewood, they pried a staple from a locked door leading to the sheriff's office, where they quickly armed themselves. When the undersheriff and the cook entered the jail with supper, they were seized and thrown into a cell, and Hays and the others began cutting through the chains of their shackles. The sheriff returned next and was also seized. Hays, Clark and Thompson split up on the outside, and the latter two, armed with pistols obtained from the vanquished lawmen, disappeared into the nearby woods. Shorty, still in leg irons, remained hidden close by the jail and watched as Clark, and later Thompson, were returned by the officers. Late that night, Hays slipped quietly into the woods.

It was bitter cold and the snow was deep, but for the next ten days Shorty followed the railroad tracks south. On December 21, about five miles above Red Bluff, a rancher asked him to come into his cabin and warm himself. As Shorty was drying his hat before a fire, the rancher suddenly jumped him from behind. After a desperate struggle the fugitive was able to pull his pistol and threatened to shoot if the rancher persisted in the attack. Giving in, the man admitted to being poor and wanting the reward now being offered for the escapees.

"I guess you'll be compelled to get along without it," growled the exhausted Shorty.

The fugitive continued on to Red Bluff, then to Vina Station where he was able to get rid of his leg irons that night in a blacksmith shop. In ten days Shorty made it to Marysville. He was nearly frozen, however, and his feet were in bad shape from an ill-fitting pair of stolen boots. Early on the morning of December 24, he walked into the United States Hotel and had his first meal since escaping.

■ Shorty found shelter for a brief time in Marysville, but he was recognized and soon found himself behind bars again. *Author's collection.*

■ San Quentin, during Shorty's time there, was becoming a tourist attraction and the prisoners were now engaged in tending to gardens and landscaping. *Author's collection.*

He found a warehouse where he could rest and was sleeping soundly on a pile of sacks when a Marysville police officer arrested him. He had been identified at the hotel.

In an interview with a reporter from the *Marysville Daily Appeal,* Shorty described his long trek south. When asked if this wasn't a bad time of year for a person to be traveling under such circumstances, he laughed and said it was "very rough"—that during five of his ten days' journey all he had to eat was the wheat he had picked up—that he lay down in barns and outhouses along the railroad track and survived the best he knew how. On being asked if he had any place in view he wished to reach, he replied he wanted to get below Sacramento and to San Francisco where he would ship out for a foreign port.

Returned to Shasta County, Hays, Clark, and Thompson were tried in early February 1874, and easily convicted for the October stage robbery. Each received a twenty-one-year sentence to San Quen-

■ After several more escape attempts, Shorty finally realized his race was run. He decided you couldn't beat the system, and he quit trying. *Author's collection.*

tin. "The prisoners," noted the *Yreka Journal*, "were not troubled at all about their liberal terms in the state institution, in fact acted as pleased as though they were elected to Congress." The prisoners were quickly on their way to "the ranch," as criminals referred to San Quentin. The three took up residence on February 16, 1874. Shorty was now No. 5884.

The following March, Shorty was taken out by order of the Placer County Court and tried for the Auburn stage robbery. Convicted, he was returned to prison ten days later with an additional sentence of thirty years added to his time.

On March 28, 1876, Shorty escaped from prison, but was captured in less than ten days at Bodega, on the coast. Governor Irwin commuted his sentence to twenty-nine years in April 1878, because of his bravery during a fire at the prison that year. But, it was still a long stretch. Shorty was working in the outside brickyard when in December 1884 he once again escaped. This time, he made it as far as Los Angeles, where he was recaptured on January 1, 1885. The diminutive convict paid dearly for this escapade, as noted in a newspaper report of the time:

Shorty Hays does not receive visitors at present owing to the fact that he is doing solitary penance for his late escape and recapture. Hays will find his short spell of freedom an expensive amusement, as it will add twelve years to his term of service.... He is said to be in a complete state of collapse over the failure of his experiment.

■ Shorty apparently finally reached the point where it was no longer acceptable to be locked up like an animal. This is the padlock that secured prisoners in their cells. *San Quentin Museum Association.*

Although Shorty lost 137 months' credits toward a parole by his escape, the credits were restored in 1889. Finally, he finished out his term. Shorty was popular in prison, and the day before his release on October 17, 1891, his convict pals threw him a farewell party. There were "speeches, songs and music," and after the program a "nice little lunch" was laid out. His pals even presented him with a nest egg of sixty dollars.

"That's the last time a lock will ever be turned on me," he told the guard when his cell door was closed.

Shorty left the next morning, but his prophetic remark to the guard proved to be premature. While strolling on the streets of Spokane, Washington, the following month, he was spotted by an ex-guard at San Quentin. Because of his record of escapes, he was thrown in jail until his story could be checked. A telegram to the prison quickly ironed out the situation, and hopefully Shorty spent the rest of his life as an honest—and free—man.

Hume and Thacker's, "Robbers' Record"; San Quentin State Prison Register, California State Archives, Sacramento; San Francisco *Daily Alta California*, October 31, 1873; *San Francisco Chronicle*, October 31, 1873; *San Francisco Daily Morning Call*, June 5, 1881, January 9, 1885; *San Francisco Examiner*, October 18, November 1, 1891; *Sacramento Record*, October 11, 1873; *Sacramento Bee*, November 13, 1873; *Marysville Appeal*, December 25, 1873; *Yreka Journal*, February 18, 1874, June 7, 1876; *Yreka Union*, June 10, 1876; *Shasta Courier*, January 20, 1877.

William H. Howard

■ Described by a local newspaper as a "rattle-brained, desperate and fearless scoundrel," young Bill Howard's pal Abe Jones (right) was no prize package, either.
Author's collection.

"**F**ather, Father, strike a light!"

It was just after midnight as the man burst through the cabin door expecting his father to respond. But his father was not home. What happened next was the culmination of clever and patient detective work at the end of a string of stagecoach robberies. It was also, probably, the ultimate tragedy of bad decisions and poor parenting gone terribly wrong.

Born in California in 1863, Bill Howard grew up on the banks of the Sacramento River. Cornelius Howard, his father, was a native of Pennsylvania and had a large farm several miles south of Redding, in Shasta County. He had married Ammie Elwell in 1881, but after their divorce, he lived with several daughters at his farm. The elder Howard owned property in Oregon, as well, and his sons Bill and Virgil grew up pampered and headstrong. After his divorce, Cornelius Howard gave his Lake County, Oregon, property to son Bill, who was his favorite. The ranch was well-stocked with cattle and horses, and young Bill Howard had little to worry about financially. Still, he had a wild streak that hard work and responsibility could not curb.

In the fall of 1891, the stagecoach running between Redding, California and Linkville, Oregon, was held up and robbed five times.

All the robberies took place in California. The first holdup, on September 1, occurred near Churn Creek. A lone highwayman stopped the coach and robbed only the Wells, Fargo box, from which he obtained very little return. Investigating officers had a good description to work with, but it was generally thought the road agent had left the country immediately after the robbery.

The second robbery occurred on September 29, near Stillwater. This time, there were two robbers. The Wells, Fargo box was taken, along with the driver's purse, but the passengers and mail sacks were not disturbed. One of the robbers had a shotgun and his partner a pistol. When the third coach was stopped on October 7 in Oregon, it appeared to be the work of the same two road agents—at least they looked the same to the driver and carried the same weapons.

On Monday, October 19, the stage was again held up, apparently, once again, by the same two highwaymen. The robbery took place two miles south of Millville. The robbers were armed with the same weapons described in the previous holdups, and the mail was

■ Bill Howard and his pal Abe Jones held up stages pretty much in the manner shown here, although most highwaymen preferred not to be mounted for fear of their horse being startled. This is a posed holdup staged near Weaverville in 1902. *Shasta Historical Society.*

not touched. The final robbery in this series of holdups occurred three days later, near Loomis Corners on Stillwater Creek and was described in the *Yreka Journal:*

> Another stage robbery.—The Redding and Alturas stage was robbed again last Thursday night, at about the same place as a few days ago, by two masked men. The robbers rifled W. F. & Co.'s box and relieved the passengers of about $200. A lady on board hid her purse somewhere about the stage, and although the highwaymen made a determined search, they failed to find it. It was not learned how much the treasure box contained. The officers are looking for "Sheet-Iron Jack" and three of his pals, who suddenly disappeared from Red Bluff several days ago. It is believed they had a hand in this and other recent robberies.

Apparently, around $600 was taken in all, but "Sheet-Iron Jack" was quickly discarded as a suspect. In the last four robberies, the highwaymen seemed to be the same two men as described by the drivers and passengers. It was also noted that in the robberies the Wells, Fargo box was opened in the same way—that is, they opened the boxes by cutting the iron straps with an ax. Moreover, the mail sacks were opened the same way each time.

■ Local officers helped John Thacker wrap up this particular series of Shasta County stage robberies. *Author's collection.*

When Wells, Fargo detective John N. Thacker went to work on the case, he discovered that a man named Jack Rice had recently returned from Oregon in a wagon. Rice had bought some goods at a store in Fall River Mills, California, and one of the coins used was a counterfeit ten-dollar gold piece. Thacker flooded the area with wanted posters, and Rice was arrested when he arrived in Redding. He maintained he had just driven down from Spokane, Washington, and knew nothing of the counterfeit coin. His wagon was searched, and three overcoats were discovered. When no other bogus coin was found on him, he was released before Thacker could arrive. Rice proceeded on the road back to Oregon.

When Thacker did arrive, he was told that Rice was a friend of Bill Howard and Abe Jones, both of whom had ranches in Lake County, Oregon. Officers informed Thacker that Bill Howard's brother, Virgil, was at this time in the Portland jail on trial for passing counterfeit money. The pieces of the puzzle were coming together now.

Rice's route to California—and his return—was on a direct line with Lake County where the Howard and Jones ranches were located in southern Oregon. Thacker sent two Oregon officers, in Redding because of the Oregon robberies, ahead on the stage to catch up with Rice. Thacker and Shasta County Deputy Ross followed in a buggy. The Wells, Fargo detective was sure now that those two extra overcoats in Rice's wagon belonged to Bill Howard and Abe Jones.

The flyer Thacker sent out offering rewards for Howard and Jones.
Courtesy Wells, Fargo.

When inquiries assured they were close to their quarry, the Oregon officers, Deputy Greene and Deputy Miles, left the stage and hunted up Constable Frowley at Alturas. A short distance out of town, they came upon Rice now traveling with the other two the suspects. At first, Howard and Jones started backing up, as if to flee, but two pistol shots over their heads changed their minds. They were returned and placed in the Alturas jail to await the arrival of Thacker.

When Thacker and Deputy Ross arrived, they found the three suspects had been secured with leg irons by the local blacksmith and were ready to travel. Thacker at this time held a deputy U.S. marshal's commission and he took charge of the proceedings. On the evening of October 31, 1891, the three suspects were placed in the stage for Redding, with Deputy U. S. Marshal Carll, of Oregon, as guard. Thacker rode on the seat with the driver, while deputies Greene and Ross followed in the buggy. The stage pulled out in the afternoon as a steady rain commenced. The muddy mountain roads promised to make for a long and uncomfortable ride.

Just east of Holcomb's station, the coach stopped to water the horses. The sun had just set, and the cloudy weather made for a pitch-black night. When the three prisoners said they were thirsty, Marshal Carll stepped out of the coach with a cup. He was gone about five minutes, during which time Howard and Jones slipped off their boots and chains, then pulled their boots back on. When Carll returned with the water, the coach resumed its journey.

About ten minutes later, Howard bolted out one stage door, while Jones leaped out the other. Carll tried desperately to hold Jones, but he broke away as the marshal yelled for help. Several shots were fired, but Carll didn't dare leave Rice, and the two fugitives quickly disappeared into the forested mountain darkness.

PLAGUED WITH STAGE ROBBERS

Redding Excited Over Two Hold-Ups Within a Week.

TWO SUSPICIOUS PERSONS ARRESTED

The Mask Used by the Robbers and the Coat From Which It Was Made Found They Were Wet and the Parties Arrested Were Dripping Wet Also— Officers Say They Are the Men.

[Special to the EXAMINER.]
REDDING, October 20.—The greatest excitement has prevailed since Monday night, growing out of the robbery of both the Redding and Weaverville and Redding and Bieber stages. The followers of "Black Bart" have had a picnic in this vicinity for over a year, and it had become quite a common occurrence for a stage to be held up.

■ Northern California residents took stage robberies in their stride, but to the San Francisco papers, they were big news. *Author's collection.*

Rice was taken on to Redding and jailed as an accessory, having brought Howard and Jones down from Oregon. Carll was able to coax a confession out of Rice, who admitted he had been aiding Howard and Jones in their stage robbing ventures. At daylight, posses and Indian trackers were sent after the fugitives, but they came back empty-handed. When a man named Vandemark spotted Jones near Montgomery Creek and tried to arrest him, the fugitive shot his horse out from under him. The outlaw vanished into the mountains, but he was soon tracked to a cave in Warner Valley. Taken by surprise by several lawmen, the fugitive was arrested and placed in the charge of a Modoc County rancher named Thompson.

Six-feet-two-inches-tall, Thompson told Jones he wasn't going to put him in handcuffs for the trip back to Alturas. Instead, he told him to observe closely. Throwing an old shoe some distance away, Thompson drew his pistol and shot, knocking the shoe into the air. Before it hit the ground, he had placed two more shots into it.

"Now, Mr. robber," said Thompson, "I'm not going to tie you up. I'll let you go anywhere within fifty feet of me, but, as my aim is a little uncertain beyond that and I might kill you instead of cutting off your ears, I think you had better be careful of your distances."

Abe Jones never left Thompson's side after that until United States Deputy Marshal Maloney picked him up at Alturas and took him to San Francisco for trial. Thompson reportedly picked up some $1,800 reward for the capture.

Thacker and the other officers knew that young Howard had been raised in the area and was an expert woodsman. They also knew that he had no weapon or horse and he would probably go straight for his father's place for help.

A watch was put on the Howard house, but when Bill had not shown up by November 3, old Cornelius was arrested and jailed in Redding. The lawmen had not given up, however. Thacker placed deputies Thomas Miles, O. P. Whitton, and S. A. Stewart in the house with orders to wait it out for several days and see if the younger Howard would show up.

The Howard house was a crude affair. A story-and-a-half structure, it consisted of four rooms, with stairs leading to a double-roomed loft above. The front door opened into a bedroom, and the three officers took up their vigil in the room behind, where there were several chairs and a lounge. As the afternoon waned and the sun went down, the deputies ate some jerky and other dried food. They lit a small candle, but kept it low, on the floor. From time to time, they would talk in quiet tones. All of the lawmen had noticed an outside ladder to the upper story, indicating surreptitious comings and goings. One of the officers kept an eye on that ladder.

About midnight, the watchers heard a horse in the distance and quickly blew out the candle. In a few minutes, the horse had galloped up to the picket fence, and a rider was heard to leap to the ground and sprint up to the house. As the intruder stepped through the front door, the three lawmen were on their feet, listening and poised for action.

"Father, Father, strike a light!"

When he received no response, the man quickly walked to the

door behind which the deputies waited. When he opened it, one of the lawmen shouted, "Throw up your hands!"

Bill Howard was startled, but only for a moment. "You go to hell!" he screamed, but before he could slam the door, a shotgun blast blew him backwards onto the floor in a sprawled heap of shredded clothes and bleeding wounds.

A coroner's jury was summoned from Redding and a hearing commenced. The Redding *Republican Free Press* reported:

> From an examination of the body it was ascertained that one charge of buckshot entered the body just below the left nipple, which caused death. One charge tore away the rim of his hat on the left side, four of the shot taking effect on the forehead and face and another charge must have missed him altogether, as a multitude of shot went through the window and riddled a portion of the sash....

After testimony from the three deputies, it was not too difficult to arrive at a verdict that the deceased had come to his death while resisting arrest.

There was some criticism of Thacker for trying to take too much credit in the affair. It seems clear that the Oregon officers were quite active in flushing out Howard and Jones and were on their trail when Thacker took charge. As usual, the San Francisco press played up Thacker's part in the case since he was a high-profile officer and well known throughout the West for his work. This was the reason reporters sought out Thacker for interviews, and he was always careful to give himself and his company the lion's share of the credit in such matters. Although this often rankled local lawmen, it was all part of Thacker's job to make the public aware that it was not safe to rob Wells, Fargo.

And Bill Howard's fate was certainly a bloody object lesson.

Redding Republican Free Press, October 31, November 7, 21, 1891; *Yreka Journal*, October 28, November 11, 1891; *San Francisco Chronicle*, November 5, 1891; *San Francisco Examiner*, November 5, December 16, 1891; Early Shasta County Marriages, 1852-1904; Shasta County Great Register of Voters, 1866-1884, 1898 in Collections of Shasta County Historical Society.

THOSE PERILOUS TRAILS...

One of the hazards of driving a stage was the presence of brown and black bears as they often spooked the horses. With switchbacks along narrow paths barely wide enough to accommodate wagon wheels, any unexpected happening could hurl wagon, horses and passengers over a cliff. On one run from Inspiration Point down to Wawona, we came down a very steep hill and had to cross a place called Artist Creek, which was in the bend of a curve. The momentum of the hill caused my wagon to climb up the back of my horses, I yelled, "Everyone get out and get out quick!" Well I turned around and saw the two men and women along side the wagon, but they left the little four-year-old boy inside. I was so darn mad that I asked them, "What kind of cattle are you to leave your young one in the stagecoach while you jump out. Not even a cow would leave her young one in that kind of situation." One of the men got up into the wagon and got the kid out. Then the other threw a rock under the wheels, so I could get my horses up off the ground. That's as close as I ever came to endangering lives.

Yosemite stage driver Artie Helm

The most terrifying experience, outside of regular road hazards, was one night in late winter between Varberrie's stopping place and Whiskey Bend on Hatchet Mountain, when I was followed by a screaming, hungry mountain lion. I was alone that night with only two very frightened horses who sensed the serious danger, had the lion decided to attack. Finally, to my great relief, he let out one awful scream and abandoned his quest that night.

Shasta stage driver A. G. J. Paine

Rufus Henry Ingram

■ For all his youthful appearance, Alban H. Glasby was a Southern sympathizer willing to rob stage-coaches to further the cause of the Confederacy.
John Boessenecker collection.

During the Civil War, California was a hotbed of Confederate sympathizers. Southerners had been in the forefront of the great Gold Rush, many bringing their slaves with them to toil in the mines. The South was prominently represented in local California government, also, while many newspapers blatantly supported the secessionist cause. As a result, there were various plots and schemes to undermine Union support in the Far West, and serious concern was voiced that California could remain loyal to the Union. Fresno County boasted only one Republican voter in 1860, and the populace was so vocally disloyal that in 1863, for a time, Company A of the 2nd California Volunteers occupied nearby Fort Miller.

Little is known of Rufus Ingram's background, but he was born about 1834 and served with William C. Quantrill's Confederate guerrillas in the Kansas border country. Notorious in Missouri as the "Red Fox," Ingram participated in the savage raid on Lawrence, Kansas, in August 1863, when all male residents were shot down and the town burned to the ground.

Fleeing to Mexico, Ingram met a young farmer, George Baker, from San Jose, California, who was on his way to join the Confederate service. Baker told Ingram that although there were large numbers of Southerners and Condederate sympathizers in California, there were no experienced leaders to organize them. The two men agreed to return to San Jose and recruit a rebel unit to serve in the war.

In San Jose, Ingram joined the Knights of the Golden Circle, a Confederate organization that met secretly to raise funds and plot the overthrow of the state government. A sympathetic local rancher helped fund the group, and meetings were held in a valley outside of town. Many of the Knights joined this group, which was planning to fight for the South. But funds were needed to equip the men, and in 1864, money was scarce in drought-stricken California.

A plan was formulated whereby Ingram and a band of carefully selected men would rob one of the treasure stages crossing the Sierra from Nevada's Comstock Lode. Ingram and some of his men rode over to Placerville where they began picking up information on the treasure coach schedules. When Jim Grant,

■ A Virginia City stage preparing to leave for Placerville and Sacramento.
John Boessenecker collection.

one of the band, tried to recruit a man in town, Ingram was afraid their plan was in jeopardy, and the group rode back to San Jose. Later, when Grant made a nuisance of himself by threatening to kill other members of the gang, Ingram expelled him.

Becoming more desperate by the day, Ingram next planned a raid on San Jose itself, in the style of his Kansas forays. All the banks and shops would be raided, after which they would be able to head

■ The daring Ingram holdup took place at this spot, about fourteen miles east of Placerville. *Author's collection.*

east to join in the war. Luckily, Santa Clara County Sheriff John H. Adams learned of the raid and made suitable preparations. When this was discovered by the guerrillas, the foray was abandoned.

Selecting as his band of highwaymen Thomas B. Poole, George Baker, John Bouldware, John Clendenning and Al Glasby, Captain Ingram again prepared to rob one of the bullion-carrying stages coming into the state from Nevada. The group left San Jose on the night of June 21, 1864, arriving at the Somerset House, thirteen miles south of Placerville, on the afternoon of June 27.

The outlaws selected a spot at a bend of the road eleven miles above Placerville and were waiting there on the night of June 30 when two Concord coaches laden with $26,700 in treasure came into view. The *Placerville Mountain Democrat* reported on July 2:

> Stage Robbery—On Thursday night last, between the hours of 9 and 10 o'clock, on the narrow grade about 2½ miles above Sportsman's Hall, six men armed with shot guns and pistols, stopped two of the stages of the Pioneer Line and took from them eight sacks of bullion. Ned Blair was driving the first team and Charley Watson the second. They ordered Blair to halt, seized his leaders and stopped them. They

■ Stage driver Charley Watson. *Author's collection.*

demanded the treasure box. Blair told them that he hadn't it. They told him to throw out the bullion and he replied, "Come and get it!" Two of them covered him with their guns, while two others took out the bullion. They didn't get the treasure box. Blair asked them not to rob the passengers. They said it was not their intention; all they wanted was the treasure box of Wells, Fargo & Co.

Observing that Blair's stage had stopped and supposing that Blair had met with an accident, Watson halted his team and hurried to Blair's assistance. As he approached, two of the robbers advanced towards him, covered him with their shotguns, ordered him back, and demanded the treasure box and bullion. Watson was forced to comply. From his stage, they took three sacks of bullion and a small treasure box from Genoa. Both stages were filled with passengers, but unfortunately none of them was armed.

After giving a receipt signed by Ingram, "Captain, Commanding, C.S.A.," the high-waymen mounted and rode off. Burying their treasure, for which they would return later, they kept several bars of bullion and some coin.

Returning to the Somerset House, the bandits were

■ Somerset House, where Ingram's raiders were discovered, and the deadly gun battle took place. *Author's collection.*

startled to be quickly discovered by two lawmen from a Placerville posse. Deputy Joseph Staples burst into a room where Ingram, Glasby, Bouldware, and Poole were gathered. In a harrowing, close range gunfight, Staples wounded Poole, but was shot and mortally wounded in a hail of outlaw bullets. Constable George Ranney was gunned down, also, and badly wounded. After robbing the officers' bodies, the outlaws quickly fled, leaving the wounded Poole be-

■ El Dorado County Undersheriff James B. Hume, later the famous Wells, Fargo detective, was very active in tracking down the Ingram raiders. *California State Library.*

hind. Taken into custody, Poole quickly "peached" on the gang.

El Dorado County Undersheriff James B. Hume brought Staples's body back to Placerville. His funeral was held at the Neptune Fire Engine House, of which he was a member. A large number of friends, family, and officials were present. A letter from his mother in the East was found in his pocket and read to the crowd. Born in Ireland, Staples was eulogized as "brave, true-hearted and generous."

Ingram and his men made their way south through the mountains, abandoning their horses when they were too closely pursued. Back in Santa Clara County, they were hiding in an out-of the-way house in a dense thicket when Sheriff Adams and a posse closed in. After another desperate fight, Clendenning and Bouldware were both mortally wounded and young Al Glasby captured. Ingram and Baker made their escape into the surrounding thickets and fled the state.

■ Jim Grant was more interested in loot than he was in causes. *San Jose Historical Museum.*

Jim Grant, who had earlier been dismissed from the gang, had meanwhile gone off on his own crime spree. He and a partner had robbed two stages on the coast road in early July 1864, then stopped the Visalia coach near Pacheco Pass a month later. Lawmen, watching a girlfriend's house, trapped him and, after weighing him down with a load of buckshot in his back, persuaded Grant to accompany them to jail. In April 1865, he began a two-year term in San Quentin as No. 2982.

Tom Poole was tried and sentenced to hang for his part in the killing of Deputy Staples at the Somerset House. Poole had a colorful history. While undersheriff of Monterey County in February 1858, Poole had hanged a prisoner who had received a reprieve from the governor. The lawman had taken advantage of the fact that the wrong name was on the reprieve, although he knew full well who the recipient was. He had also been captured as one of the Chapman "pirates" who had outfitted a Confederate ship in San Francisco Bay to raid coastal shipping in 1863.

On September 29, 1865, Tom Poole calmly ascended the Placerville scaffold. "He smiled on all and seemed perfectly resigned," noted the local newspaper. "While the cap was being drawn over his face and his arms and legs were being pinioned, he stood perfectly composed. He died almost without a struggle in a few seconds." It was just five months after the Confederate surrender at Appomattox. When Glasby and various others of the conspirators were released for cooperating with the authorities, the great Confederate stage robbery saga had come to an end.

■ Thomas B. Poole, the ex-Monterey lawman, was the only member of Ingram's group to be executed. *John Boessenecker collection.*

San Quentin State Prison Register, Governor's Reward Files, California State Archives, Sacramento; Boessenecker, John, *Badge and Buckshot*; Dillon, Richard, *Wells Fargo Detective*; *Santa Cruz Pacific Sentinel*, March 13, 1858, October 7, 1865; *San Francisco Daily Alta California*, July 2, 3, September 10, 1864; *Placerville Mountain Democrat*, July 2, 9, 1864; Sacramento *Daily Union*, July 2, 9, 10, 13, 19, 1864.

THAT'S ENTERTAINMENT...

We are told that pioneer days were nothing but work from dawn to dusk. It was another time, and life was indeed hard, but modern Californians might be surprised at the great variety of entertainments our frontier forebears had available to them. Here are just a few...

San Francisco Bulletin, October, 1856.

California Police Gazette, January, 1868.

Stockton Herald, May, 1874.

Mariposa Gazette, September, 1865.

Mariposa Gazette, September, 186

San Francisco Herald, May, 1859.

PRIZE FIGHT!!
BULL AND BEAR FIGHT FOR FIVE HUNDRED DOLLARS!! The *South American Cinnamon Bear*, which has beaten three grizzlies, will fight *R. Riddle's celebrated Bull*, Santa Anna, for the above sum, on *SUNDAY, the 22d inst., on the Stockton Race Course.* The attention of the sporting public is requested, as from the well-known fighting qualities of both, rare sport can be relied on.   SPENCER, DAY & CO.

Stockton San Joaquin Republican, February, 1852.

California Police Gazette, January, 1868.

Thomas Jackson

■ Rustler, burglar, and stage robber, Tom Jackson was as versatile as he was dangerous during his wild career.
Author's collection.

A native of Ireland where he was born about 1835, Jackson and his parents were probably immigrant victims of the great Irish potato famine of the period. Nothing is known of Tom prior to 1865 when he was operating with John A. Toney and one William Joslyn in a cattle stealing operation. A newspaper recap of his rustling experiences at this time reads like a chapter from a matinee cowboy movie serial:

> ...Thomas Jackson will be remembered as having been arrested two or three years ago on several charges of horse stealing in Sacramento and Yolo counties. On one occasion, when acquitted on a charge in this county he made his escape from the courtroom without waiting for a trial in Yolo county. He was subsequently arrested and imprisoned at Marysville, but broke jail. More recently he was arrested in El Dorado county after a severe fight between him and his friends on the one hand and the El Dorado county officers on the other, and taken to Yolo for trial on the old charge. He soon managed to escape from the Woodland jail and has been at liberty ever since, until the last few days.

According to the Yolo press, Tom had obtained a chisel from friends, tunneled through the jail wall, then scaled a fifteen-foot wall to escape. After the brawl with the El Dorado County lawmen, Jackson was charged with assault to kill an officer. He was tried for attempted murder and sentenced to state prison for two years in early November, 1865. As No. 3128, he served his term and was released early for good behavior on February 27, 1867.

A laborer by occupation, Jackson may have worked for a time in the San Francisco Bay Area until an opportunity for plunder presented itself. It was late in the year when he joined forces with Bill "Jersey" Gregg, or Gray, a highwayman and burglar of odious record. Gregg had been picked up for burglary of the What Cheer House in 1861, then served a brief term in San Quentin the following year before he escaped. He was in and out of prison for the next few years and was considered to be a dangerous thief who was always armed. Teaming up with Jackson, the two held up lone pedestrians in San Francisco and Oakland, and committed burglaries at every opportunity.

On the night of December 28, 1867, Gregg and Jackson stopped Nathan W. Spaulding on an Oakland street. As one held a pistol to Spaulding's head, the other "went through him," taking a fine watch and some coins. The crime was of particular notice, since Spaulding was a prominent San Francisco businessman, as well as mayor of Oakland. After he described the two thieves to the San Francisco police, Detective Captain Isaiah W. Lees was certain the robbers

■ San Francisco was the financial center of California in the 1860s and was the playground for highwaymen, con-artists, and burglars from around the world. Tom Jackson and Bill Gregg were right at home.
Author's collection.

were "Jersey" Gregg and Tom Jackson. He had recently talked to Gregg on the street, and the robber assured him he would never again submit to arrest by an officer.

Captain Lees was a famous sleuth whom William Pinkerton would later refer to as the "greatest criminal catcher the West ever knew." A fourteen-year veteran of the police force, Lees was on his way to a dinner engagement, accompanied by one of his men, when he decided to take a look around inside a local train depot. Lees and Detective Fred Fuller entered and were startled to spot Gregg and Jackson talking over in a corner. As they walked toward them, the two

■ Captain Isaiah Lees had many physical contests with criminals during his long career, but few were any rougher than his fight with Bill Gregg. *Author's collection.*

thieves edged away from each other. Lees, recovering from a broken ankle, was on crutches, but he hobbled right up to Gregg. Fuller approached Jackson, but as he warily closed in, the thief dodged around him and raced out the door with the detective right behind him.

■ Lees' battle with Bill Gregg. *A contemporary newspaper sketch in author's collection.*

As Lees grappled with Gregg, Fuller pursued Jackson, as described in the *San Francisco Bulletin*:

...Jackson sprang past Fuller and broke for the street. Fuller pursued and called to him to stop, but he had gained Market street, and only quickened his pace, the officer right at his heels. As they ran past a sand hill Fuller saw him fling some object away from him over the fence, and then draw a revolver from his holster. Fuller then drew and fired...but did not hit him.... An old unoccupied house lay in their way, and Jackson ran into that, the officer going round it with a large crowd of citizens at his heels....

After a brief struggle, Fuller captured Jackson as he emerged from the back door of the house. Returning to the depot, Fuller

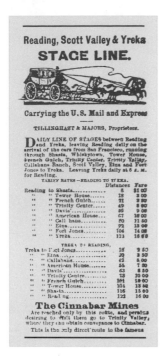

acquired the watch Jackson had tried to discard. At the depot, Lees had subdued Gregg after a desperate fight, and the two thieves were taken to police headquarters. The watch proved to be Mayor Spaulding's, and the two men were easily convicted. Gregg received a ten-year sentence, while Jackson entered San Quentin on January 21, 1868, to serve an eight-year term as No. 3736.

Discharged in September 1874, Jackson promptly backslid into his life of crime. In less than a year, he was back in San Quentin on a San Mateo County burglary conviction, sentenced to five years. Governor William Irwin commuted his time to four-and-one-half-years and he was again a free man on July 3, 1878. Within a month, Jackson was making plans with Martin Tracy, an ex-convict he had met in San Quentin. The two gambled together for a time, then had a chance meeting with Andy Marsh, another ex-con who was traveling from town to town in Shasta County as a shoemaker—a trade he had learned in prison. Marsh was already weary of going straight. It probably didn't take his pals very long to talk him into tackling a stagecoach robbery with them. Why, the way they told it, all that easy money was already almost burning a hole in their pockets.

Heading north to Siskiyou County, the trio lay in wait for the Yreka to Redding coach on the night of September 7, 1878. It was 3:30 in the morning and the shotgun guard was riding inside the coach.

■ The Tower House was a favorite stopping place for stages and other travelers between Yreka and Redding. Such places usually had a store, saloon, and rooms for overnight stops. *Author's collection.*

■ The three bandits stopped the coach as planned, but only two would walk away. *The Wasp,* November 4, 1876.

The team was toiling towards the summit of the Scott Mountain grade, when a man with a flour sack over his head stepped out in the road and called for the driver to halt. Two other highwaymen appeared out of the roadside brush. R. G. Dunn, Wells, Fargo's agent at Redding, wrote to the company's detective, Jim Hume, and described what happened next:

> ...Within four hundred yards of the top, the team was on a walk, Reynolds was inside and no one was with the driver, when three men stepped out and told them to halt. Two men stepped forward, one on each side of the leaders, and one came up to the driver, covered him with a six-shooter, and told him to throw up his hands. He put whip and lines in his right hand and raised it, and asked the robber to drop his pistol as he had no arms. He did this to give Reynolds a chance. The robber lowered his pistol and Reynolds shot him in the breast killing him instantly. His pistol went off when he fell. With this the others commenced firing and the team started. They fired several shots. The team went about seventy-five yards and the near wheeler fell dead....

Leaving Andy Marsh sprawled in the road, Jackson and Tracy fled into the dark brush- and pine-covered mountains. While Jim Hume caught the first train north, Jack Conant, a French Canadian who had scouted with Custer, took two men and headed north on the outlaw's trail. When a dispute arose regarding the direction the robbers took, Conant pressed on alone and at Yreka caught the stage for Sisson's. There he hired Dick Hubbell and Sisson Jim, an Indian tracker, and again sought the highwaymen's trail. They had gone some thirty-five miles towards Picayune Lake when they heard a rifle shot at about eight o'clock in the evening. Waiting till dawn, the possemen saw a light and a spiral of smoke in a canyon below and began working their way towards it. Conant described the action that followed:

> I used every precaution to arrest the fugitives unawares, which I did, as I had them covered and within twenty foot before they were aware of my presence—Hubbell and the Indian being immediately behind. They (the robbers) were well armed. Mitchell attempted to draw a pistol he had on his person while lying in bed, when I told him "hands off," which he did like a wise man. They had an improved Winchester, model 76, a double-barreled shotgun and two cartridge revolvers....

Giving their names as Charles Brown (Jackson) and Charles Mitchell (Martin Tracy), the outlaws were escorted to Callahans, a small community that had grown up around a local ranch and stage station. From there, they were driven to Yreka by a sheriff's deputy. Andy Marsh's body was brought to Callahans also, on the evening of the holdup. He was buried there the next day, "unwept, unhonored and unsung," as one correspondent put it. He had died instantly with a full load of buckshot hitting him in the neck at short range, "making a ghastly wound."

While waiting for his trial in the Yreka jail, Tracy became ill and was diagnosed with heart disease. He complained of a pain in his side, and the sheriff had him placed in one of the wooden cells which were more comfortable than the iron ones. "In a short time," reported the *Yreka Journal*, "it was discovered that he had a couple of

■ The cellblocks at San Quentin were looming up before Tom Jackson once again. *California State Library.*

bricks loose towards making a hole in the jail wall, when the sheriff removed him to an iron cell until he became so sick that the sheriff moved him back again."

Jackson obtained the highly-respected Elijah Steele as counsel and the trial began on December 17. A stream of witnesses testified for the prosecution and certified copies of Jackson's prior convictions in both El Dorado and Alameda counties were allowed to be read in court, effectively estab-

■ Rancher and attorney Elijah Steele was appointed Jackson's counsel, but little could be done. *Author's collection.*

lishing Jackson's violent past. The defendant testified in his own defense, but it was a lost cause. On December 30, 1878, it took the jury only five minutes to convict him of the attempted robbery. He was sentenced to another ten-year stretch as No. 8607 at San Quentin. He was released June 30, 1885. Martin Tracy pleaded guilty and began serving a five-year term on January 14, 1879.

Instead of his sad fate, Andy Marsh would have happily settled for either, or both, terms.

Hume and Thacker's, "Robbers' Record"; San Quentin State Prison Register; California State Archives, Sacramento; *Byram Journals,* John Boessenecker collection; *Oroville Weekly Union Record,* July 15, 1865; *San Francisco Daily Alta California,* January 3, 1868; *San Francisco Daily Evening Bulletin,* January 2, 1868; *Redding Independent,* September 12, 1878; *Shasta Courier,* September 14, 1878; *Yreka Journal,* September 11, 18, 25, October 9, November 27, 1878; *Yreka Union,* September 14, 21, November 30, December 21, 28, 1878; *Marysville Daily Appeal,* September 3, 1904.

WELLS FARGO SHOTGUN GUARDS

They were called "Shotgun Messengers," because of those deadly shotguns they carried. Contrary to a popular conception, guards did not accompany every stage, only the ones carrying a large amount of treasure. Guards rode next to the driver, but if there were no passengers, they sometimes rode inside the coach, hoping to catch any bandits unawares. And sometimes they did.

■ Shotgun messenger William J. Hendricks killed John Keener during an attempted stage holdup. *A contemporary newspaper sketch in author's collection.*

Samuel P. Dorsey, Wells, Fargo's Grass Valley agent, claimed to have originated the guard system on the run between Nevada City and Colfax. Apparently a May 3, 1858, robbery as reported in the local press at the time was the impetus:

The Telegraph Stage left Nevada City shortly after one o'clock in the morning with $21,000 in treasure being conveyed via Wells, Fargo. The coach was stopped a mile and a half out of the city by five men armed with shotguns and pistols. The driver handed down the Alta Express box, but the highwaymen weren't taken in. After demanding the Wells Fargo box, it was thrown down and the driver was told to "Git up and git!" Daniel Ludington, One-Eyed Jack and several other characters, all of Nevada City, were quickly picked up, while Wells, Fargo, promptly made good the loss.

Jim Hume said that shotgun messengers "are the kind of men you can depend on if you get in a fix," and that is as good a description as any. In 1861 there were 16 messengers on duty, 35 in the early 1870s, 110 in the early 1880s, and 200 by 1885. These included guards on trains, boats, and ships.

Although many a stage robbery was discouraged by the presence of a shotgun guard, there were never any guarantees. Early on the morning of April 30, 1892, shotgun messenger Mike Tovey climbed aboard the stage leaving San Andreas. The stage carried the Sheep Camp mine payroll, and a drizzling rain promised an uncomfortable ride. Dave Raggio, the driver, sat next to Tovey as the stage headed out of town. Some four miles down the road, a masked man stepped out from behind a tree and opened fire on the passing coach. Raggio took some buckshot in a shoulder and his breast, while Tovey was hit in the arm. The other barrel of the assassin's weapon blasted through the side of the coach and instantly killed fifteen-year-old Johanna Rodesino. A veteran guard, Tovey jumped from the coach and went after the killer, but when Raggio cried out, Tovey climbed back onto the seat and drove to a nearby ranch. A year later, Tovey was shot and killed in the same kind of attack, the killer in both cases making a clean getaway. Tovey and the innocent young girl were both widely mourned.

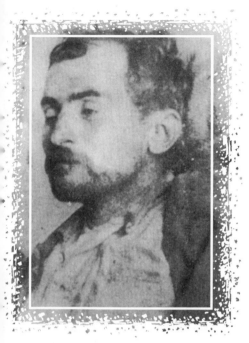

John Keener

The tragic story of Johnny Keener was another vivid reminder of the terrible fate that sometimes awaits those who take to the highwayman's road. His father, John D. Keener, was born in North Carolina, but migrated to Missouri at an early age. He was married to Ellena in the mid-1840s, and their first child, Emily, was born in 1845. Henry came along two years later, just prior to the family's move to Texas. Daughters Elizabeth and Sarah arrived in 1849 and '51. The father brought the first herd of Durham cattle to California in 1852 and the family settled in Tulare County. The elder Keener made other trips east for more stock. In California daughter Francis was born, along with sons James and William. To this large brood, John E. Keener was added in 1859.

It is thought that the parents moved about a good deal, their children staying in Tulare County with relatives and the oldest boy, Henry. The Keener girls married, and several of the boys eventually acquired their own farms. Johnny Keener was content to work for his brother William, however, who farmed ten miles south of

■ John D. Keener was not around when young John needed him most.
Tulare County Historical Society.

Visalia. All were regarded as honest, hard-working pioneers of the period.

By the early 1890s, Johnny Keener was in his early thirties and was no longer happy with his situation. He was getting by, but was spending an inordinate amount of time in saloons drinking and playing cards. He was apparently a poor gambler, continually losing his money, and, no doubt, was criticized by his brother for his poor judgment. It was a strained situation which Johnny resolved sometime in 1893 by leaving home to visit an old friend near Tucson, Arizona.

■ Keener and Dowdle's binge was taking them down a one-way road to destruction. *Author's collection.*

Rancher William E. Dowdle was undoubtedly glad to see an acquaintance from Visalia. He and his parents had lived in California some years earlier and had known the Keener family. Although Dowdle was some three years younger than Keener, they were quite similar in their social habits. Both were adept at drinking, gambling, and living beyond their means. And, apparently, Keener was all the incentive Dowdle needed to indulge in his worst traits.

There are few details known of the Keener-Dowdle rendezvous in Arizona, but after some prolonged drinking bouts, both men were involved in some trouble and narrowly avoided being jailed. Dowdle sold his ranch, and after telling his wife he would send for her later, he and Keener engaged in more drunken binges. Finally, they made their way back to Visalia.

Keener's brothers begged Johnny to stay away from Dowdle, who they felt was a bad influence. He refused, and the two men continued their drinking bouts until Dowdle had gone through all his ranch sale funds. In their carousing, Dowdle and Keener had met a kindred spirit named Amos Bierer, and the three men joined in a wood chopping venture to make some drinking money. Dowdle's wife, Tillie, and child, had joined him by now, but when

■ Angels Camp as it appeared when Keener and his two pals hit town. Trouble soon followed. *Author's collection.*

she became aware of his dissolute life, she left for the coast to visit some friends. Dowdle and his two pals, meanwhile, continued their drinking.

Wood chopping was hard work, and the three souses now decided there must be an easier and better-paying way to make their drinking money. Perhaps there was some truth to rumors that Dowdle had been mixed up in some prior Arizona stagecoach robbing scheme. There was even talk of there being a reward on his head. In any case, the three men now decided the way to get some big money was to hold up a stage, and they began making plans. It was quickly realized, however, that the local coaches would not be carrying any significant amounts of money. Agreeing that the mining country to the north would be much more profitable, Dowdle,

■ William Dowdle.
California State Archives.

Keener, and Bierer misleadingly left word that they were heading south to the Red Rock mines in Kern County. They reportedly left on April 25, 1894, and headed north for Calaveras County. There is evidence, however, that they left earlier and on March 7, held up their first coach. Five other stage robberies followed, the sixth taking place on May 7.

Although Keener and Dowdle had planned to keep a low profile, they continued drinking and gambling in the Sonora saloons, while Bierer stationed himself in Angels Camp and picked up information on stage shipments. A coach carrying a heavy treasure box was reportedly leaving on May 19 and, while Bierer remained in Angels Camp, Keener and Dowdle positioned themselves on opposite sides of the stage road, about twelve miles east of Milton.

Fred Wesson, who had driven several of the previously robbed coaches, handled the reins on the stage that now rumbled down the road and approached the ambush site. Keener stood up with his weapon at the ready. This was going to be so easy. William J. Hendricks, the guard, was sitting inside the coach with five other passengers. He had given up his seat beside the driver to a lady passenger, but he was as alert as ever. When he spotted the armed

■ Contemporary newspaper sketch of the crime scene. Dowdle is behind tree at extreme left, while Keener lies dead on the right. *Author's collection.*

Keener, he quickly fired twice, and the outlaw fell over backward, his own weapon being discharged into the air.

The highwayman was dead, riddled from head to foot with two loads of buckshot. "He presented a ghastly sight as he lay there in the chaparral," reported a witness later, "torn and mangled by the death-dealing load of the messenger's gun."

■ In this photograph taken shortly after the aborted robbery, Johnny Keener lies where he fell. He holds a pistol in his hand, a rifle lying nearby. *Courtesy Wells Fargo.*

The stage had never stopped moving and, as the frightened horses plunged on, Dowdle fired from the other side of the road, slightly wounding two passengers. The coach careened wildly down the road, as the passengers huddled in their seats. Lillie Stowell, who had taken Hendricks' seat next to the driver, later commented that it was "the wildest ride I ever want to take, rounding curves on a rough mountain road, the stage threatening every second to be upset."

After stopping at a nearby ranch to check on his passengers, the driver then drove on to Milton and spread the news. The novice robbers had made a bad mistake. There had indeed been $15,000 in bullion on the coach, but because Reason McConnell, the regular guard, was not sitting next to the driver, it was assumed there was no guard. By sitting inside, Hendricks had taken the bandits completely by surprise.

Lawmen were quickly on the scene, and the dead outlaw was identified by a former Visalian. There was no clue to the other ban-

■ Amos Bierer. *California State Archives.*

dit, however. When a description was sent to Henry Keener in Visalia for a verification of Johnny's identity, Henry telegraphed back that it was indeed his brother and that William Dowdle was probably his partner. As a dragnet spread out over the area, it was now thought that Keener and Dowdle were responsible for the other stage robberies in the past month. The fugitive had vanished, however, swallowed up by the rolling, oak-studded hills.

On May 30, a farmhand on the Ed Moore ranch east of Copperopolis was searching for a shovel. Walking behind an old shed, he saw a man lying on the ground. The fellow was moaning and crying in a pitiful way, and the farmhand asked what the trouble was. The only response was even more agonized cries. William Dowdle had been found.

Filthy dirty and half-starved, Dowdle was recognized immediately by the local constable. He was treated kindly in the town jail, and some food had him back to normal in a few days. He quickly blew the whistle on Bierer, who was captured in Angels Camp. The two men were tried in the Calaveras Superior Court and convicted of the attempted robbery. Sentenced to fourteen years each in state

■ California State Prison at Folsom. *California State Library.*

prison, the two convicts were escorted into Folsom on August 6, 1894. Dowdle as No. 3223 and Bierer as No. 3222.

Both Bierer and Dowdle were paroled in 1902, after much pressure had been exerted by the Dowdle family in Arizona. William Dowdle met his long-suffering wife at the gate. Most of his years of marriage had been squandered, and there was not much left. Tillie Dowdle died three years later, and her husband followed her in 1906. Their dreams, however, had died long before.

San Quentin State Prison Register, California State Archives, Sacramento; Boessenecker, John, "John Keener Cashes In," *Old West*; Edwards, Harold L., "The Story of John Keener and William Dowdle," *Los Tulares*; United States Federal Census Schedules, Tulare County, 1860, 1870, 1880; Mitchell, Annie, *A Modern History of Tulare County*; *Stockton Independent*, May 31, 1894; *Visalia Weekly Delta*, May 24, 31, June 7, 1894; *Calaveras Prospect*, June 2, 30, July 7, 1894.

Frank Kellett

alias "Tex" and "Frank Tex"

■ Kellett was a rustler, horse thief and stage robber who outlived his time.
California State Archives.

At different times, Frank Kellett gave both Louisiana and Texas as his birthplace, but perhaps the latter is more accurate, since that was the derivation of his nickname. He was born about 1847. Nothing is known of Kellett's antecedents, but he may have migrated west from Utah. He first shows up in a dispatch from Fresno Flats to the *Fresno Weekly Expositor* in early July 1881:

> Information was received last Friday that two men named Billie Bender and Frank Kellett, alias "Tex," were driving stolen cattle across the mountains east of here. A counsel of the stockraisers was immediately held, and a posse of citizens, accompanied by Deputy Sheriff Pickett, who happened to be in the neighborhood, set out for Mammoth, calculating to intercept the thieves at Mono Lake....

At the lake, the posse found that the thieves had sold the stolen cattle some five or six days previously, several already having been butchered. Rancher Jonathan Lewis, the posse leader, identified the stolen stock by their various local brands.

Kellett and Bender had by now doubled back and began drinking in the Fresno Flat saloons. According to a newspaper report, the two thieves "defied arrest, cursing the constable, shoving their pistols into men's faces, and parading the streets with a whoop, a threat, and a wild halloo." In short, they pretty much treed the town. Before leaving at a wild gallop, the two rustlers left word where they were going if anyone wanted to arrest them.

The Lewis party galloped into Fresno Flats too late to arrest their quarry, but they obtained good information and headed for Jim Bethel's ranch and saloon, where Kellett and Bender said they could be found. After a tough pursuit through the mountains, Deputy Pickett split the group and with the other party under Lewis, they pursued two different courses. Lewis's posse caught up with the fugitives near the summit of the Sierra and a spirited gun battle

■ Shown in its declining years, Fresno Flats, now known as Oakhurst, was a supply point for local miners and stockmen, as well as a stage stop for the Yosemite tourist coaches. *Author's collection.*

took place. Armed only with pistols, the rustlers were pinned down, as the posse remained out of range and kept up a withering rifle fire. Kellett and Bender slipped away on foot, abandoning their horses and gear. When the posse discovered the outlaws were gone, it was getting dark, and they gave up the chase. The *Expositor* remarked:

> The pursuing party brought back the money, knives, horses and other personal effects of the thieves, but they, unfortunately, escaped. As Deputy Pickett was not with the party that found the thieves, and the pursuers brought back so much, we feel certain that these "cow-boys" won't bother anybody in the future.

If the *Expositor* reporter had hoped a lynching had taken place, it was wishful thinking. Still, the two "cow-boys" were apparently scared out of the area for a time. Another three-man posse took the trail soon after the Lewis posse returned, but they too came back empty-handed. The outlaws, it seems, had decided to lie low for a time in Nevada.

Making their way to the eastern side of the Sierra, Kellett and Bender probably stole some horses and fled to the lower, southwest corner of Nevada.

The Moapa Valley area had originally been settled by Mormons who had left after a boundary dispute with Arizona in 1871. Others had settled in the area by 1880, among whom were various fugitives from the law. Kellett may have had friends or family there and he is thought to have worked on several mining claims, probably for room, board, and shares.

Tex made friends with the Gentrys who established a hotel at Saint Thomas in 1881. When a local killer and thug named Jack Longstreet got drunk and began cursing in front of Gentrys' hotel, Kellett knocked him down. The two outlaws had a vicious, rough-and-tumble brawl in the street, Kellett beating Longstreet to his knees and making him apologize to Mrs. Gentry.

After lying low for a time, Kellett undoubtedly took up rustling again. When he returned to California in the spring of 1887, it was probably with a Nevada lawman sniffing at his trail. For a time, he was greatly feared by the Indians and mountain ranchers when he lived among them in Fresno County. Soon, Kellett made the mis-

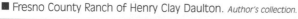

■ Fresno County Ranch of Henry Clay Daulton. *Author's collection.*

take of stealing a horse from the ranch of Henry Clay Daulton on June 27, 1887, then selling it on the eastern side of the Sierra.

■ Constable, later Fresno County Sheriff John M. Hensley. *Fresno County Sheriff's Office.*

Returning to Fresno County, Kellett stopped for the night at one of cattleman Henry Miller's bunkhouses, where an alert rancher spotted him as a suspect in the Daulton horse theft. Constable John Hensley was put on his trail and organized a posse of ranchers and Indians. Heading into the mountains, Hensley sent most of the posse to cut off the outlaw, while he took along Tom Beasore, a half-blood Indian tracker, and several others. They soon spotted the outlaw's horse staked out on a high meadow. Cautiously working his way around the meadow, Hensley saw Kellett hiding in some brush by a water hole. When he called out for the outlaw to surrender, Tex broke for his gun, and both Hensley and Beasore shot him in the leg and brought him down. Hensley had to talk hard to keep his posse from lynching the outlaw.

■ Kellett did time in the Fresno County jail, which also housed the local sheriff's office. *Fresno City and County Historical Society.*

After reciting the story of Tex's capture, the *Expositor* gave a brief history of Kellett and Bender and brought their story up to date:

Tex is one of the gang of thieves known as "Tex & Benton," [sic] who operated in this territory about seven years ago, and whom the citizens pursued into the mountains.... Since then they operated over in Nevada. Some time ago it is said that Benton was found with a bullet hole in his head, and Tex would have been buried at Beasore Meadows but for the effort of Constable Hensley....

■ Kellett was a hard-looking customer, but he knew when to give up. *California State Archives.*

Hauled into a Fresno justice court on September 2, 1887, Kellett was held for trial in the superior court in November. After pleading guilty, he was sentenced to ten years at San Quentin where he was logged in as No. 12782 on December 14, 1887. Tex's stay at the prison was uneventful and, with good behavior, he was discharged on June 11, 1894, and again drifted south to Fresno County.

Fresh out of prison, Kellett rode into the Upper Kings River ranch of John W. Rice and asked for work. Rice had been having trouble with sheepmen encroaching on his property, and Tex, with a six-shooter at his waist and a Winchester rifle on his saddle, looked like just the man for the job. There was some shooting that summer and fall, but nothing serious, and the sheepmen quickly learned to keep their stock off the Rice range.

Kellett was a skilled cow handler and after helping move the Rice cattle to their summer range in the spring of 1895, he again set out to guard against any sheep encroachments. But the sheepmen had learned their lesson well, and Tex had little to do that summer. With time on his hands and a ready-made alibi, Kellett rode north and took up a position on the stage road about six miles west of Snelling on August 1, 1895. He stopped the Coulterville to Merced coach and obtained $290.67 from the treasure box, not bothering to rob the passengers.

On October 1, the coach was stopped again near the same spot as reported in the *San Francisco Daily Morning Call*:

■ The type of mountain stagecoach that Kellett robbed. *Author's collection.*

The Coulterville stage was held up again today near the spot where it was stopped in August. The stage had been driven upon a small bridge over a gulch, when a man rose up from the road side and commanded Bert Campbell, the driver, to hand down Wells Fargo's box. The robber was told that the box was iron and was screwed to the bed of the wagon. At this response the highwayman reached down at his feet and produced an ax and a monkey-wrench. These he gave to Campbell and told him to go to work.

■ Merced Constable Tom Mack. *Contemporary newspaper sketch in author's collection.*

The passengers had been directed by Tex to hold the horses, but he didn't rob them. Driver Bert Campbell soon had the box opened, and the highwayman filled his pockets, then told the coach to move on. Officers were promptly on his trail.

On the night of October 29, Constable Thomas A. Mack opened the door of a roadhouse at Robert's Ferry on the Tuolumne River. From descriptions, he recognized Kellett sitting across the room and quickly had his prisoner cuffed. There was good evidence of Tex's guilt, particularly since he had the Rice family mule with him at the robbery, packed and ready to cross the Sierra. The Rice brand had been duly noted by the stage driver. At his trial in November, Kellett gave in and made a full confession, hoping to receive a reduced sentence. He still received a ten year term in San Quentin.

Discharged on July 14, 1902, Kellett is reported to have traveled east, disappearing in Utah. He was fifty-seven years old now and perhaps decided to seek a job and go straight. In any case, we will probably never know Tex's fate.

San Quentin State Prison Register, California State Archives, Sacramento; Wells Fargo History Room, San Francisco; Zanjani, Sally, *Jack Longstreet, Last of the Desert Frontiersmen*; Fresno *Weekly Expositor,* July 6, 13, August 3, 1881, October 30, 1895; Fresno *Morning Republican*, October 2, 1895; San Francisco *Daily Morning Call*, October 2, 31, 1895; San Francisco *Examiner*, October 31, 1895; *San Francisco Chronicle*, January 14, 1896; Rice, Lee, "Ashes from Dead Campfires"; Justice Court and Trial records from Fresno County Court Archives, Fresno, California.

Charley Meyers

■ Charley Meyers was just another working man who thought he could turn his life around with the proceeds of a stage robbery. "Lord, what fools these mortals be!" *Hank Johnston collection.*

"**I**f any man moves I'll shoot him, or woman either!" Writing from England in 1885, an erstwhile passenger on a Yosemite stage that was robbed some months earlier complained bitterly of the rough language and tactics of the two highwaymen. "The robber actually had the cowardice," continued the passenger, "to hold his revolver to the face of each lady as he searched her." This may or may not have been true, since newspaper accounts reported the women were not bothered, even though one was wearing diamond earrings. Still, the fact that a complaining passenger could be heard from halfway around the world was in itself a curious facet of our frontier stagecoach history.

Born in the early 1860s, Charley Meyers was the son of David Meyers, a prominent rancher of the Coarsegold-Fresno Flats area, on the road to Yosemite. Charley was good with tools and had received the limited schooling available to the mountain children.

When he came of age, Charley worked his own small piece of land, supplementing his income with carpentry and painting jobs around the nearby village of Fresno Flats. When Charley married the sister of his friend, William Prescott, David Meyers helped his son build a small cabin near his parents' home.

Willie Prescott, the brother-in-law, worked off and on in the local sawmill. Like Charley, he barely scratched out a living, and the two men probably discussed various schemes to increase their net worth. But it took money to make money and the two boys finally began talking about other means of boosting their incomes. The Yosemite stage road wound right through their area. People from around the world rode those coaches, stopping in Fresno Flats for meals and a change of horses. And many of the travelers were quite wealthy.

Late on the night of May 22, 1885, the railroad agent at Madera, California, telegraphed Fresno County Sheriff O. J. Meade to tell him the Yosemite stage had been stopped and robbed. The first account of the affair appeared in the *Fresno Weekly Expositor*, May 27, 1885:

Late Friday night last two of the Yosemite stages were robbed at about 5 o'clock on the road near Buford's place, by two men; one a short man, the other a man of lighter build, but taller. The short one was armed with a rifle and pistol, the other with a shotgun and pistol. There were a number of passengers aboard the stages, and the robbers divested them of their money, watches, sleeve buttons, charms and jewelry of all kinds.... They also took Wells Fargo & Co.'s treasure box. The robbers were evidently well acquainted with the drivers

■ A posed photograph of a stage holdup on the road to Yosemite, showing how it was done in the days of Meyers and Prescott. *Author's collection.*

as they told the first driver, Phillip Toby, to "Drive on, Phil," when they had got through stripping his passengers…

Sheriff Meade caught the first train for Merced, where he picked up Merced Deputy Sheriff Hiram Rapelje and the two proceeded to Fresno Flats. Mariposa County Sheriff John Mullery and his undersheriff, William J. Howard, proceeded to the scene of the robbery also, as did various local officials and lawmen.

■ Fresno County Sheriff O J. Meade tried too hard to obtain the reward. *Fresno County Sheriff's Office.*

At the robbery scene, lawmen prowled the area, finding various bits of evidence. Tom Beasore, a local half-blood Indian, found tracks nearby, which were followed to the home of Charley Meyers,

■ William Prescott was the other accused stage robber. *Author's collection.*

a few miles from Fresno Flats. Rapelje, Meade, Beasore, and Howard found Willie Prescott sleeping at the Meyers' house, Charley having gone to Coarsegold. Prescott was arrested and left with Howard, while Sheriff Meade and Rapelje rode over to Coarsegold, where they took Charley Meyers into custody. The suspects had been arrested in less than three days.

Besides a standing Wells, Fargo reward, the Washburn brothers, operators of the stage line, had offered an additional $200 reward. Sheriff Meade had expended a good deal of his own funds in the investigation and hoped to recoup it with some reward money. The deputies involved also looked forward to a share in the windfall. When the two suspects were brought to Fresno for a preliminary hearing, it looked like the case would be quickly wrapped up. The superior court trial was set for early September, and the defense and prosecution began marshalling their forces.

James Daly, the newly-elected Fresno district attorney, was inexperienced in such matters and solicited George Goucher, the Mariposa County district attorney, who was also a state senator, to aid in the prosecution. Fresno lawyer Walter D. Grady was employed as defense counsel. Grady was a local farm owner and opera house entrepreneur whose brawls, marital spats, and gunfights had often enlivened the local newspaper columns. One of his exploits involved biting a chunk out of a San Francisco waiter's ear in a saloon brawl. Aligned in the defense with Grady was Pat Reddy, who had lost an arm in a Nevada gunfight in earlier times. Undoubtedly the best criminal lawyer on the coast, Reddy was himself a state legislator as well. All but Daly were noted drinkers and brawlers.

On September 2, 1885, much of the day was spent in jury selection, followed by Senator Goucher's opening statement. The following day, Phil Toby, one of the stage drivers, became the first in a long series of witnesses. Toby testified that the robbers called him by name, indicating the suspects, as well as all the local inhabitants, knew him.

The main alibi of the two suspects was that they had been looking for wild hogs in the mountains at the time of the robbery. William Howard testified that he had taken Charley Meyers into the

■ A stagecoach stop in the mountains. *Author's collection.*

mountains to point out where the suspects had gone during their hunt. Although he had grown up in the area and knew it well, Meyers became disoriented and couldn't find the spot where they

had supposedly slept. Next, Deputy Rapelje told of finding some hidden clothes in the Meyers barn that matched the clothes worn by the bandits. The two outlaws had blackened their faces under their masks, and one of the discovered shirts had a black stain around the collar.

Tom Beasore had measured the tracks of the outlaws at the robbery site and testified that one track had a noticeable worn spot. The posse then followed the tracks up to the outskirts of Charley Meyers' house just prior to arresting both men. John Washburn, who operated the Wawona Hotel, also testified as to the tracks and stated that he was not prejudiced against the defendants, but thought they were guilty. Various witnesses testified that Meyers owned shirts similar to the one worn by one of the robbers. Significantly, the two defendants fit the description of the robbers and admitted to taking a rifle on their hog hunt. Later, it was brought out that Meyers had also borrowed a shotgun from his father-in-law.

Day after day, Pat Reddy objected to, ridiculed, questioned, and harassed the witnesses, but slowly a strong case was built against the two ranchers. When a tin of blacking found in the Meyers' barn was introduced into evidence as what was used to darken the highwaymen's faces, Reddy insisted the same material could be found in any paint shop in the country.

"Mr. Reddy," commented the *Fresno Expositor*, "continued in an

■ Pat Reddy was an imposing figure in the courtroom, with his long sideburns and waving his one arm. *A contemporary newspaper sketch in the author's collection.*

outburst of oratory on the point of his objection, when he was asked by Mr. Goucher of the opposing counsel if he were through with his speech?"

"You don't call that a speech, do you?" responded the bombastic Reddy. "If you call that a speech you will be astonished when you hear one."

And so it went. The trial lasted twenty-two days, the jury bringing in a verdict of "guilty" after deliberating some ten hours. Judge J. B. Campbell fixed October 22, 1885, as the time he would pronounce sentence on the defendants. For Charley Meyers, it was a particularly difficult day. The same hour the jury brought in the verdict, his only child died.

On the designated morning, the prisoners faced the court as the judge asked if there were any reason sentence should not be pronounced. With a smile playing about his heavily-whiskered lips, Pat Reddy stepped forward. He asked for a new trial based on affidavits showing that the jury did not obey the admonitions of the court to remain in a body and not to communicate with outside persons. Reddy produced a sworn document by saloon owner J. Bernstein that on or about the eighteenth of September, the jury had been drinking at his bar and were freely discussing the case with strangers as the sheriff stood by. Sheriff Meade had been trying to ensure a conviction to collect the rewards.

Judge Campbell was furious. He ordered the sheriff to subpoena the jury again for a new hearing on October 27. The crestfallen sheriff and the other lawmen all saw the rewards going out the window. After interviewing the jury at length, however, the judge surprisingly denied the request for a new trial and sentenced the two defendants to twenty years at San Quentin.

But Pat Reddy was just getting warmed up. He appealed to the State Supreme Court, where the request languished until August of the following year. When the appeal was granted, the court directed that a new trial take place, and on January 3, 1887, the second trial commenced in the Fresno County Superior Court.

Pat Reddy again appeared for the defense, while a new district attorney prepared to prosecute. Aurelius "Reel" Terry was chief

■ Fresno's courthouse, shown here at the end of Mariposa Street, was the scene of the Meyers and Prescott trials. Fresno was growing out of its frontier days, but the hills behind town were still quite wild. *Fresno County Public Library Collection.*

prosecutor for the second trial, assisted by S. J. Hinds. Terry was a nephew of the noted judge David S. Terry, who, in 1859, had killed Senator David Broderick in a duel. At the time of the trial, the elder Terry was practicing law in Fresno. During his youth, Reel had lived with his uncle and was every bit as combative.

Hopes that new evidence or witnesses would liven up the retrial were quickly dashed, the *Fresno Expositor* reporting, "The trial upon robbing the Yosemite stage drags along in the Superior Court with nothing new...." It "dragged" on for the next two weeks. When the jury was sent out late in the evening of January 18, it quickly became apparent that a hung jury was in the offing. After being out some thirty-five hours, the jury foreman did indeed announce a hung jury, and the jury members were dismissed by Judge Campbell. When both defendants were granted a reduced bail, they were promptly released to their families to await further action by the court. Pat Reddy was on the evening train for San Francisco to attend to other business.

■ Although good with his fists or a law book, Reel Terry was just not in Pat Reddy's league. *A contemporary newspaper sketch in author's collection*

The third trial commenced on November 30, 1887. Reel Terry and George Goucher conducted the prosecution this time, but they had nothing new to offer. Pat Reddy was as intimidating and cocky as ever. During jury selection he suggested to the judge as he looked at several wistful jurors, "as two or three of the jurors like a toddy, I move the sheriff allow them to have one, whenever convenient." This, of course, was a direct reference to the reason for the retrial, and the sheriff must have done a slow burn.

The trial lasted nearly a month, and Reddy succeeded in again hanging the jury. Five jurors were for conviction, and the balance disagreed. When they were discharged on the afternoon of December 25, 1887, the saga came to an end. The *Fresno Daily Republican* commented:

> It is safe to say that the three trials these men have had have cost the county fully $25,000 and probably more. District Attorney Terry and Senator Goucher made as strong a case as could have been made from the evidence at their command and it was generally thought that a conviction would result. In cases of this kind it is always the prosecution that suffers....

The county could afford no more trials, and Charley Meyers and Willie Prescott went free. Public opinion was something else again. It seemed that much of the evidence was contrary to the end result. Pat Reddy had just worn down the prosecution and the jury, and once again upheld his reputation as the best criminal attorney on the coast.

Weary of being pointed out as stage robbers, both Prescott and Meyers disappeared for a time. Willie Prescott was using the name Hatch when he returned to live in Fresno some years later. In May of 1899, he was convicted of assaulting his wife and did a stretch in San Quentin after all.

Charley Meyers and his wife moved to Portland, Oregon. When Hattie, his wife, divorced him, Charley married Kitty Wittle in 1899. Charley and his new bride returned to Fresno Flats when his father died, but things had not changed. Kitty Meyers disliked hearing constant references to Fresno Flats "being the home of Charley Meyers, the stage robber," and she decided to do something about it. In 1912, she obtained enough signatures to petition the state to change the name of Fresno Flats to Oakhurst. The state complied, the name was changed, and it all happened because of a stagecoach holdup on the road to Yosemite.

Correspondence with Shirley Sargent, Yosemite, California, and Hank Johnston, Palm Springs, California; trial records and documents in Superior Court Archives, Fresno, California; Mason, Ruth and Bill, "An Overview of the History of Fresno Flats and the Surrounding area, 1850-1934," typescript in Fresno County Public Library, California Room, Fresno, California; San Francisco *Daily Morning Call*, August 30, 1885; *Mariposa Gazette*, May 30, June 6, 1885; Fresno *Weekly Expositor*, May 27, June 10, 17, September 9, 16, 22, October 22, 27, 1885, January 12, 19, February 20, 26, December 7, 8, 9, 12, 13, 16, 24, 25, 1887; *Fresno Morning Republican*, May 19, 1899.

William A. Miner *Various aliases*
(real name Ezra Allen Miner)

■ Stage robber, train robber, ladies' man, jail breaker...Bill Miner looked every inch his legendary persona.
Robert G. McCubbin collection.

Although he told so many tall tales about himself, it was many years before the real story of outlaw Bill Miner could be told, and by then he did not need these tales. He really was one of the wildest desperadoes of our American frontier days. He robbed stagecoaches all over the West, but when the frontier days were coming to a close, he robbed trains, also. In between, he shot his way out of tight situations and spent a good part of his adult life in prison. He was Bill Miner, the movies' legendary "Grey Fox," and few Western characters can match his story.

Ezra Allen Miner was born in Michigan on December 27, 1846. His father died ten years later, and the mother and three younger children moved to California in 1860. Young Ezra grew up in the mining town of Yankee Jims in Placer County. Indications are that he left home at an early age and was picked up for stock theft in Southern California in late July 1863. Escaping prison on a technicality, he fled north to Sacramento. When eighteen-year-old Ezra enlisted in a California cavalry regiment in April 1864, he signed up under the name William Allen Miner and was known as "Bill" for the rest of his life.

■ The beginning of a life of crime. Young Bill Miner's first mug shot.
San Jose Historical Museum.

A few months of army regimen was all that young Miner could stand, and he deserted. He went to work in a mine, but spent what money he made in Sacramento saloons and brothels. When he was broke, one of the "girls" suggested he steal money from his employer. Caught in this crime, he was released because of his youth, but failed to learn any lesson from the incident.

Young Miner next stole a horse and robbed a store in Auburn. Returning home, he rented another horse and in early January left for San Francisco, where he sold both horses. On the way, he picked up a seventeen-year-old thug at Stockton named John Sinclair, who had the same larcenous ideas as Miner.

■ John Sinclair, an early partner of Bill Miner.
Author's collection.

After nearly two weeks of riotous living on the Barbary Coast, the two boys crossed the Bay and rented two saddle horses at Oakland. They traded off the two horses near Georgetown, then headed west. On January 22, 1866, they stopped and robbed a ranch hand named Porter who was driving to Stockton. Lawmen were already on their trail, seeking the two Oakland horses, and they now knew the same pair had robbed Porter. The fugitives were picked up early the following morning while sleeping in a Woodbridge hotel. The two boys were hauled before a Stockton justice of the peace, as the *Daily Evening Herald* reported:

> They have started young, neither apparently being twenty years of age. They are fine looking boys, and it is painful to see what they are, and to observe from their appearance what they "might have been."

Little did Justice Baldwin realize he was witnessing the debut of one of the most noted and legendary outlaws of the Old West.

Miner and Sinclair made several attempts to escape before their separate trials, but were convicted and sentenced to three years each at San Quentin. Miner's attorney was James H. Budd, later governor of California. Both defendants acted like a pair of smart alecks in court and on the boat taking them to prison.

Miner entered San Quentin on April 5 as Number 3248. There were some seven hundred convicts occupying the three cell block buildings within the walls. Many worked in the brickyards outside the walls, while the balance labored in various shops inside the prison for private owners.

After being taken out to be tried for his Placer County transgressions, Miner was returned to prison with more time to serve. He was finally released on July 12, 1870. A free man again due to time off for good behavior, Bill Miner was wiser only in the ways of crime.

In prison, Miner had met a character named James "Alkali Jim" Harrington. Jim was a third-timer, his current sentence being for burglary. They were released within a month of each other and were suspected of several burglaries in San Jose and the robbing of a Calaveras County stage. The two met up with an ex-convict pal, Charles Cooper, and talked him into participating in robbing the San Andreas stage.

■ Alkali Jim Harrington.
Author's collection.

Early on the morning of January 23, 1871, Miner waved down the stage as it was crossing Murray's Creek, a mile-and-a-half outside San Andreas. Asking for a ride, Miner was unbuckling the straps on the door when driver Billy Cutler noticed two shotgun-wielding men at the head of his horses. As he threw down the box, the driver remarked that there were no passengers, which led the three highwaymen to rob him instead. They took some five dollars in coin,

■ Stagecoach at Angels Camp. This was probably the type of coach stopped by Miner and his pals.
Author's collection.

but returned his watch when he stated it was a gift from his mother. They tried to take Cutler's boots also, but when found to be too small, they too were returned.

"It is not known how much money was in the box they took," noted the local press, "as Wells, Fargo & Co. have received no word of the amount forwarded on the stage from Murphys this morning. The driver thinks there were four men engaged in the robbery, although he saw but three."

■ Charles Cooper. *Author's collection.*

When Miner and his cohorts sent Cutler on his way, they chopped open the box and found two hundred dollars in gold coin and twenty-four hundred dollars in gold dust. The trio made their

■ The streets of old San Jose where Miner and Alkali Jim exchanged shots with a local lawman. California *State*

way to the outskirts of Stockton, Cooper was sent into town on an errand. Miner and Alkali Jim promptly left for San Francisco with the loot.

When the two outlaws were spotted in San Jose as ex-convicts, police officer Mitch Bellow tried to talk to them, and a shooting scrape commenced, as noted in the *San Jose Daily Patriot*:

It appears that when the officer ordered the fellows to stand, each drew a pistol — Clifford [Jim Harrington] a derringer and Miner [Bill] a heavy navy revolver — both covering the officer, who stepped back a few paces, not fearing the derringer, but having conscientious doubts about the revolving ordinance....

Bellow got off several quick shots as the two outlaws' weapons misfired and they disappeared into the fog. When Miner stopped behind a telegraph pole, Bellow nicked his coat with a shot and Bill again took off running.

Cooper was meanwhile picked up and could not "peach" on his pals fast enough. Alkali Jim was picked up at a girlfriend's house in Mayfield, north of San Jose, while Miner was spotted in San Francisco. He was walking down Third Street when two detectives "drove on top of him " in a hack, grabbing and disarming him before he knew what was happening.

■ Bill Miner, as he appeared at the time of the 1001 stage robbery. From a contemporary Sacramento police mug book.
Author's collection.

George W. Tyler, a notorious criminal attorney, was retained as counsel for Miner and Harrington and was outraged when San Francisco Police Chief Patrick Crowley would not allow him to see the prisoners. The robbery loot had not yet been recovered and Crowley, from past experience, knew that once Tyler talked to the prisoners, the loot was gone.

Years later, the story of Tyler and a law partner defending two other stage robbers was still being told. When the two lawyers discovered where the individual caches of stolen treasure were buried, they sought to dig them up. The partner returned with his loot and when Tyler came back empty-handed, his generous partner split his loot with him. Later, Tyler admitted to a friend that his partner was too gullible. Tyler had found his loot after all and had half his partner's loot as well.

Crowley knew with whom he was dealing. When Tyler's habeas corpus writ was served on him, Crowley brought Alkali Jim into court. When the judge agreed with the chief, however, Tyler was left sputtering about Crowley having more power "than Napoleon ever had."

Chief Crowley and an escort of officers took the prisoners to Stockton and Calaveras County to collect witnesses and evidence. They were very successful, but at the last stop to eat, Miner stole a steel table knife and concealed it in his coat sleeve. When the knife was discovered, the prisoners were weighed down with forty-five pounds of manacles and chains in the San Andreas jail.

Not at all discouraged, Harrington had almost cut through his new chain with a bucket handle when he was caught and re-ironed. On June 6, they were brought into the Calaveras courtroom in chains, despite the strenuous objections of both Tyler and the tenets of common law. The judge overruled the defense, and the two defendants were convicted and sentenced to ten years in San Quentin.

■ George Washington Tyler. *A contemporary newspaper sketch in author's collection.*

Tyler, of course, appealed, but his clients had spent some ten months in prison before a new trial was granted. The two convicts were returned to San Andreas for trial and when searched, a wire saw was found sewn into Alkali Jim's trousers. The trial was brief and disastrous. Quickly found guilty again, the defendants were sentenced to thirteen years by an angry judge, this time with no credit for time served.

Miner was in trouble at various times during his long confinement, but he finally gave up on his attempts to escape. Instead, he took up a letter-writing campaign to the governor and to various Calaveras County officials. With time off for

■ A cell in the "Stones," the first cellbock building at San Quentin. *San Quentin Museum Association.*

good behavior, Miner was released in July 1880. He headed for Colorado where a sister lived, but a family reunion was not uppermost in his mind.

In Colorado, Miner made the acquaintance of one Arthur Pond, also known as Billy LeRoy. The two held up several stagecoaches in the southern part of the state, but with meager results. Stopping the Alamosa to Del Norte stage on October 14, 1880, they ripped open the registered mail pouch to discover a four-thousand-dollar haul. The two bandits separated after dividing their loot, Miner catching a train to his home town in Michigan. Here, under an assumed name, he posed as a wealthy miner and wooed a young local socialite until his money ran low. It was time to move on and, taking on a partner named Stanton Jones, Miner then headed back to the Rocky Mountains.

With various other outlaws, Miner held up several Colorado stages and was closely pursued by posses. Captured once, Miner escaped after shooting and wounding the Saguache County sheriff and a deputy. One of Miner's partners had identified him, however, and Bill thought it prudent to scamper back to the West Coast, where he and Stanton Jones arrived sometime in the fall of 1881.

Jim Crum, horse thief and stage robber. *John Boessenecker collection.*

In California, Bill looked up some of his old prison pals. Jim Crum was just settling in for the winter after a successful summer of large-scale horse theft. Bill Miller, another San Quentin alumnus, was a Yolo County ranch owner, but the smooth-talking Miner soon had him signed on. In a short time the new crew was ready for the road.

It was just after five o'clock on the morning of November 7, when Miner, Crum, Miller, and Stanton Jones gathered along the Tuolumne County stage road, between Sonora and Milton. The coach was just pulling up a grade when Miner stepped out and commanded the driver to stop. Clark Stringham duly pulled up, as reported in the *San Francisco Chronicle*:

> The chief of the quartet, who was a very tall man, called his men off by numbers and they took the places assigned them. One of them covered the driver with his gun and other two took charge of the three passengers who were ordered out of the stage and compelled to stand with their backs to

■ Yuba County Sheriff Henry McCoy was part of the corps of lawmen who pursued Miner's stage-robbing gang. *Author's collection.*

him and with their hands behind them. The chief took a sledge and broke open the two wooden boxes of Wells, Fargo & Co., and their iron safe which was bolted to the stage. The safe had a considerable amount of money in it, just how much is not known.

Besides thirty-three hundred dollars in coin and gold dust, the bandits obtained over five hundred dollars from the passengers. Afraid he would miss the Milton train, Stringham asked if he could leave, and Miner waved him on saying, "Ta, ta, my boy!"

A massive manhunt was inaugurated to track down the robbers. Besides Wells, Fargo detectives, lawmen from Stockton, Oakland, Marysville, and other cities were in the field, looking for clues to the highwaymen. Miner had stopped at Chinese Camp, a few miles west of Sonora, when he had first arrived from Colorado. He was probably getting a line on stage schedules and in his usual, smooth-talking way, he became quite popular. He had called himself William Anderson, but descriptions and the investigation of the robbery convinced lawmen that Bill Miner had returned to California.

By expert detective work and luck, a posse tracked Miner, Crum, and Miller to the latter's ranch in Yolo County. Yolo County Sheriff Rahm, Wells, Fargo detective John Thacker, and Yuba County Sheriff Henry McCoy were closing in on the ranch house when they saw three men run from the back door. Seeing he had no chance, Crum tried to make a stand behind a tree, but was overwhelmed by the lawmen. Miner and Miller escaped into the brush.

The next day, Miner and Miller were spotted some ten miles north of Sacramento. After a desperate flight on foot, they were captured and soon locked up in the Sacramento jail. Both had been armed with two new Smith and Wesson double action pistols, but after a few shots from the officers had thought better of shooting it out, and they surrendered. Only Stanton Jones had somehow escaped the dragnet.

Crum was the first to break down under questioning, in the Sonora jail. Miner and Miller had little choice but to confess also, hoping for minimum sentencing. At their Tuolumne County Superior Court appearance on December 17, 1881, Crum was given a twelve-year sentence, while Miner and Miller were sentenced to twenty-five years each. Four days later, Bill Miner entered San Quentin, as No. 10191.

Miner had already spent thirteen years of his life in San Quentin, and he knew he was in for the long haul this time. Although in his mid-thirties, Bill was an old-timer in prison and knew the ropes well. He was cocky at first. Ex-Wells, Fargo detective Charles Aull, who was now yard captain at San Quentin, reported Miner was the inseparable companion of Buck English, Black Jack Bowen, and other noted criminals.

Over the years, Miner was continually in the limelight at San Quentin. When he maintained a high profile by advocating prisoners' rights, Bill was interviewed by various San Francisco reporters. In April 1884, he made an ineffectual attempt to escape. He had his cellmate place a dummy in his bunk that would be mistaken at lock-up time for Miner. The plan fell through, and Bill was found hiding in one of the work houses, from where he had hoped to go over the wall that night.

Miner had lost many of his credits for early release through his shenanigans, but when he helped fight a fire in the door and sash factory, he signaled that perhaps he was turning over a new leaf. But the "old" Bill Miner still resurfaced from time to time. He was stabbed by another convict in a personal squabble in 1885 and nearly died.

■ Miner and Marshall were ambushed by guards stationed at the window marked 1. Their cell door is marked 2 and the two convicts fell at the spot marked 3. *Contemporary newspaper sketch in author's collection.*

■ Bill Miner's pardon application cover. *California State Archives.*

On a night in November 1892, Miner and cellmate Joseph Marshall had just broken out of their cell when they were greeted by a shotgun blast that dropped Marshall dead on the stairs. Miner tried to crawl back toward his cell, but another blast sent several buckshot through his cheek, ripping out some teeth. An investigation showed that guards were aware of the escape plan and had been watching Miner and Marshall's cell at the time of their breakout. When the two men were spotted out of their cell, they were brutally gunned down. The incident was effectively whitewashed by the prison authorities, and Bill Miner gave up all plans for escape in the immediate future. He did pursue legal means of release, however, but his record was so bad, the prison board found it difficult to take him seriously anymore.

Nevertheless, on June 17, 1901, Miner was discharged after serving nearly twenty years of his sentence. He was fifty-four years old and had wasted almost thirty years of his youth in prison. Heading north for Washington State, he worked for a time at an oyster-packing operation, but he had no intention of going straight. In September 1903, Miner and two accomplices failed in a train-robbing venture near Portland, one of the gang being badly wounded. The other accomplice was captured, but Miner escaped to Canada. Working with Jake Terry, whom he had met in San Quentin, Miner engaged in smuggling operations in British Columbia, but he soon yearned for more excitement.

■ The shadows were growing long for old outlaw, but he never gave up. This his Canadian prison mug shot. *British Col Provincial Archives.*

Another train-robbing venture—the first in Canada—took place near Mission Junction in September 1904. This time, Miner, Terry and a cohort named Shorty Dunn got away with seven thousand dollars in gold

■ Miner died in this building at Georgia's Milledgeville State Prison. *Mark Dugan collection.*

dust, and some U.S. and Canadian bonds and securities. There were more train robberies, and Miner was finally captured and did time in British Columbia's New Westminster Penitentiary.

After a sensational escape from the Canadian prison, Miner spent the next few years in Denver living off his recovered loot. When the money ran out, he held up another train, this time near White Sulphur Springs, Georgia. Bill and his two young accomplices were quickly captured. When he received a twenty-year sentence, Miner politely thanked the judge.

The old outlaw died at the Milledgeville, Georgia, state prison farm on September 2, 1913, his death hastened by a dramatic escape attempt that summer. It is only the old man's bones lie in that forgotten prison cemetery, however. The books, films, and articles extolling Bill Miner's legend will keep his colorful story alive forever.

Hume and Thacker's "Robber's Record"; San Quentin State Prison Register; California State Archives, Sacramento; Dugan, Mark and Boessenecker, John, *The Grey Fox*; San Francisco *Daily Alta California*, August 7, 1863, Stockton, *Daily Evening Herald*, January 24, February 22, March 12, 1866, January 23, 1871; San Francisco *Daily Evening Bulletin*, February 4, 6, 11, November 11, 1871; San Jose *Daily Patriot*, February 1, 27, January 27, 1871; Stockton *Daily Independent*, February 7, 1871; *San Francisco Chronicle*, September 18, 1879, November 8, 1881; San Francisco *Examiner,* May 21, 1889, November 30, 1892; Milledgeville *Weekly News*, September 5, 1913; Detective Edward Byram's journals, John Boessenecker collection.

HOW TO ROB A STAGE?

In the summer and fall of 1884, there were a spate of stage robberies in central and northern California. Some were the work of two young San Francisco "loafers," as one newspaper characterized them. John Dwyer, a twenty-two-year-old and his pal, nineteen-year-old William Corbett, were typical amateurs who thought they would stop a few stages and then loaf and party all winter long. On October 9, 1884, they robbed the Mendocino stage out of Cloverdale, obtaining $3,600 from the Wells, Fargo box. The next morning they were quickly arrested by several Wells, Fargo detectives and the loot was recovered. The boys were deposited in the Cloverdale jail and eventually shipped to San Quentin with five-year prison terms.

Characterized as "asses in lions' skins" by the *Mendocino Beacon*, the two youthful highwaymen behaved as though they were in the same class as Black Bart. Their bragging to the local press was hilarious:

NEW

Daily Mail and Stage Line.

On and after June 1st, 1884, J. L. Sanderson will run his Daily Mail and
Stage Line between

MENDOCINO & CLOVERDALE,

on schedule time as follows:

Leaving Mendocino at 8:00 A. M., arriving at
Cloverdale at 1 A. M. and at San
Francisco at 8:50 A.M.

Returning, leave San Francisco at 5 P. M., ar
riving at Mendocino at 3 P. M. next day

FARE:

Mendocino to San Francisco, - $9.60
Navarra Ridge to   "   -   9.00
Mendocino to Cloverdale, - -   7.00

Return Fare the same. Tickets for sale at
the Postoffice.

— HILL,   J. L. SANDERSON & Co.
   Agent at Mendocino.   Proprietors
J. L. SANDERSON, Jr., Gen. Sup't, Cloverdale
              vii-19 tf

"My partner and I," said young Corbett, "saw by the papers that stages were being held up in all parts of the state, and we concluded to try it. The first one we tackled was down in the mountains, 100 miles south of here, and we got nothing but a little silver from the driver—and some good advice. He says: 'See here, you fellers. You're green at the business and I know it. When you order up a stage, just you remember also to call for 'em to throw off the box. The box is the thing that's got the dust in. I don't happen to have any just now, but that's what you're after.' We tried it next time on the Oroville line, but it so happened that that driver didn't have any box, and we had to stand the passengers up."

Dwyer now piped up with his own insightful words of wisdom:

"It's just as my partner says. You have got an awful sight to learn. I am thinking of writing a book on the staging business. I could give some of the fellows a few points. There ought to be some authority which the young might use as a guide. All the old road agents are gone, and the only way a newcomer can get along is to learn by experience.

"In the first place, never appear to be in a nervous hurry or scared at all. There is no danger. Second—Just keep your weapons handy, and don't take your eye off your victims. Third—Remember that the big haul is generally in the treasure box or the mail sack and that neither the driver or the passengers care for either of them. Fourth—Don't be too hoggish in going through the passengers themselves. If you exasperate a passenger he may fight. Fifth—If there are ladies abroad assure them the first thing that they will not be disturbed. Watch them , of course, for they are treacherous, but when you come to them in the line just say that you never rob the fair sex, and hand them back their things. Sixth—Look out for yourself every minute you are at the job. Some of the most harmless-looking men I ever saw had the hardest and heaviest fists. One fellow down here on the big tree road told me he was a consumptive, and five minutes afterward, when he hit me back of the ear I thought a tree had fallen on me."

"That's all true," chimed in Corbett, "every word of it. We learned a good deal one day coming over the mountains. We had been off for a little recreation and coming back here in the stage three big fellows with shotguns stopped us. We stood up in a row with the rest of the passengers and when one of them came along to me I whispered, 'I'm a member of the profession.' He looks at me sharp like, and says loud, so all could hear him, 'Is that so! We never rob preachers.' And he handed back the little roll of bills which he had taken from me. Well, I rather admired the chap for his geniality, but it cut me up dreadful to be called a preacher."

Mendocino Beacon,
February 14, 1885.

■ The Cloverdale stage, ready to begin another trip through old Mendocino County.
California State Library.

Charles and John Ruggles

■ John Ruggles (left) and his brother were misfits, hurtling through their lives toward an inevitable destination. *Author's collection.*

It was an ugly scene. Two men were hanging from a hoist positioned between two cottonwood trees in Redding, California. A large railroad woodshed stretched across the background, and crowds of men milled about chatting and occasionally looking up at the bodies that slowly turned to the tune of the groaning, stretching hemp. It was the end of a tragic story that should have been so different.

Twenty-two-year-old Lyman Ruggles had joined the great California Gold Rush in 1850. He had worked in the mines for a time, but like so many others had concluded that the real gold in the new country was the rich, untilled earth. He bought a farm near Woodland, in Yolo County, and married young Martha Dexter in 1857.

Ruggles prospered, and his family grew. A daughter, Gertrude, was born in 1858, John in 1860, Mattie in 1865, Charles in 1871, and Clarence in 1875. As a prominent farmer of the area, Lyman Ruggles was also elected to the Yolo County Board of Supervisors. In 1875, he saw opportunity in the rolling farmlands opening up in Tulare County, to the south. A new railroad spanned the fertile San Joaquin Valley, greatly facilitating travel and the shipping of crops. The elder Ruggles purchased 160 acres in the Mussel Slough area, near Hanford, in what is now Kings County, and began new farming operations. In 1880, Ruggles bought 320 more acres, twenty miles east of his property. Life had been good to Lyman Ruggles, but cracks had already appeared in his well-ordered world.

The Ruggles children went to school, helped out on the farm, and lived normal lives. The older boy, John, had problems, however. He was sickly and did not fit in somehow. Telling his parents he was going to Stockton for medical attention and to look for work, John left home in 1878. He worked on a farm for a time, then obtained a position as a stock tender for Dr. E. A. Stockton, who also began treating him. But John was still troubled—"addled," his mother would call it—and his next experience was reported in the *San Francisco Chronicle*, November 1, 1878:

> Stockton, October 31—This evening, at 9 o'clock, a young man named Avey, accompanied by a young lady, was returning to the lady's home, and when near the St. Agnes Convent they were stopped by a masked man, who demanded their valuables. Avey said he had nothing and the man asked for the lady's rings on her fingers. These were given, and the fellow…told them to go on, and as soon as Avey turned the footpad did likewise. Avey then turned around, drew a revolver and shot the man in the back. He then fired three shots at Avey, none of them taking effect. Avey discharged five shots at the fellow, the first being the only one that hit him…

The parties then ran in different directions, the wounded thief making his way to the local police station. He asked for medical attention, telling the jailer his name was John Dexter Ruggles and he had been shot while robbing a man. He also confessed to a prior robbery.

Young Ruggles' wound was serious, the bullet having entered his back and lodged in the right lung. "He will probably die before morning," noted a newspaper report. He quickly showed signs of recovery, however.

■ A San Joaquin Valley farm of the 1870s. *Author's collection.*

Promptly tried and convicted for robbery and assault, John was sentenced to state prison for seven years. He entered San Quentin on November 16, 1878, as No. 8540. His parents were terribly upset by his criminal actions and incarceration. To make matters worse, the Stockton press published interviews in which John admitted he had saved up money for medical attention while working, but had squandered it in the local red light district and had taken to the road for ready cash. Embarrassed and hurt over his son's actions, Lyman Ruggles nevertheless initiated a campaign to obtain a pardon by the governor.

Dr. Stockton, who had employed John, stated that he had been treating him for sexual addiction and that his state of mind was such that he was nearly an "imbecile" at the time of the robberies. Dr. G. A. Shurtleff, superintendent of Stockton's state mental facility, had examined John during his trial and agreed with Dr. Stockton's diagnosis. Both physicians recommended that the young man be pardoned.

Keeping up a steady campaign, augmented by John's good behavior while in prison, Lyman Ruggles' efforts finally began to pay off. On February 24, 1880, Governor George C. Perkins granted him a pardon, and John returned to live with his parents near Hanford. And he seemed to have gotten a new lease on life. In 1883, he acquired farm land near Dinuba and some unimproved property in the nearby Sierra Nevada. He was married on April 22, 1886, to Ida May Henderson, and the following year a daughter was born to the union. When Lyman Ruggles sold his properties and retired to manage a warehouse in Traver, he hoped his son's troubled early years were far behind him.

But adversity was never very far away from John Ruggles. When his wife died in 1889, John was devastated and asked relatives to look after his daughter until he felt he was able to do so. He was soon ignoring his mortgaged property and spending time hunting in the mountains.

For the next few years, John worked his property off and on, but mostly traveled about the state living off the land. In early 1892, his younger brother, Charley, visited him. Charley had been working at a mine in Shasta County and had apparently been in some trouble himself, since he was using an alias at the time, calling himself Howell. His best friend at the mine was a character named "Arizona Pete," and it was later thought the two had either robbed stagecoaches, or had planned to so. There had been some sixteen stage robberies in Shasta County since 1887, and the public was very thin-skinned on the subject.

Both brothers were hard up for money, and they discussed various schemes to fatten their wallets. John finally leased his farm, and the brothers left for San Francisco and took a room at a Jessie Street boarding house. They left town in early May 1892 and headed north. Charley's stories of gold shipments from the Shasta mines had struck a chord with John. Their larcenous natures now in full bloom, the brothers had decided to rob the Weaverville stage as it traveled to Shasta.

On the evening of May 10, John and Charley lay in wait for the stage along the road to Shasta. There was plenty of cover, the surrounding hills being cloaked in pine trees and chaparral thickets of scrub oak and manzanita. The two bandits were wearing red bandana masks and long linen dusters, and they had tied sacks over their feet. Johnny Boyce was driving the stage carrying four male passengers and a little girl. He quickly pulled up when the masked figures told him to stop. In another moment, the express boxes had been thrown down, and the coach was waved on. To the disgust of the robbers, there was little of value in the boxes. It had been so easy, however. The brothers lay low for a few days, then picked a time and place on the same route for another robbery.

■ Johnny Boyce driving the Shasta stage on the Weaverville to Redding road about the time of the robberies.
California State Library.

■ Redding as it appeared during the time of the Ruggles boys excitement. *Shasta Historical Society.*

This time they picked a spot five miles north of Redding, just after the crest of a long grade. As the stage, again driven by Johnny Boyce, began its ascent, the other two passengers relaxed. Amos "Buck" Montgomery, the shotgun messenger, rested his weapon across his knees inside, while George Suhr, who had just climbed aboard at Shasta, shared the driver's seat with Boyce. It was a little after five o'clock in the evening. Suddenly, a masked man stepped into the road and yelled for the coach to stop. Johnny Boyce described what happened next:

We arrived at the scene of the robbery about 5:15 o'clock. Just as we started down the grade of the cut, the highwayman stepped out from behind a clump of low oak brush and said, "Stop, Stop!" I instantly pulled the horses up and brought the stage to a standstill.

He next said, "Passenger, throw up your hands!" in a most pleasant manner and tone of voice. He then commanded me to throw out those boxes.

All this time he had his bristling shotgun, with both hammers cocked, leveled directly at myself and the passenger, Suhr. He seemed to be as pleasant and affable as a French dancing master. Just as the second box struck the ground I heard a pistol shot, and the messenger shot almost at the same instant. I am sure the robber fired just a little bit in advance of the messenger.

The shot from the messenger's gun dropped the robber who held the shotgun on me to his knees and his gun fell from his left hand, but he still held it in his right. He raised off one knee onto one foot and shot at me. He sent fifteen buckshot into my right leg just above the knee and three into my left leg. Three pistol shots were fired in rapid succession immediately following the first of the messenger.

As the bandits made their getaway, the scene at the stage was awful. The wounded Boyce was desperately trying to calm the frightened stage horses, which had bolted from a cloud of dissipating gunsmoke. Passenger Suhr had received several shotgun pellets in the leg, also, but was trying to stop the bleeding of the groaning Montgomery inside the blood-spattered coach. In shocked disbelief, John Ruggles had seen from his hiding place what happened and rushed to the coach. He shot Montgomery in the back with his pistol as the messenger looked out the opposite window. Montgomery's wounds were mortal, but it was to be a lingering death.

As the coach left the scene to seek aid, John Ruggles later described his movements:

"Buck" Montgomery, shotgun guard. A contemporary newspaper sketch. *Author's collection.*

> As I finished shooting and run for the axe, I saw poor brother reeling and struggling down the hill to the gulch, still holding his gun in his left hand. Charley pulled off his disguise and with the bloody handkerchief in his right hand he pointed toward the damned boxes and waved me away from them and pointed away across the hills and mumbled something like—"Go, you have got me done for," but not much, I said, it will take something more than one man's death to keep me from getting inside of the boxes. Charley…reeled around awful and as he got clear to the bottom of the gulch he let go his gun and stumbled and rolled down into the water with his face down and his right arm under him.

> I…grabbed him and turned him over on his back and looked at him and oh, what an awful sight. His head literally

■ Charley Ruggles in the Redding jail. The three Xs on his face mark buckshot wounds. *A contemporary newspaper sketch in author's collection.*

shot full of holes and the blood just running all over his clothes…

Thinking his brother was dying, John broke open the express boxes, stuffed the contents in a sack, and, making Charley as comfortable as possible, said good-bye and disappeared into the dusk with some $3,300 in gold and coin. The wounded bandit was captured the next day and taken to the Redding jail. He was found to have thirteen buckshot in his face and breast, but his heavy overcoat had saved his life. One slug had entered his mouth, knocked out two teeth and exited the back of his neck. He refused to say who his partner was, but when he was identified by a friend, Wells, Fargo detective John Thacker quickly tracked down Lyman Ruggles and gave him the sad news.

Taking the first train north, Lyman Ruggles visited Charley in his Redding jail cell. It was the sad meeting of a heartbroken father and his errant son. The wounded outlaw was finally convinced to identify John as his partner in the robbery, and the manhunt was on.

Governor Henry H. Markham offered a special $500 reward for Montgomery's killer, which was added to a standing state reward of $300 and Wells, Fargo's $300 offer. John, meanwhile, made his way south and worked a few days for a farmer along the way. When he turned up in Woodland on June 18, several relatives who lived there reported the fugitive's presence to the

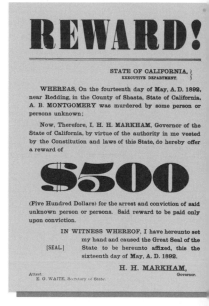

REWARD!

STATE OF CALIFORNIA, }
EXECUTIVE DEPARTMENT.

WHEREAS, On the fourteenth day of May, A.D. 1892, near Redding, in the County of Shasta, State of California, A. B. MONTGOMERY was murdered by some person or persons unknown;

Now, Therefore, I, H. H. MARKHAM, Governor of the State of California, by virtue of the authority in me vested by the Constitution and laws of this State, do hereby offer a reward of

$500

(Five Hundred Dollars) for the arrest and conviction of said unknown person or persons. Said reward to be paid only upon conviction.

IN WITNESS WHEREOF, I have hereunto set my hand and caused the Great Seal of the [SEAL.] State to be hereunto affixed, this the sixteenth day of May, A.D. 1892.

H. H. MARKHAM,
Governor.

Attest
E. G. WAITE, Secretary of State.

sheriff. A store clerk had also recognized him and officers were already on the lookout. At nine o'clock the next night, John sat down at a table in the Opera Restaurant to order his meal. The *Woodland Mail* reported what transpired next:

■ Yolo County Deputy Sheriff David Wyckoff, pictured here, captured John Ruggles after a desperate struggle. *Author's collection.*

Deputy Sheriff Wyckoff walked leisurely into the restaurant, and sat down near Ruggles, who held up a paper as if reading. At this moment the officer leveled his pistol within a foot of Ruggles' face, commanding him to throw up his hands. Ruggles did not heed this request, but reached for his pistol, when the officer fired and pounced upon him, and had a desperate struggle, until the Sheriff and two constables came to his aid. [Only when] several were choking him and the pistol was wrenched from his hands, was he overpowered....

John had received a bullet wound in the neck and was patched up in a nearby drugstore as large crowds gathered in the Woodland streets. Cursing at the onlookers, John yelled, "Hurrah for Hell," as he was carried to the local jail. A long confession was found in his pocket, giving a description of the robbery and blaming society and his father for his troubles. After resting up for several days, John was put on the train, escorted by two deputy sheriffs and Wells, Fargo's detective, John Thacker. They arrived in Redding on the evening of June 23, and John had an emotional meeting with his brother.

"Charley, I thought you were going to die," John tried to explain as they seized each other's hand. He broke down before again making attempts to explain his conduct, but Charley cautioned him that it was not the time to talk of such things. Explaining that the brothers would be allowed to talk again later, officers now led them off to separate cells.

Charley's preliminary hearing was on June 30, and John's was set for July 28, 1892. A brief item in the Redding press announced that the Ruggles' trial strategy was to involve Montgomery in the stage-robbing plot. "Of course all this," responded the *Republican Free Press*, "in the way of a defense, is the worst kind of bosh, but they hope to get a juror or two who will believe it." The article stirred up more than a passing interest. There had already been talk of a local vigilance committee meeting, and the time for action had now arrived. Buck Montgomery was well-liked and highly respected in

■ "Ruggles Raised Right Royally" headlined the Redding newspaper. It was the end of a long, sad trail. *Author's collection.*

the area. Many locals had witnessed the tragic weeping of Buck's widow and children as they had boarded the train with his body. They were not going to stand by now as the Ruggles brothers dragged Buck's name through the mud.

Early on Sunday morning, July 24, 1892, early risers could see the slowly twisting bodies of John and Charley Ruggles hanging from a makeshift gallows near Etter's blacksmith shop. A well-organized mob had entered the jail just after midnight and broken into the two prisoners' cells. John put up a fight and tried to take the blame and save Charley. But it was too late. There would be no expensive trials, appeals, and legal fees. There was no sympathy.

It was generally agreed that the Ruggles boys had obtained a well-deserved change of venue: to Hell.

San Quentin State Prison Register; Governor's Pardon Files, California State Archives, Sacramento; Secrest, William B., *Lawmen & Desperadoes*; Edwards, Harold, "A Footnote in Tulare County History," Los *Tulares*; *Redding Republican Free Press*, May 14, 21, 28, June 18, 25, July 2, 30, 1892; *Yreka Journal*, May 18, June 22, 1892; *San Francisco Chronicle,* November 1, 1878; *San Francisco Examiner,* May 15, 21, 1892; *Visalia Weekly Delta*, June 9, 1892; 1880 Tulare County Federal Census.

AND THE GUNS THEY USED...

We take our guns for granted today, but their importance in our history is exemplified in the many expressions imbedded in our language that derives from weapons. An expression dating back to colonial days is "lock, stock and barrel." This refers to the three major parts of a rifle, and means all of anything. In purchasing a business and all the merchandise, you are buying it "lock, stock and barrel."

To "go off half-cocked," refers to the half-cock of a pistol trigger action and "flash in the pan" dates back to when the powder was ignited in a flintlock's pan, but it did not fire. "The whole shooting match" and "shot in the dark" are other expressions dating back to our frontier days, and there are many more.

Loading a cap-and-ball revolver of the 1850s-1870s.

Photos: Joseph G. Rosa

■ A measure of powder is inserted in each of the six cylinder chambers.

■ Lead ball is rammed on top of powder in each chamber by lever under barrel.

■ Ready to fire when copper percussion cap placed on nipple at rear of cylinder.

Photo: Wells, Fargo

■ The sixteen-shot, .44 calibre Henry Rifle was popular throughout the 1860-1880 period. The weapon shown here was presented to Steve Venard by Wells, Fargo for killing three stage robbers near Nevada City, in May 1866.

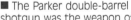

Photo: Charles G. Worman

■ The Parker double-barrel shotgun was the weapon of choice for many of the stagecoach guards in old California.

PARKER'S
BREECH LOADING DOUBLE BARRELED
SHOT GUN
BEST IN THE WORLD.
PARKER BROTHERS WEST MERIDEN.
SEND FOR A CIRCULAR. CON!
New York Office, 27 BEEKMAN ST
an 19-4y°

Grass Valley Union, January 9, 1873.

■ The famous single-action Frontier-model Colt, Remington, and Smith and Wesson pistols were very popular, but the Merwin, Hulbert & Co., double-action, .44 calibre Pocket Army shown here was favored, also. This particular pistol was presented to popular Sheriff John J. Bogard, the captor of stage robber Milton Sharp.

Photo: Richard L. Henry

Ramon Ruiz

■ Born to be hanged?
Well, maybe, if he wasn't shot
stabbed, trampled or beaten
to death first. *Author's collection.*

"Years ago," commented a contemporary, "nobody rode better horses, could ride harder, dance longer or shout louder than Ramon Ruiz." To which he might have added "Fight longer and shoot quicker."

A native Californian, Ramon was probably born in Los Angeles about 1837. Even as a youngster, there were dire predictions that he was born to be hanged, or at best, to die in a penitentiary. And, for much of his life, he seemed to be living up to these expectations.

There were stories that Ruiz was a member of Joaquin Murrieta's marauders, but no evidence to prove this has surfaced. His first criminal conviction was for assault with a deadly weapon in Los Angeles when he was twenty years old. Listed in the prison register as Jose Ramon Ruiz, No. 1243, he was received at San Quentin to serve a one-year term on October 27, 1857.

There is no indication what Ramon, who was released on October 22, 1858, did for the next few years, but he probably worked as a vaquero and indulged in some rustling. He was operating in the San Ramon Valley, near San Francisco, in July 1860, when his temper got the best of him again, as reported in the *Contra Costa Gazette*:

A Mexican named Guadalupe Tapia was mortally wounded with a knife by Ramon Ruiz, on Wednesday last.

They were seen together near Alamo, each having a horse, though dismounted, and just previous to the attack deceased was observed to be reclining upon the ground, holding his animal by the bridle. What the provocation was we have not been able to ascertain, but Ruiz suddenly rushed upon him with a knife, inflicting a terrible wound in the abdomen, from which death ensued in a few hours.

Ruiz leaped on his horse and fled, but he was arrested by the Alamo constable and lodged in the Martinez jail. Convicted of manslaughter in May 1861, Ruiz was back in San Quentin as No. 2165. He knew the routine and settled in for his three-year stint.

On July 22, 1862, a carefully orchestrated prison break took place. A group of prisoners seized Warden Chellis, obtained keys from the gatekeeper and rushed out through the entrance with their hostage. Hundreds of other convicts, seeing what had transpired, now ran through the gate shouting "Freedom!" Ramon Ruiz was among the prisoners who splashed through swampy creeks and brushy forests while watching helplessly as pursuing guards closed in from the rear. Careful not to hit Chellis, the guards began picking off convicts, who soon abandoned their hostage. After running into posses from nearby San Rafael, the weary and bullet-riddled convicts were forced to surrender, although various individual prisoners scattered into the countryside. By nightfall, a long line of prisoners was being herded back within the hated walls.

■ The main entrance to San Quentin as it looked at the time of the 1862 outbreak. The convicts ran around the walls to the right, fleeing across the brickyard at the rear and towards the mountains to the west *California State Library*

First count showed three dead convicts and a great many wounded, some of whom died later. Several dozen were missing. Ruiz, who had been shot in the hand, had his injury treated before being locked up again. The cries of the wounded in their cells could be heard throughout the night.

Ruiz was glad to be free again when he was released on June 1, 1864. He had learned nothing, however, and was convicted of horse theft in Contra Costa County in November 1867. This time it was a five-and-one-half year term, but he had established a pattern. The prison was a second home to him now. Friends greeted him as he came in the gate. The days were long, but they passed. He regained his freedom on July 2, 1872.

Under the heading "Wholesale Horse Stealing," the *Los Angeles Star* of December 14, 1872, reported Ramon's latest operation:

> It seems that the gang carried on their operations from Santa Clara County to this place, and that they had run a band of sixty-five animals they had gathered in their forays to San Juan Capistrano. Some of the animals were vary valuable, and

■ Stock ranches, such as the San Luis Obispo operation shown here, were the constant prey of Ruiz and other rustler
Author's collection.

> there they traded 40 head of horses for 33 head of cattle; and to a man at the Ballona they gave a fine stallion and three colts; and after they made the trade at San Juan they gave the same individual two cows. In the original ramada there were nine good American mares. The Sheriff of Santa Clara telegraphed information to Sheriff Rowland, which led him to take active steps to ferret out the thieves. On Tuesday night, an ex-convict named Ruiz was identified and arrested by Marshal Wolf. He is known as the man who acted as selling agent for the gang...

For some reason, Ruiz was not tried and convicted until December of the following year. The San Luis Obispo court sentenced him to three years in San Quentin on July 8, 1873. According to the prison register, Ruiz was released on July 8, 1876, but this seems to be an error and should read 1875. Ramon promptly fell in with some ex-convict pals who had assembled a stage-robbing gang.

■ Killer, rustler, and Highwayman, Ysidro Padilla was the most ruthless of Ramon Ruiz' pals. *Author's collection.*

Ysidro Padilla was the worst of the group. A native Californian, Padilla had been a principal suspect in the brutal murder of five men during a store robbery in 1869. He was convicted of the murders, but on appeal won a new trial. By that time, many witnesses had disappeared, and he escaped conviction. More recently, he had been a member of Tiburcio Vasquez' gang before that murderous bandido was hanged in San Jose. Ruiz's new pals had already robbed the Sonora-Milton stage, once in November 1874 and again in March of the following year.

On August 3, 1875, Ruiz, Ysidro Padilla, and Jose Lenaris stopped the stage running between LaPorte and Oroville. Joining with fellow gang members "Old Joaquin" Olivera, "Little Mitch" Brown, and "Big Mitch" Ratovich, Ramon and his pals attempted to rob the Wells, Fargo express box on the Sonora to Milton stage on October 12, 1875. When the robbery fell through, Ramon was thoroughly

■ The LaPorte to Marysville stage. *Author's collection.*

disgusted, as well he might be. According to the *Calaveras Weekly Citizen*, these rough, tough highwaymen had behaved like rank amateurs:

Road Agents Again—On Tuesday morning the Sonora and Milton stage on its way down, was brought to a stand by three masked highwaymen, who were after the express box and treasure. The driver told them the cash box was not on board...another stage coming along had it. With child-like faith in humanity characteristic of road agents, they took him at his word; took leave of him and took up position again, no doubt, to stop the coming stage...which, however, did not come, there being but one on the road that day. Wonder if those road agents are profane men?

A furious Ramon determined to rob the Sonora to Copperopolis stage by himself. Just before dawn on December 1, 1875, Ruiz rode up behind the Sonora coach that was driven by Jack Gibbons. The *Sonora Union Democrat* reported:

The first intimation that Gibbons had of any trouble was a command from the rear to halt. He obeyed, and a man, unmasked and armed with a pistol, rode alongside.

"Put out your lights" was the next order, and Gibbons was not slow in attending to the matter.

■ Ruiz, the dangerous and dashing bandido, in his prime. *Author's collection.*

"Throw down the box," was the next polite request of the road agent.

"I tell you what it is," replied the driver as he passed the box over to the gentleman on horseback, "I don't think you'll find much in it, it's mighty light. If you don't believe it just heft it."

Ramon waved the coach on and went to work opening the box in which he found some $600. Gibbons drove into Copperopolis, where he spread the alarm and gave a good description of the outlaw, which turned out to be a clear picture of Ramon Ruiz.

Wells, Fargo quickly offered a reward, plus one-fourth of any portion of recovered treasure. Calaveras Sheriff Ben Thorn tracked the outlaw to a secluded cabin. Carefully working his way up to the door, Thorn surprised the badman, preventing him from snatching his pistols. Faced with a certain conviction, Ramon offered to "peach" on his comrades in exchange for immunity for certain robberies, an offer that was gleefully accepted by Wells, Fargo's Jim Hume and Sheriff Thorn. The outlaw was convicted in July, 1876, and sentenced to a moderate four years at his old alma mater, San Quentin. All his stage-robbing pals were eventually caught, also. As No. 7083, Ramon served out his term and was released on July 25, 1879.

Stepping through the San Quentin gate, Ramon was startled to find Tuolumne County Sheriff Tryon M. Yancey waiting for him. When the lawman proceeded to show him a warrant for the robbery of Jack Gibbons' stage, Ramon protested vigorously that he had immunity for that crime. In court, the judge ruled that Hume and Thorn had no power to offer him immunity, and he was promptly convicted and sentenced to another two-year prison stretch. He was released on June 14, 1881.

Ruiz lost no time in stealing some Merced County horseflesh and was chased back to Tuolumne County as a result. After stealing the Stanislaus County sheriff's prize gray mare, Ramon decided it would

be safer on the east side of the Sierra. In Mono County, he fell in with some Paiute Indians and promptly wore out his welcome by killing one of the tribesmen in a dispute. He hightailed it

■ The cellblocks at San Quentin had been home to Ramon for much of his life, but in the winter of his years he knew he would have to change. *Author's collection.*

back over the mountains, only to be captured and indicted for stealing the sheriff's mare.

Returned to San Quentin on May 22, 1885 for a four-year term, Ruiz did some serious thinking. He was forty-eight years old, and this was his sixth prison term. He had been through many desperate situations, and his luck wouldn't hold out forever. By the time he was discharged on May 22, 1888, he had decided to move to lower California and go into the butcher business. Surprisingly, this is what he did. What is more, he was a decided success. But he was Ramon Ruiz, and when the local rancheros finally figured out that he was selling much more beef than he was buying, a vigilance committee quietly formed. According to report, Ramon was warned of their mission, and when they showed up at his shop, he appeared in the doorway with a blazing sixshooter in each hand. He was hit several times, but various vigilantes went down also, with the balance running for cover. Bleeding from his wounds, Ramon leaped onto his horse and made a dash for the border.

■ The last prison mug shot of Ramon Ruiz. *California State Archives*

Returning to California, Ruiz recuperated from his wounds, then called on the sheriffs of Tuolumne and Calaveras counties and told them that he intended to settle down and bother them no more. And he didn't. He vaqueroed for a time, utilizing his natural rapport with horses. When he became too old for that work, he took to selling tamales in the streets of Sonora and the nearby foothill towns.

The "Tamale Man" was working the streets of Angels Camp on the night of August 30, 1899, when he suddenly collapsed and died.

"It is said," noted an obituary, "that even in his old age and while pursuing his legitimate calling, his natural instincts never deserted him and he was easily startled, but was ever found ready on the defensive until the situation was understood."

Hume and Thacker's "Robbers' Record"; Boessenecker, John, *Badge & Buckshot*; San Quentin State Prison Register, California State Archives, Sacramento; Carlo M. DeFerrari, "Ramon Ruiz, The Road Agent,"; *Sacramento Daily Union*, July 9, 1860; *San Francisco Daily Alta California*, July 22, 23, 24, 1862; *Los Angeles Star*, December 14, 1872; *San Luis Obispo Morning Tribune*, December 13, 1873; *Calaveras Weekly Citizen*, October 16, 1875, July 22, 1876; *Sonora Union Democrat*, December 4, 1875, October 18, 1879, June 13, 1997; *Calaveras Weekly Prospect*, September 2, 1899; various legal documents in Calaveras County Archives, San Andreas, California.

Milton A. Sharp

■ Milton Sharp's mild appearance concealed a desperate character and an ingenious jailbreaker.
John Boessenecker collection.

ne of an influx of California stage robbers claiming a Missouri nativity, Milton A. Sharp stated he had been born near Lee's Summit about 1840. He had four brothers and three sisters, all apparently raised by their mother, Elisabeth. After receiving a moderate education, Milton left home about 1866. Making his way to the Pacific Coast, he worked for some twelve years as a miner in both California and Nevada.

In 1879, Sharp was working for farmer Peter Ahart near the town of Auburn, in Placer County, California. His employer recalled him as a hard worker whose pleasant manners earned him lodging with the family. Although he scrupulously saved his money, Sharp "had a mania for speculating in cheap mining stocks in which he invested and lost every cent of his earnings," recalled Wells, Fargo detective James B. Hume. When ex-convict William C. Jones went to work on the Ahart farm, he and Sharp became close friends. And because Sharp had recently lost money on another bad stock investment, he was very susceptible to his new friend's suggestion that they make some easy money. Late that year, the two men left the farm and disappeared.

After holing up in a deserted cabin for a time, Sharp and Jones stopped the stage on the Auburn to Forest Hill run on May 15, 1880.

Holding rifles on the driver, the outlaws commanded the passengers to dismount and line up along the road. After robbing them, the robbers waved on the coach and headed east into Nevada. They robbed the Carson City stage on June 8, rifling the Wells, Fargo express box, as well as the passengers' pockets, before telling the driver to move on. Officers were quickly on the trail of the bandits, but were unsuccessful in their search.

On June 15, the Bodie stage was stopped and $300 taken from the express box, the passengers being spared. The outlaws lay low for a time, but when their money ran low, they crossed back into California. With a $600 reward on each of their heads, Sharp and Jones again stopped the Forest Hill stage on August 7. After first robbing the passengers, the outlaws broke open the treasure box and took $1,500. The driver was then told to move on. Jim Hume and local officers were quickly on the scene, but the outlaws had vanished into the wild and rough country.

■ Sharp and Jones were on a stage robbing spree when they met up with Mike Tovey, who was guarding one of the Nevada coaches, such as is shown here. Even in the face of tragedy, the nervy Sharp managed to get away with the loot.
California State Library.

On September 4, 1880, Sharp and Jones stopped the Bodie to Carson City coach, but the robbery was interrupted and they fled with nothing. The following day, they waited for the return stage in the same area. At 2:30 in the morning, the coach stopped when the guard, Mike Tovey, saw some footprints in the road. Following the tracks, the coach rolled along until Tovey thought he saw where the tracks left the road. Climbing down, the guard was examining the prints when a voice called out, "You're trying to sneak up on us!" Then, two shots were fired, killing one of the horses, and Tovey retreated behind the coach lights to grab his shotgun. As Jones advanced into the light, Tovey shot him in the head, and the outlaw dropped dead in the road. Another guard on the coach had fired ineffectively at Sharp, who was on the other side of the stage. Tovey now ran to aid his partner, but received a bullet wound in the arm from Sharp as the outlaw retreated into the brush.

■ Mike Tovey, the shotgun messenger who killed Sharp's partner. *John Boessenecker collection.*

Having dropped his shotgun, Tovey retreated also and noticed that he was bleeding badly. While the other guard and a passenger took Tovey to a nearby farmhouse for treatment, Sharp returned and ordered the driver to throw down the express box.

"This order was naturally complied with," recalled Jim Hume later, "and the cool rascal broke open the box and took $750 from it while his companion lay dead in the road. After pocketing the money, he started off without appearing to notice the body of Jones…"

Jim Hume found a San Francisco bank book on Jones' body and promptly sent the information along to Captain Lees of the San Fran-

■ Sharp was captured in San Francisco at his Minna Street boarding house, perhaps the very one shown above. Note police officer in the street. *Author's collection.*

cisco police. Detectives John Coffey and Ray Silvey were put on the case, and after a few days of surveillance, Sharp was picked up in his boarding house room on Minna Street. Property taken in the robberies was found in the room. Returned to Aurora, Nevada, for trial, Sharp was prosecuted by Patrick Reddy, the famous criminal attorney who had been retained by Wells, Fargo. Sharp was convicted on October 30, 1880, but when Reddy presented a $5,000 bill to the express company, there was trouble. When the company offered to pay half, Reddy blew up and refused anything. From then on, Reddy took any case he could find against Wells, Fargo, and over the years the company lost many times the amount it had refused to pay. Meanwhile, during an exciting election day, Sharp managed to tunnel through a jail wall and make his escape.

■ Pat Reddy. *Eastern California Museum.*

Staggering across the desert with a fifteen-pound "Oregon Boot" on his ankle, Sharp stopped after traveling some twelve miles to take time to break the "Boot" with rocks. He then resumed his journey. But man hunters were everywhere, Jim Hume later stating that some $1,100 was expended by Wells, Fargo to recapture the outlaw. The fugitive was spotted and captured in Candelaria, and the officers lost no time in transferring him to the Nevada State Prison at Carson City, where he was admitted on November 12, 1880, as No. 158.

■ The Oregon Boot. *Author's collection.*

Although described in his prison record as "quiet and gentlemanly," Sharp was determined to escape. At various times, he was caught making tools and files, and did time shackled by a ball and chain in the dungeon. In the late 1880s, he finally contacted his family, urging them to write letters in his behalf. When a pardon was refused, he immediately began devising a new escape plan.

Sharp had been elevated to "trusty" status when he escaped from prison on the night of August 15, 1889. Returning to California, he did menial jobs in Calaveras County, using the name of Wiser. Under a variety of names, the fugitive worked on ranches near Sacramento for a time, then moved to Mendocino County and later to the Red Bluff area in Tehama County.

Sharp's undoing was the murder of Mike Tovey, the guard who had killed his partner Jones during the Carson stage holdup in 1880.

■ Newspaper sketch at the scene of Mike Tovey's murder. The killer stood where the ① is shown. *Author's collection.*

On the evening of June 15, 1893, the Ione to Jackson stage in Calaveras County was ambushed. Tovey was shot and killed as he sat next to the driver. Several more shots hit the driver and crippled two of the stage horses who had run some distance down the road. The killer then fled without attempting to rob the coach. The primary suspect was the fugitive Milton Sharp, with revenge for Jones' death considered to be the motive. Tovey was popular and highly esteemed and a massive manhunt was promptly underway.

Sharp later claimed that during this period he had worked as a cook in Trinity County for several years and then quit to buy an interest in a farm near Redding. He had caught a ride with a farmer and arrived in Red Bluff early on the afternoon of September 28, 1893. Incredibly, he was seen by a blacksmith in town, an ex-convict named Randall, who had known Sharp in the Nevada State Prison. Randall contacted Tehama County Sheriff John J. Bogard, who surprised the fugitive as he was buying a pair of shoes. The fugitive was quickly taken into custody. Sharp had two pistols and over eight hundred dollars when he was captured.

■ Sheriff John J. Bogard. *Courtesy Mrs. Jeanne W. Henry.*

In a long letter detailing his whereabouts for the past four years, Sharp provided names and addresses to James B. Hume verifying his account of leading an honest life. After confirming the outlaw's alibis, Hume and other lawmen believed him, and different suspects were pursued. A man named William Evans was convicted of Tovey's killing, but the evidence was conflicting and he was later released. The murder was never clearly resolved. Meanwhile, Sharp was returned to the Nevada State Prison to finish out his sentence.

On the recommendation of Hume and various other officials, Sharp was paroled on July 10, 1894. Like so many of the early California stage robbers, he promptly disappeared. If he again resumed his highwayman's career, it apparently was not in California.

Hume and Thacker's "Robber's Record"; Boessenecker, John, *Badge & Buckshot*; Dillon, Richard, *Wells Fargo Detective*; O'Dell, Roy, "Milton Sharp, Scourge of Wells Fargo," *National Association for Outlaw and Lawman History*; *San Francisco Chronicle*, September 14, 1880; *San Francisco Daily Morning Call*, February 5, 1885, August 17, 1889; *San Francisco Examiner*, October 4, 1893; Nadeau, Remi, *The Silver Seekers*.

WHAT THEY WERE READIN' AND SINGIN'...

Popular national magazines in California from the 1850s to the turn of the century were *Frank Leslie's Illustrated Newspaper*, a weekly collection of news, music, drama, fine arts, sports and serial fiction. The cost was ten cents a copy, or four dollars per year. Other popular magazines of the era were *Good Health*, *Farmer's Home Journal*, *Illustrated Police News*, *Harper's Bazaar*, *Scribner's Monthly* and *Sporting Times*.

California magazines during this period were *The Pioneer*, *Hutchings' California Magazine*, *The Hesperian*, and *The Californian*.

Anton Roman's ground-breaking *Overland Monthly* was inaugurated in San Francisco in 1868. It was not only a showcase for California talent, but also quickly boosted the fame of its first editor, Bret Harte. Other noted *Overland* writers were Ina Coolbrith, J. Ross Browne, George Sterling, and Prentice Mulford.

Books that captured Californian's interest during this period were George Eliot's *Silas Marner*; Jules Verne's *From the Earth to the Moon* and *Twenty Thousand Leagues Under the Sea*; Louisa May Alcott's *Little Women*; Thomas Bailey Aldrich's popular children's book, *The Story of a Bad Boy*; Lew Wallace's *The Fair God* and *Ben Hur*; Mark Twain's 1876 novel *The Adventures of Tom Sawyer* and his many later works; Anna Sewell's *Black Beauty*; Arthur Conan Doyle's *The Adventures of Sherlock Holmes*, and Robert Lewis Stevenson's *The Strange Case of Dr. Jekyll and Mr. Hyde*.

In 1865, Anton Roman also published *Outcroppings*, an important collection of local authors edited by Bret Harte. Roman was a good friend of San Francisco's famous police detective, Captain Isaiah W. Lees. Although a man of little institutional learning, Lees was a self-schooled intellect known across the country as one of the great detectives of his age. Roman helped Lees accumulate one of the finest private libraries of the period, one that was a good cross-section of California reading at that time. A fine, rare collection of criminal and legal books filled the walls of his office in police headquarters. A list of Lees' books has survived, but his library was destroyed by the earthquake and fires of 1906.

Songs Californians were singing included "Eating Goober Peas," an 1866 Confederate soldier ditty that originated during the war. Another popular Southern song was "Nobody Knows the Trouble I've Seen." In 1868 "The Flying Trapeze" was introduced and the following year "Little Brown Jug" gained lasting fame. In the 1870s "Silver Threads Among the Gold" and "I'll Take You Home Again, Kathleen," were nostalgic favorites, while the 1880s brought "Oh My Darling Clementine" and "Johnny Get Your Gun." The 1890s introduced "There is a Tavern in the Town" and "A Hot Time in the Old Town," one of the first songs recorded for the new phonograph machines.

Milton D. Shepardson

alias "Mathews" and various other names.

■ Like other highwaymen of his day, Milt Shepardson discovered the hard way that lawyers ate up most of a stage robber's profit.
Author's collection.

"He was a man of kind companionable nature, hospitable and generous in all his dealings, and was well liked wherever known. His death removes another of the old and well known residents of the county."

Or so said the obituary of Milt Shepardson when he died in 1915. He had apparently come a long way, in time as well as character.

Reportedly born in Baker County, Kentucky, in 1832, Milt Shepardson probably came to California during the Gold Rush. He and his brother, Dudley, settled in Colusa County. The brothers worked at odd jobs, but Dudley was the more ambitious of the two and in his spare time studied for the law. Dudley was a practicing attorney in the 1860s, Milton preferring to dabble in mining and gambling in the northern part of the state, although the 1870 census showed he still resided in Colusa. Eventually, "Milt" became involved with some tough characters bent on mischief and easy money.

There seemed to be a wildness in both Shepardson brothers. In late April 1865, Dudley and other Confederate sympathizers were rounded up in Colusa by the military for cheering when news was received of the death of Abraham Lincoln. On December 14, 1870, "Dud" discharged employee Levi Stevens—then had to shoot and kill him when Stevens became violent and abusive. The killing was judged to be justifiable and Shepardson was later elected district attorney of Colusa County.

In January 1878, Dud became involved in a feud with Town Marshal John T. Arnold. In a shoot-out on March 4, Shepardson killed Arnold with four well-placed pistol shots. He was acquitted of a murder charge the following May. Milton, however, had already preceded his brother into the dubious realm of notoriety.

Perhaps it was a streak of bad luck at gambling and mining that got Milt thinking along other lines of endeavor. His mining claim in Trinity County had not been paying much, and in late summer of 1871, he gathered some of his ne'er-do-well pals—Johnny Grant, Ziska Calmez, Billy Fugate, and a fourth man thought to be Charley Kyle—around him and made plans to hold up the Yreka to Red Bluff stage. Shepardson and his men took up a position about twenty miles north of Red Bluff. It was eleven o'clock on the night of August 21 when they stretched a rope across the road after hearing the stage off in the distance. One man stayed out of sight with a pack mule as four masked men stepped out into the road brandishing Henry rifles. On August 26, the holdup was reported in the *Shasta Courier:*

> Four men suddenly came out of the bushes, three of them armed with rifles or shotguns, commanded Lynch, the driver,

■ The village of Shasta, shown here, was on the route of the robbed stages. After capture, Cullen and Grant were lodged in the Shasta jail. *Author's collection.*

■ The Yreka to Red Bluff stage was robbed twice at the same spot by Shepardson and his men.
Shasta Historical Society.

not to attempt to move. One of them approached the stage and demanded the treasure box—Lynch handed out the smallest one upon which he demanded the others. The driver said there was no other, to which he replied—

"You're a damned liar" and climbing up took out the box and threw it down along side the road. He then went and examined the hind boot and finding it empty, came back and asked Lynch who the passenger was inside. Upon being told it was a white man, he told the driver to go on.

Shepardson and his pals quickly disappeared into the night with some $4,300 in gold bullion and coin, which they packed on a mule. The coach rolled on into Red Bluff and spread the alarm. The next day, an Indian came upon five men, three of whom had Henry rifles.

■ Shepardson and his men held up stages in pretty much the manner shown in this old posed view made around 1900. *Author's collection.*

When they scattered at his approach, he reported their actions to the authorities. Later, the Indian identified a suspect who was brought in but was later released.

Keeping out of sight for the next month, perhaps at Milt's mining claim, the outlaws replaced Kyle with Billy Cullen, a Canadian hardcase. The gang struck again on the night of September 26. It was at the same spot as the previous robbery, with the same driver at the reins. The robbers secured about sixty dollars from the Yreka box, while the Shasta box contained some $240. Seven men and two women on the stage were not bothered, but several Chinese passengers were robbed of about $160. "Wells, Fargo & Company," announced the *Shasta Courier*, "have issued handbills offering a reward of $500 for the arrest and conviction of each of the parties engaged in the robbery of the stage on Tuesday night."

Two officials of the California and Oregon Stage Company were promptly on the scene and began following the distinctive hoof prints of the outlaws' pack mule. The next morning, the stage men were joined by Shasta County Undersheriff Jackson, John Shedd, George Kingsley, Tehama County Deputy Sheriff Vickers, and a man named Long. The trail led eastward toward Mount Lassen, and the posse soon found a camp where the robbers had burned letters from the express boxes. Farther along, a teamster told of seeing five men on the road, and the posse soon spotted its quarry at some distance across a treeless plain, about eighteen miles west of Susanville. Unfortunately, the outlaws spotted them at the same time, although they were unaware that any lawmen had followed them so closely.

As the posse approached, Shepardson and his men became suspicious, and three of them dodged into a rocky area in back of their camp. Riding slowly toward the outlaws, the lawmen suddenly

$2,000 REWARD.

A Reward of $500 each will be paid for the arrest and conviction of the parties concerned in the robbery of our

TREASURE BOXES!

on the night of *September 26th, 1871, near Cottonwood, Shasta Co.*

WELLS, FARGO & CO.

Shasta, Sept. 27th, 1871.   "Shasta Courier" Print.

■ *Trinity County Historical Society.*

spurred their mounts and in a moment had the two remaining fugitives disarmed and cuffed. Captured also were five horses, the mule, four Henry rifles, and some camp paraphernalia. The two prisoners were Billy Cullen and Johnny Grant, Shepardson and the other two making a clean getaway.

■ Sheppardson's pal, John Grant, was kicked to death by a mule some years after his prison sentence. *Author's collection.*

Grant and Cullen were tried and convicted, both receiving seven year terms in San Quentin. Shepardson, Fugate, and Calmez remained at large, although Fugate was later captured and pardoned after "peaching" on his pals. In 1879, Fugate did some time for an assault charge in Merced County.

Shepardson fled to Oregon, where he laid low for a time, apparently in Baker County. He gambled and prospected intermittently, apparently with little luck at either. When his funds began running low, the stage lines once again began tempting his baser instincts.

Milt and a pal named Charles Darnell met a Gem Town blacksmith named T. D. Phelps in early July 1871. Shepardson was known by several different aliases in the area, and Phelps soon found out why. Milt proposed he help them in a stagecoach robbery. When the blacksmith refused, Shepardson approached him again a few days later. Shepardson had the location and robbery all planned out, and he soon won over the dubious Phelps. The three men headed west with a pack horse, the plan being to rob the stage running between Canyon City and The Dalles, Oregon.

Phelps later described taking up positions in a brushy canyon on July 12, 1872, and waiting for the stage:

When the stage came up the three men stepped out into the road simultaneously and Shepardson called out, "Halt, throw up your hands," and passed around the heads of the lead horses and the mail sacks were thrown out. The witness and Darnell still kept their guns bearing on the stage driver and passengers. Shepardson had a short Henry rifle, Darnell had a shotgun and witness had a Henry rifle.... The parties wore masks over their faces made of blue cloth. After the sacks were thrown out, Shepardson ordered the driver to go on and Darnell and witness stepped out of the road, the passengers got in and the stage started…

After loading their loot on the pack animal, the three outlaws rode all night, stopping at daylight to divide up their treasure and burn any letters or material of no monetary value. Phelps here left his partners and made his way to Pendleton and Walla Walla, while Shepardson rode on to Lewiston.

While the real highwaymen had eluded detection, four suspects named William Bramlette, Frank Tompkins, John White, and Ed-

■ Re-enactment of a stagecoach holdup in Oregon, taken probably around 1900. Shepardson and his men robbed at least two, and probably more, stages in Oregon in the 1870s, but ultimately paid the price for the crimes. *Josephine County (Oregon) Historical Society.*

ward Hansen, who lived in the area, were picked up for the robbery and nearly lynched by an angry mob. The stage driver, Ad Edgar, had noticed one of the robbers had an ivory-handled pistol and since no such weapon was in the possession of the suspects, the driver believed they were innocent and so confided to Deputy U.S. Marshal J. H. Boyd. Moreover, Edgar was a friend of Tompkins, who was well known and had a good reputation.

In August 1872, while Boyd set out to investigate the case, the four hapless suspects were tried and convicted of the robbery on what appeared to be strong—but purely circumstantial—evidence. Because the mail had been robbed, it was a federal crime with punishment set at life imprisonment.

Soon afterwards, another Baker County outlaw, named Fulford, was picked up. He confessed to various robberies and asserted that Shepardson, Darnell, and Phelps were the real robbers of the Canyon City stage. After comparing Fulford's statement with that of the stage driver, Marshal Boyd was fully convinced he was on the right track. He next arrested Phelps at his ranch in Washington Territory, then picked up Darnell at Iowa Hill, near Colfax in Placer County, California. While traveling to Portland with Phelps, Marshal Boyd hinted that Shepardson was in custody and might "peach" on his pals. Phelps then confessed, implicating Shepardson and Darnell. Meanwhile, the clock also was running out on Shepardson, as reported in the *Shasta Courier*, September 13, 1873:

> On the first day of September, Wm. Harper, Deputy Sheriff of Baker County, Oregon, armed with a requisition from the governor of California and other convenient articles, drove into the town of Sparta situated on the Eagle Creek mines in Union County, Oregon. On his advent into the place, he visited a saloon and invited the inmates, among whom were Shepardson, to take a drink, but Shepardson declined on the ground that he "never drank." Harper carelessly threw himself outside of "forty drops" of Webfoot benzine and suddenly turned around and covered Shepardson with a cocked revolver, telling him to keep still or suffer the consequences.

After placing Shepardson in irons, the deputy relieved him of a derringer and an ivory-handled revolver. Harper then set out for Shasta, traveling some nine hundred miles in nine days. There, the outlaw chief was admitted to bail in the sum of $2,400, and on September 23, 1873, took the stage for Colusa to visit his brother.

In early March 1874, Milt surrendered for his trial in Shasta. His principal defense was that he was in Oregon at the time of the Shasta robbery, and when he was convicted, Creed Haymond, his attorney, promptly appealed for a new trial, which was granted on the basis of an erroneous instruction to the jury. When a second trial also found him guilty, a second appeal was also sought and won on the same basis. This time the jury determined that he was "Guilty, but not proven." The trials had cost the county $30,000, and county officials were glad to see him catch the stage for Colusa, even though he was a free man. Or was he?

On January 26, 1876, Deputy U.S. Marshal Boyd of Oregon arrested Shepardson at his hotel room in Colusa. When the warrant was read, the indignant outlaw said, "There must be some mistake about this. Haven't you got the wrong man? That is not my name." Although "Mathews," one of Shepardson's aliases, was on the warrant, a "John Doe," had been included, and the warrant was served.

■ Early day Portland, Oregon, where Shepardson was tried, but found not guilty on a technicality. But the law was not yet through with Milt. *Northwest and Whitman College Archives.*

The outlaw immediately contacted attorney Haymond, but was told nothing could be done and that he must stand trial. Shepardson now faced the prospect of having to confirm his being in Oregon, since he had previously used his Oregon residence as his defense during his California trials.

On June 21, 1876, the Shepardson trial was called in Portland's U.S. District Court. The trial lasted over a week, and strong evidence was produced by a great many prosecution witnesses. Phelps' long and detailed testimony was particularly damning.

After closing arguments on June 29, Judge Deady charged the jury to bring in a verdict of "not guilty," since conviction had been barred by the statute of limitations. The jury could, however, amend its verdict with a statement indicating that Shepardson had indeed robbed the stagecoach as charged in the indictment. The jury brought in an incorrectly worded verdict of "guilty," but with an acquittal based upon the statute of limitations. This was not the verdict the judge had asked for, and he instructed the jury again and sent them out. When the jury returned with the correctly worded verdict, the trial was over. The verdict immediately initiated a tumult over the four previously imprisoned men, who would now soon receive a pardon. Shepardson, meanwhile, was rearrested on another stage robbery charge in Baker County, Oregon.

If Judge Deady thought the case was over, however, he was to be rudely awakened. President Ulysses S. Grant's administration in Washington, D.C., was in its waning days but was still under attack by Democrats hoping some of the Grant scandals would splash onto Hayes, the 1876 Republican nominee. The Credit Mobilier, whiskey ring, and other scandals had been horrendous detriments to Grant's administration, and the Democrats were eager to add to the charges. When a Washington, D.C., correspondent learned of the four innocent men serving their third year for a stage robbery they didn't commit, there were newspaper repercussions. A long article in the *Chicago Times* on October 6, 1876, was copied into the *San Francisco Chronicle* of October 15. The *Portland Daily Oregonian* reprinted the same story, but then demolished it editorially, point by point.

The gist of the *Chicago Times* story was that Judge Deady was just another bad political appointment by "Ulysses" (Grant), and therefore the President was somehow responsible for the four innocent men in the Oregon prison. Actually, Deady had been on the federal bench in Oregon for the past twenty-four years and was not a Grant appointee. Many other aspects of the trial were similarly exaggerated, or invented, to show that Deady was prejudiced against the defendants and was profane and abusive in court during and after the trial. Other "facts" in the *Times* article on the trial were just as wrong. The *Oregonian* had covered all aspects of the trial at the time, and both the *Times* and *Chronicle* stories were refuted. When President Grant signed a pardon for the four men in late October, the matter quickly dropped from the news.

Convicted of robbing the Baker County stage in 1873, Shepardson was finally sentenced to ten years in the Oregon State Penitentiary. Newspapers throughout California and Oregon heaved a collective sigh of relief, a sample of which appeared in the *Marysville Daily Appeal:*

> Convicted at Last—Milton Shepardson, known commonly as "Shep," has just been convicted and sentenced to ten years in the Penitentiary in Baker County, Oregon. "Shep" is an old offender…

As No. 693, Shepardson was admitted on November 13, 1876, and served his time quietly. He was well-behaved in prison, and for his good conduct was released early on August 23, 1883.

So far as is known, Shepardson returned to his Trinity County mine and only troubled the law of California, or Oregon, one more time. In October 1898, he was hauled into the Weaverville Justice Court and charged with threatening to kill a neighbor, one Robert Crews. He was granted bail, but the final disposition of the case is not known. Other neighbors concurred that Shepardson was taciturn and unfriendly, and when he died at his home at Peanut, on November 14, 1915, there were few to mourn his loss, despite the laudatory obituary in the *Trinity Journal.*

Giles, Rosena A., *Shasta County, California, A History*; Rogers, Justus H., *Colusa County*; Boggs, Mae Helene Bacon, *My Playhouse was a Concord Coach*; Trinity County Historical Society Archives; Red Bluff *Independent,* August 24, October 5, 1871; *Weekly Shasta Courier*, August 26, September 30, October 7, 1871, February 21, April 4, 11, 25, 1874; *Trinity Journal*, November 27, 1915; *Yreka Journal*, September 17, 1873, February 9, 1876; *Sacramento Daily Bee*, January 27, 1876; *Portland Daily Oregonian*, June 21, 22, 23, 24, 26, 27, 28, 30, July 12, October 24, November 6, 15, 1876; California Supreme Court Reports, *People vs. Milton Shepardson*, 49 Cal. 629 (April 1875); Oregon State Prison Register, Oregon State Archives, Salem.

Francisco and Santos Sotelo

■ Santos Sotelo, alias Chico Lugo, was bad, but he and his brother never gained the stature of a Murrieta or Vasquez. Still, it wasn't from a lack of trying. *Author's collection.*

In early California, Sotelo was a prominent name in the ranks of soldiers and settlers scattered from San Francisco to Santa Cruz and over to Los Angeles and environs. As in all families, there were those who brought shame to their relatives. There were hot-blooded vaqueros in the Sotelo clan. Some could not forget the days of the vast ranchos, before the Gold Rush changed their lives. Others scorned hard work and yearned for a wild and free life in the mountains and on the plains. Ramon Sotelo, an 1805 settler at Los Angeles, was a noted outlaw who was killed at Purisima in 1824. His descendants, probably grandsons, headed down the same dark trail.

The family is hard to track, no one by the Sotelo name showing up in the 1850 census of Los Angeles County. Francisco Antonio Sotelo is a likely candidate as the founder of the California family, being born in Sinaloa, Mexico, about 1753. He was living at Mission San Gabriel in 1782, near Los Angeles, where he was married the following year. The 1860 Los Angeles census lists a Jose Sotelo family, but the names do not include the two later bandidos, who perhaps lived on isolated ranches, not on the route of the census enumerators.

Whatever the family status was, there were reportedly five brothers in all, Santos Sotelo being born in Los Angeles about 1851, while brother Francisco came along around 1858. As they grew older, the boys were in trouble at times, and Santos used the alias "Chico Lugo," while Francisco sometimes operated under the name "Francisco Olivas." They may also have been half-brothers, as noted in various accounts.

The three other brothers are all shadowy figures, with the exception of Miguel, who may have been the oldest. He was a convicted horse thief, sentenced from Los Angeles County to a five-year term at San Quentin in November 1869. As No. 4270, he did his time and was released in February 1874, but the Sotelo family had not learned its lesson. The family violence gurgled to the surface again in Francisco Sotelo one night in mid-June 1876.

There was some personal difficulty between Francisco and a cousin, Ramon Tapia Sotelo. One insulted the other and Ramon knocked Francisco down. That night Ramon attended the funeral of a dead friend in Los Angeles' Negro Alley. Later, Ramon and an acquaintance named Francisco Garcia left, but while they navigated a narrow passage in the alley, two pistol shots rang out, and Ramon dropped dead. Garcia shouted for an officer, crying "Murder," but when a policeman arrived he took Garcia into custody.

"…It is thought," reported the *Los Angeles Star,* "the latter [Garcia] enticed the murdered man into the dark alley where [Francisco] lay in waiting." Despite a widespread manhunt, Sotelo could not be found. When his horse returned to town, it was assumed he had stolen a fresh animal. Francisco hid out in the San Bernardino Mountains until the posses became discouraged.

■ A murder in the notorious Negro Alley pushed the Sotelo brothers into a wild crime spree in Southern California. The alley was filled with saloons, gambling halls, and tough characters.
Author's collection.

When it seemed safe, Santos joined his brother, bringing along a friend named Jose Tapia. Francisco was now a hunted man and could not return home. He was an outlaw and didn't hesitate to take his brother and a friend along on his perilous journey.

In late December 1876, the trio rode northwest, past Mojave, where they lay in wait for the Darwin stage. On January 6, in Red

■ Spreads such as the Crocker ranch, shown here, just south of Bakersfield, were prime targets of the Sotelo gang. *Author's collection.*

Rock Canyon, they stopped and robbed the stage, then moved swiftly, backtracking into the Tehachapi Mountains. On January 20, they held up the Newhall to Ventura stagecoach. The trio, no doubt, celebrated at the Mexican cantina near Elizabeth Lake.

Making their way north over the Tehachapis again to the Mexican settlement of Panama, near Bakersfield, the bandits added Francisco Romero to the gang. Six horses were stolen at an isolated ranch, then on February 25, they stopped at a store on the edge of Tulare Lake. The owner, S. A. Lovell, was knocked unconscious and robbed of $500 and some goods. Driving their stolen stock ahead of them, the outlaws headed south. Nearing Bakersfield, they had a shoot-out with some canal workers who recognized some of the stolen stock. Looping around to the south of town, the bandits now made for the Tehachapis with a posse already on their trail. Constable Harry Bludworth and two men pressed the bandits so closely that they abandoned the stolen stock, and one of the outlaws left his horse and scrambled into the brush.

Returning to Bakersfield with the recovered stock, Bludworth and his men were again in the saddle the following morning, relentlessly pursuing the bandits, who seemed to have been swallowed up by the country. They did manage to locate and arrest Romero, the new gang member, who had abandoned his horse the previous day. Sending the captive back to Bakersfield, the lawmen pressed on. The trail of the other two outlaws was too cold, however.

Weary after a week of hard riding, the posse rode back toward Bakersfield, stopping for a meal at the ranch of George Reig. When a call went unanswered, they entered the house and found Reig dead with a bullet through the head. There was little doubt in the lawmen's minds who had committed the murder.

The bandit brothers did not pass up other robbing opportunities during the chase. On March 2, they tied up some fourteen Chinese miners in San Francisquito Canyon and got away with $260 in gold dust.

■ Los Angeles in 1877 was no longer a frontier village, but the plaza, church and Sonora Town, as shown here, dated back to the early days. *Author's collection.*

After a brief rest, Bludworth and his men joined the Kern County sheriff in further pursuit of the outlaws. Tapia had meanwhile been captured, and Los Angeles posses were now in the field, keeping up the relentless pressure on the outlaws.

Acting on a tip in late April, a posse consisting of Luis Lopez, Guadalupe Lugo, D. Bustamente, San Bernardino Constable Thomas, and Thomas Warden tracked the two Sotelo brothers to a valley in the San Bernardino Mountains. They surprised Francisco Sotelo and took him without a fight. "He was surrounded before he had a chance to use his weapons or fly," noted the *Los Angeles Star.* "He had on his person two revolvers, one of which, now is in the Sheriff's office."

■ A Californian fandango.
Author's collection.

The posse then proceeded to a cantina where Santos was reported to be attending a fandango. Sotelo was present, but was not recognized since he had recently shaved off his shaggy beard. The outlaw made his way to the door and escaped into the night.

Pleading guilty in Los Angeles to robbing the Newhall stage, Jose Tapia was sentenced to seven years in San Quentin. He was admitted on March 21, 1877, as No. 7463. Francisco Sotelo was also tried in Los Angeles for stage robbery and sentenced to ten years. He entered San Quentin on May 29, 1877, as No. 7602. Although his identity was known, he was admitted under the name Francisco Olivas. Francisco Romero was sent to Tulare County where he was tried for

■ San Quentin was hard on the old time Mexican vaqueros, some dying cooped up in tiny cells such as this one, when they were used to a wild, free life. *San Quentin Museum Association.*

the robbery of the Lovell store at Tulare Lake. Convicted, he was given a five-year term and was received at San Quentin on June 25, 1877, as No. 4647.

The murderous gang was now effectively broken up, but Santos Sotelo still roamed the Tehachapi mountains. His string, however, was quickly running out. On July 19, the *Los Angeles Star* reported:

The Last of the Sotelo-Tapia Outlaws—Santos Sotelo in the County Jail.

The last member of a desperate gang of horse thieves, stage robbers and suspected murderers, Santos Sotelo, has at last fallen into the clutches of the law, and will doubtless do the State some labor for the next few years of his life...On Friday last, while riding in the mountains near Elizabeth Lake, Rafael Lopez, a young Californian, espied a horse hitched to some bushes quite a little distance ahead of him, and a closer observation showed the form of a man lying in the shade of a tree, quietly smoking a cigarette. Lopez recognized the outlaw at once, and quietly made preparations for his capture...Lopez softly crept toward the robber, keeping the tree on a line between them, until he had approached within a few steps, when he suddenly presented the muzzle of a formidable six-shooter at Sotelo's head....

■ Francisco Sotelo, alias Pancho Olivas, as he appeared during his second San Quentin sojourn. *California State Archives.*

Lopez was accompanied by the same posse that had captured Francisco Sotelo. During the trip into Los Angeles, it was reported the captive kept up a continual banter about his robbing exploits. Insisting his name was "Chico Lugo," the prisoner was tried in Kern County on stage robbery charges and was easily convicted. He was sentenced to a fifteen-year term and, as No. 7763, was admitted to San Quentin on September 23, 1877. Although the Sotelo gang, as such, was now history, the brothers had not quite finished their saga.

In late June of 1878, the *Fresno Morning Expositor* ran the following brief item:

Miguel Sotelo, a noted horse thief and desperado, and a former member of the Vasquez gang, was shot and killed last Tuesday night in Verdugo Canyon, Los Angeles County, while resisting arrest by Sheriff Mitchell and Deputy Adolph Celis.

"Chico Lugo," or Santos Sotelo, was discharged from prison in February 1887. When he was released from San Quentin on November 20, 1883, Francisco Sotelo returned to Los Angeles. But the old days died hard. He was convicted of grand larceny in the spring of 1886 and again admitted to San Quentin to serve a three year term on April 13, as No. 12090.

Hume and Thacker's "Robbers' Record"; San Quentin State Prison Register; California State Archives, Sacramento; Northrup, Marie E., *Spanish-Mexican Families of Early California: 1769-1850,* Vols. I and II; Edwards, Lee, "Mob Violence in Bakersfield," *Historic Kern*; Bancroft, Hubert H., *History of California,* Vols II-V; *Bakersfield Courier Californian*, March 8, 15, 22, May 13, June 7, 27, 1877; *Southern Californian* and *Kern County Weekly Courier,* July 19, 1877; *Los Angeles Weekly Star,* January 17, 1876, April 28, May 5, 1877; *Los Angeles Daily Star*, March 15, June 17, July 10, 1877; *Los Angeles News*, November 7, 13, 1877; *San Francisco Daily Alta California,* July 13, 1877.

Ormstead Thurman

alias Bill Early, Charles Thompson and other names

■ A murderous hardcase and lifelong criminal, Thurman still could not let an innocent man go to prison if it could be prevented.
Author's collection.

One of the worst of old California's stage robbing fraternity was a character named Ormstead Thurman, if indeed that was his real name. Born in Kentucky about 1828, Thurman came to California during the Gold Rush in the 1850s. He had no trade and apparently soon grew tired of low-paying menial labor jobs. He was living in El Dorado County in August 1856, when he was arrested for grand larceny and sent to San Quentin for one year.

As No. 975, Thurman looked around at the prison. The San Francisco press made much of the constant graft, bad food, and escapes from the place. There were from 500 to 600 convicts on register at this time, and overcrowding had been a problem from the start. John H. McCauley was the current private lessee of the prison, and he ran it like a forced-labor camp. He rented his chained convicts out on various county labor jobs, then cut meals back to two a day to sweeten his profit margin. Since neither the convicts or their guards wore uniforms, it was sometimes difficult to tell one from the other.

At this time, there was one stone cellblock building and a new brick cellblock that had just been completed. A substantial wall had been added in 1855. It was not a happy place, the guards grumbling over their low pay of $50 a month and the convicts complaining about short rations, overwork, and crowded cells. Convicts were not supposed to be happy, but Thurman began looking for a way out as soon as possible.

Thurman found an opportunity in a little over a week. His means of escape is not known, but on September 4, 1856, he disappeared and was not heard from again for some time. He was picked up in Solano County on another grand larceny charge and returned to San Quentin on January 12, 1858, under the name Early Thurman. With a two-year sentence this time, Thurman again looked around for an opportunity to escape. On July 3, 1859, he vanished with only six months of his term left to serve.

Once outside, perhaps Thurman tried to work and keep a low profile, fearing to be apprehended again. If he did, his plan did not work. Captured on September 14, 1859, he was promptly returned

■ An early sketch of San Quentin as it appeared in the later 1850s when Thurman was an inmate there. *San Quentin Museum Association.*

to San Quentin. This time, he served out his term and was discharged on February 26, 1860.

Again dropping from sight for a time, the ex-convict was arrested in Colusa County on a grand larceny charge in late 1861. As No. 2281, he entered prison as William Thurman on November 22 and began a two-year term.

San Quentin had a more stable atmosphere at this time, primarily because the state was in control, rather than private parties who were only concerned with profits. The food had improved and the crowded conditions had been alleviated somewhat by the addition of a third cellblock building. A long structure housed various work facilities, including blacksmith, wheelwright, cooper, tin and machine shops where the convicts could learn a trade. Another building contained the dungeons, kitchen, dining room, and hospital, while brick offices and quarters outside the walls housed officers and guards. It was a tough, functioning prison, filled with a constantly expanding population of desperate men.

So far as job appointments went, however, the prison remained in the hands of inept politicians, and floggings and dungeons were still being utilized. Beginning in January 1862, the new prison directors were Governor Leland Stanford, Lieutenant Governor John F. Chellis, and Secretary of State William H. Weeks. That month, some twenty-four inches of rain soaked the Sacramento and San Joaquin valleys, causing widespread flooding. At the prison, convicts were locked in their cells, since it was impossible to work outside. Thurman huddled in his crowded cell day after day, listening to the rain and trying to ignore the stench of the toilet bucket.

At noon, July 22, 1862, there was a massive break at the prison. A swiftly moving group of convicts kidnapped Acting Warden Chellis, and using him as a hostage, forced the guard to open the front gate. Some three hundred convicts going to their jobs after lunch now turned and, screaming—"Liberty!"—rushed out the gate. With hastily assembled posses from surrounding towns in front of them and mounted, rifle-wielding prison guards at their rear, the escaping convicts and their hostage did not get far. By eight o'clock that night, a long line of crestfallen convicts was filing back through the prison gates. Among the casualties were ten dead or dying cons and some thirty wounded. First reports listed Thurman as missing during the escape, but he apparently was with the captured convicts herded back that night. The groaning of the wounded as they were brought in was a sobering sound to all.

Released on November 16, 1863, Thurman must have been grateful to leave the stench of those cells, and that surrounding wall, behind him. He turned up in Mariposa County early the following year. The ex-con was sharing a cabin with Charlie "Stiffy" Boyle, when he proposed holding up the Coulterville stage that was re-

■ A Mariposa stage stops midstream to pose for the photographer. This is probably the type of coach Early and his pals robbed. *Author's collection.*

ported to be carrying a valuable shipment of amalgam. The date selected was the night of May 29, 1864, as later described by Boyle:

> At 1 o'clock, A.M., the stage came along when within 50 yards of us, we hailed for it to stop; when it got to us it stopped. Early [Thurman] covered the driver with his gun, and I went to the doors of the stage to open them, but they were fastened on the inside. I said to the driver that I would fire into the stage if the passengers did not open the door; the driver replied there were only Chinese passengers, and do not understand English; he then told the passengers to come out. I then requested a man who was sitting with the driver to come down. I took $500 from him, and on his pleading poverty, and that it was all he possessed, gave him $50 back. I then requested the driver to give me Wells, Fargo & Co's box, which I broke open and took $1,500 dollars in dust and $150 in coin, then told the driver to go on.

Prior to and after the stage robbery, indications were that the two outlaws plundered the area, as noted in the *Mariposa Free Press* on June 11, 1864:

During the past two weeks a series of bold robberies have been committed in the neighborhood of Coulterville, and even in the town itself. The robbery of the stage and passengers two weeks ago has been followed up by a number of others...

The two bandits then split up, Thurman heading for Sonora where he engaged in what a local newspaper termed "sporting and otherwise exhibiting and spreading cash in a style indicating that he had found it in the road...." When Thurman caught the stage for Coulterville, a suspicious Tuolumne County Sheriff Bourland followed. After questioning some of the locals, the sheriff arrested the suspect as one of the stage robbers. Thurman, who now called himself Bill Early, had made the mistake of retaining a pistol stolen from

■ In the 1860s, Mariposa was still very much a frontier town and retains this flavor even to this day. *Author's collection.*

one of the passengers in the stage robbery. Denying his guilt initially, Early was terrified when a lynch mob surrounded the jail, as he later reported:

When I was arrested and put in jail at Coulterville, I first denied the robbery, but when the sheriff found the pistol on me which I had taken from one of the men on the stage, it compelled me to own up. But this alone did not satisfy the

The old granite Jail at Mariposa that housed Bill Early, as it appeared in more recent times. *Author's collection.*

blood thirsty cowards who had assembled around the jail; they wanted no less than to give me a taste of lynch law. Finding myself in such a precarious position and knowing they would not be content by mere truth, I implicated Thos. R. Brazier, with myself and Boyle, which seemed to have had the effect in allaying danger of being immediately mobbed....

Brazier was a young man who had innocently stopped by Early and Boyle's cabin one day looking for work. For a time he was employed in a local mine with them, then proceeded to Cherokee Camp where he had a claim. Brazier had nothing to do with the robbery and had only been implicated by Early in an effort to pacify the lynch mob.

Mariposa County Sheriff Joshua D. Crippen, like other lawmen of the time, believed in the perks of his office. *Bob Grycel and Sheriff Pelk Richards.*

Brazier was quickly picked up, and the three suspects were placed in a wagon and began the trip, under guard, to Mariposa County. Within three miles of the town of Mariposa, Thurman had slipped off his handcuffs and, grabbing a shotgun, jumped from the vehicle and disappeared into the brushy forest. Deputy Sheriff McGowan didn't dare leave the two other prisoners to chase the third, and "Early" Thurman made good his escape. Boyle and Brazier were tried and convicted in late August 1864, the former receiving ten years and Brazier five. In January 1865, the *Sonora Union Democrat* reported Thurman's arrest in Placerville and he was promptly returned to Mariposa. The *Mariposa Free Press* noted on February 11:

Early, the stage robber, who is at present confined in the

County Jail, it appears has been making arrangements to leave. He managed to saw his shackles in two with the blade of an ordinary pocket knife, but was discovered in time by McGrann, the Jailor, who furnished him with a new set of an improved and more substantial pattern.

In Sonora, Thurman had told Sheriff Bourland where some of the stagecoach loot had been buried near Coulterville, and the lawman recovered $117.50 which he turned over to Wells, Fargo. They, in turn, told Bourland that he might keep any of the loot he could further recover. When Thurman later told Bourland where the rest of the loot was hidden, the lawman was unable to find it. Thurman had deliberately misled Bourland, furious that the officer had returned the money to Wells, Fargo—which was contrary to the outlaw's expressed wishes.

Thurman next wrote to Sheriff James B. Hume of El Dorado County. When Hume visited him, he told the sheriff the correct hiding place of the loot. Hume and Mariposa Sheriff Joshua Crippen successfully recovered some ten or eleven hundred dollars. The two sheriffs apparently kept the money for themselves, much to the consternation of Sheriff Bourland and the *Mariposa Free Press*. Wells, Fargo undoubtedly told the two lawmen they could keep any of the loot they could find, just as they had told Sheriff Bourland. The express company was impressed by the officers' work and a few years later they would make Hume their chief detective.

As No. 2994, on April 8, 1865, Thurman, under the name William Early, was again ushered into San Quentin prison to serve a ten-year sentence. Depressed to be back in prison, he immediately began organizing plans for a breakout. There were probably only three or four in on the plot, one of them being young Fred Engles who was doing an eleven-year stretch from Fresno County for assault. When the plot was discovered, Thurman and several of the others were given a vicious flogging, but Engles was, curiously, exempted from any punishment.

■ Louis Dreibelbis. *John Boessenecker collection.*

Certain that Engles had turned them in, Thurman vowed vengeance. On May 20, 1865, he caught Engles in one of the prison shops and split his head open with a hatchet, killing him instantly. The murderer was quickly seized by guards, but only convicts had witnessed the incident, and convicts at that time could not testify in court.

Thurman was held in the Marin County jail for trial, but the authorities didn't know how to prosecute the case. Finally, a convict was found who agreed to testify if promised an immediate pardon from the governor. A deal was made, but at Thurman's trial the convict refused to talk and the killer was acquitted. This incident later resulted in a reversal of the law forbidding court testimony by convicts.

There had meanwhile been a movement by friends to secure a pardon for Thomas Brazier. Hardened criminal that Early was, he wrote a letter to the *Mariposa Gazette* from San Quentin explaining Brazier's total innocence. A letter from Boyle accompanied Early's plea. Petitions signed by many Mariposa residents were sent to Governor Frederick Low, but apparently a pardon was not forthcoming. Brazier was released on October 19, 1868.

■ Mickey Delaney.
Author's collection.

Thurman couldn't wait to get mixed up with another band of hardcases when he was released on June 9, 1873. He had met stage robber Louis J. Dreibelbis while in San Quentin, and the two men promptly began planning a stagecoach holdup. On June 23, they robbed the Downieville stage, then planned another stage robbery in Nevada County. Along with two characters named Nat Stover and George Lane, they held up the Colfax to Grass Valley stage on the night of July 27, 1873.

Thurman was picked up the next day. The others were in custody by the following month. Convicted and sentenced to fifteen years in San Quentin, Thurman entered the prison for his fifth commitment as No. 5903, on March 5, 1874. This time, he was in to stay. After spending nearly nine years behind those massive brick and stone walls, Thurman was released on August 5, 1883. He was fifty-five years old now and, no doubt, offered a wry smile if the gate guard asked about his plans for going straight.

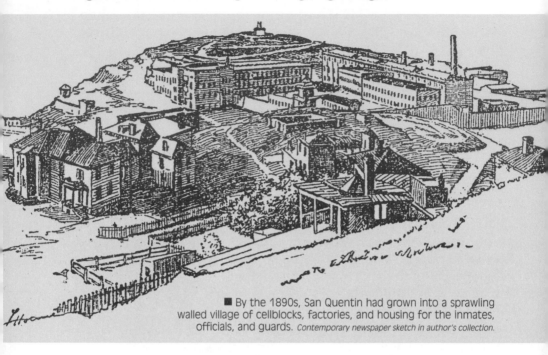

■ By the 1890s, San Quentin had grown into a sprawling walled village of cellblocks, factories, and housing for the inmates, officials, and guards. *Contemporary newspaper sketch in author's collection.*

Thurman probably pulled a few small burglaries while looking for a big job to turn up. In mid-October 1884, Thurman and a pal named Mickey Delaney broke into the Wells, Fargo office safe at Drytown in Amador County. When he was arrested some time later, he gave the name of William Harris, but Detective Jim Hume immediately recognized Thurman, as noted in the *San Francisco Chronicle:*

William Harris was brought to the central police station Sunday evening by Detective J. B. Hume of Wells, Fargo & Co., and the Sheriff of Amador county, en route to San Quentin to serve a term of seven years…. He was jointly interested in the robbery with Mickey Delaney, who will be tried by the Federal authorities, as the United States mail was robbed at the same time. Both are well known convicts. Harris, whose real name is Ormstead Thurman, has escaped several times and is considered a very desperate man….

Released on December 9, 1889, Thurman probably dug up some stolen loot, then enjoyed San Francisco's night life for a few weeks. Prison didn't bother him any more. He was a veteran con, accepted by the lifers and guards alike as an old friend. San Quentin was just a place he went to relax between robberies. The prison had improved greatly since the 1850s and '60s, but the new cons still complained about everything. Thurman knew better.

On September 8, 1890, Thurman stopped the Georgetown stage, between Greenwood in El Dorado County and Auburn. Telling the driver to throw down the box, the highwayman motioned him to move on, and, dragging his prize, Thurman disappeared into the brush- and oak-filled countryside. He was picked up the next day, some eight miles east of Placerville, by Undersheriff Winchell. The suspect gave his usual false name and insisted he knew nothing of the robbery. When Jim Hume arrived on the first train, Thurman knew the jig was up. The *San Francisco Evening Post* considered the old outlaw's career to be virtually at an end:

> He protested his innocence until Detective Hume identi-fied him. He then told the story of how he robbed the stage and when he is called for trial in the Superior Court he will plead guilty in the hope of getting a light sentence. Thurman is now quite an old man and it is probable that when he again enters the penitentiary he will never leave it alive.

The prison records for Thurman's final years have not been located, but his end was likely to have been as the *Post* predicted.

Hume and Thacker's, "Robbers' Record"; San Quentin State Prison Register, California State Archives, Sacramento; Boessenecker, John, *Badge and Buckshot*; Dillon, Richard, *Wells Fargo Detective*; Lamott, Kenneth, *Chronciles of San Quentin*; Sonora *Union Democrat*, June 25, 1864, January 14, March 25, August 26, 1865; *Mariposa Free Press*, June 25, July 23, 1864, February 11, June 11, August 19, September 2, 1865; *Mariposa Gazette*, April 20, 1867; *Mariposa Mail*, March 23, 1867; *Fresno Times*, February 15, 1865; *Grass Valley Union*, March 11, 1885; Nevada *Daily Transcript*, September 18, 1890; *San Francisco Evening Post*, September 16, 1890.

GOING DOWN IN FLAMES...

We've all seen war films and documentaries that depicted aircraft going down in flames. Likewise an occasional automobile will begin smoking or catch fire on the road nowadays. And, of course, we've all seen structures on fire.

But what are the odds that a stagecoach could catch fire on the road in the nineteenth century? Well, it happened, and the story is just as funny as one would imagine:

Stage on Fire. *On Friday of last week, as Charles Sherman was carrying Professor Taylor, the Wizard, with his party and paraphernalia to Chico, the stage was found to be on fire. The party had gone about four miles from town. The north wind was blowing fiercely. Inside the stage were the trunks, a carpet sack and one passenger, the musician. Professor Taylor said to Sherman that he thought something was burning, as he could smell smoke. Sherman stopped, got out and examined the inside of the stage. Between the musician's feet was the carpet sack on fire. The horses were immediately unhitched and tied to the fence, and the trunks taken out as fast as possible, But in less than five minutes time two trunks and all the wood and leather work of the stage burned, except the running gear, and of this one wheel is nearly destroyed. The stage had just been taken out of Cordy's shop and was newly covered and painted in good style. Sherman's loss will not be much short of $400 and that of Professor Taylor about the same. The cause of the fire is unknown. The musician declared that he did not smoke or use matches, but he is an inveterate smoker. There may have been matches in the bottom of the stage among the hay, but this is not probable. Prof. Taylor said the carpet sack did not contain chemicals that would cause a fire. Sherman came back to town, got a new stage and took the party to Chico.*

Oroville Weekly Mercury,
January 19, 1877

Tiburcio Vasquez

■ Horse thief, lover, gunman, stage robber, killer and jail breaker, Tiburcio Vasquez was nothing if not versatile. *Author's collection.*

With the exception of Joaquin Murrieta and Black Bart, Tiburcio Vasquez was the most colorful of the early California bandits. Certainly, his career was the longest. There were those of his race who overlooked Vasquez' crimes because his victims were usually Americans and there was still much hard feeling toward the Anglos because of the Mexican War.

Those familiar with the real Vasquez, however, knew better. Jose Jesus Lopez, a prominent ranch man, recalled that "Vasquez was a man of no principle at all. When he was not robbing some honest, hard-working person, he was busy seducing some wife or a young girl, not sparing even his own niece…"

A native Californian descended from the earliest California settlers, Tiburcio Vasquez was born in Monterey, California on August 11, 1835. He and his five brothers and sisters all attended school and learned to read and write both Spanish and English.

Young Tiburcio was mixed up in bad company at an early age. When he and Anastacio Garcia engaged in a saloon brawl in 1854, a Monterey constable was killed, and Vasquez and Garcia fled. Jose Higuera, one of their pals, was lynched the following day, and the nineteen-year-old Vasquez fled to the south and took up a life of crime, as noted in the *Los Angeles Star* on July 25, 1857:

On the 17th ult., Mr. Wm. H. Peterson, our active and efficient undersheriff, arrested a gentleman who has been dealing quite extensively in horse flesh. His name is Jose Tiburcio Basquez [sic], and he has stolen no less than ten head of horses and mules from San Buenaventura [Ventura]....

Tried and sentenced to five years in San Quentin, Vasquez was constantly on the lookout for a means of escape. His first opportunity came during a mass breakout in June 1859. He escaped, but

■ The 1859 San Quentin breakout as pictured in the contemporary California Police Gazette. Author's collection.

was recaptured the following July and returned to his cell. That September, he and a group of fellow prisoners again attempted an escape in a boat. After a number of convicts were killed and wounded in a hail of bullets and buckshot, Vasquez found himself returned again to his hated cell.

Finishing out his term, Tiburcio was released in August of 1863. The following year, he and a cousin, Faustino Lorenzana, were prime suspects in the murder of a butcher in Santa Clara County. Sheriff John H. Adams could find little evidence, however, and the two killers promptly headed north. After various larcenous ventures in Mendocino and Sonoma counties, Vasquez found himself back in San Quentin once again in January of 1867.

■ Abelardo Salazar outdrew Vasquez one night in old San Juan. Author's collection.

Released from prison in June of 1870, Vasquez had an affair with the wife of his friend, Abelardo Salazar. When he later encountered Salazar in San Juan (present day San Juan Bautista) one night, the two exchanged pistol shots, and Tiburcio was badly wounded. Fleeing to the Coast Range of mountains, the outlaw recuperated at a hideout near Cantua Creek.

On August 17, 1871, Vasquez, Narciso Rodriguez, and Francisco Barcenas took to the road, near a place called Soap Lake, between

■ An old photograph shows how a stage robbery looked in operation. Usually it was on an upgrade, so the driver would be busy with the horses. *John Boessenecker collection.*

San Jose and Pacheco Pass. The *San Francisco Bulletin* reported:

> The first thing they did was to capture a gentleman named Moore… He was riding in a buggy. They took him aside privily, near the road in the field, tied and blindfolded him, and robbed him of $55. By this time the two-horse stage came along. The robbers then fell upon it, and ordered the driver to go through an opening they made in the fence. The stage was stopped at the point where (Moore)…lay *horse de combat*. The passengers were four men and a woman. The men were compelled to alight, keep their eyes on the ground, while each was securely bound, searched and blindfolded…. The robbers secured something over $500 from the stage company, and a gold watch or so… .

Lawmen were quickly on the bandit's trail. A posse led by Santa Cruz County Sheriff Charles Lincoln trapped the outlaws in the

Lorenzana barn at Branciforte, near the town of Santa Cruz. When Barcenas was flushed from the barn, a deadly gunfight took place in which he was killed. Badly wounded, Vasquez managed to escape, while Rodriguez was arrested the next day and was soon on his way to San Quentin.

After recuperating in the Coast Range, Vasquez assembled a new gang. He selected

■ Abdon Leiva would learn a bitter lesson from his chief about "honor among thieves." *Author's collection.*

217

Clodoveo Chavez, a San Juan resident, as his first lieutenant. Abdon Leiva, Teodoro Moreno, Romulo Gonzales, and several others were also recruited for this new band of outlaws. The bandit leader had in mind a raid on prominent cattleman Henry Miller's payroll, which he had learned was to be deposited at the store at Firebaugh's Ferry on the San Joaquin River. Using Abdon Leiva's Cantua ranch house as a headquarters, Vasquez plotted his next robbery, utilizing any spare time in seducing his host's wife, Rosario.

Vasquez and four of his men appeared at the ferry just after dark on February 26, 1873. The $30,000 payroll hadn't arrived as planned, so the bandits proceeded to rob and tie up twelve people in Hoffman's store, then plundered the safe. When the stagecoach stopped at the settlement, it too was ransacked. After the robbery, the outlaws faded into the nearby hills and lay low.

When he thought it was safe, Vasquez planned new raids, including a train robbery. When the train job fell through in July, 1873, he robbed the Twenty-one Mile House, a hotel and restaurant on the rail line. The gang next rode

■ Hoffman's store, at Firebaugh's Ferry, is at top, center, while the ferry is at lower left. *Author's collection.*

into the tiny settlement of Tres Pinos on August 26. While robbing Snyder's store, they shot and killed three men. Packing all the plunder they could carry on eleven stolen horses, the outlaws fled south. Closely pursued by posses, the gang narrowly avoided capture, but some of their stolen loot was recovered by the officers.

Rosario Leiva had accompanied the gang, and at this time her husband discovered his wife and Tiburcio in a compromising situation. The cuckolded outlaw immediately turned himself in to the authorities, detailing the operations of his treacherous leader.

■ A distant view of Jones' Ferry, looking across the San Joaquin River at the hotel, store-saloon and the large barn at far right. *Fresno City and County Historical Society.*

Vasquez struck Jones' store, another isolated San Joaquin River ferry settlement, on November 10. Located some two miles below the town of Millerton, the store was a two-story affair, the upstairs being a hotel, with accompanying barns and corrals for stage animals. The robbery was a typical Vasquez operation. This particular evening, nearly a dozen men were in the place, six or eight playing cards at two tables, while others watched or talked at the bar. Clerk Smith Norris was busy behind the counter. At six o'clock in the evening, six Hispanic bandidos, flourishing pistols, burst through the doors yelling, "Put up your hands!"

Everyone was told to get down on the floor onto their faces while their hands were tied behind their backs. After all the men were robbed, Norris was made to open the safe, from which some thousand dollars was taken. The bandits stayed for an hour-and-a-half, drinking at the bar and stealing whatever goods appealed to them. With a salute of "Adios, caballeros," the outlaws filed outside and disappeared into the cold, dark night.

■ Ramon Molina, one of the Vasquez raiders at Kingston. *Author's collection.*

Sheriff Scott Ashman was alerted at Millerton, but after a fruitless chase, the bandits were again lost to the Coast Range hills they knew so well.

A little over a month later, on December 26, Vasquez and his men tied their horses just outside the small village of Kingston, on the Kings River. The Vasquez band at this time consisted of Blas Bicuna, Clodoveo Chavez, Ramon Molina,

Ysidro Padilla, Manuel Gomez, Ignacio Ranquel, and three or four others. Walking across the toll bridge, the bandits entered several stores, tying up and robbing some thirty-five victims and looting safes and other property. Alerted to what was happening, local rancher John Sutherland grabbed his Henry rifle and opened fire. The bandits were forced back across the toll bridge, where they hastily mounted and spurred their horses out of the area. Several raiders were captured, while others were wounded, Chavez taking a bullet in the leg.

Frustrated lawmen and impromptu posses were quickly in the saddle. The Mexican settlements at Las Juntas and the California Ranch were visited by the officers, who threatened and roughed up the residents while searching for suspects. Complaints resulted in Governor Booth telegraphing the sheriff at Millerton, insisting that he protect the innocent. The Millerton *Fresno Weekly Expositor* was full of exciting news:

■ Fresno County Sheriff J. Scott Ashman. *Fresno City and County Historical Society.*

We could fill the entire local department of the paper this week with the thousand-and-one rumors floating about…. Rumor says one of the members of a party now hunting Vasquez found a gold watch belonging to himself in the possession of a suspicious-looking Mexican…. 'Tis said that a Mexican has been suspended from a limb…. Rumor has hanged two Mexican thieves near Kingston….

The frightened residents of the California Ranch settlement captured Ignacio Ranquel, one of the Kingston raiders, and escorted him to Millerton. The prisoner had a nasty cut on his hand, suffered during his capture. He was promptly tried and sentenced to ten years in state prison, where he was enrolled on February 15, 1874. Teodoro Moreno, Ranquel and another of the Kingston raiders were interviewed by a *San Francisco Bulletin* reporter the following month:

Ronkel [sic]… is a tall and compact young man of about 25 years… He held a position in the prison from 1866 to 1869, on account of his inability to prove

■ Ysidro Padilla had a bloody career both before, and after, he rode with Vasquez. *Author's collection.*

a legal claim to certain horses found in his possession. He... had the palm of his hand sliced open with a cheese knife. The wound is still fresh and in bandage and looks as though it might be very painful. Ronkel hazards the opinion that Vasquez will never allow himself to be captured alive and is prodigal in his praise of the Bandit's accomplishments. The youngest and brightest of the trio is Procella Anamantoria of Fresno, who is only seventeen years of age. Anamantoria is handsome in form, and has a face feminine in its delicacy... The appearance of the youth naturally awakens sympathy among those who are unacquainted with the fact that he has fought under Vasquez...

■ Los Angeles County Sheriff William Rowland. *California State Library.*

The gang scattered, Vasquez hiding out with friends in Southern California. By late February, Chavez had rejoined his old commander with another recruit, and on the twenty-fifth they held up the Bakersfield stage at Coyote Holes in the Mojave Desert. Here, some twenty men were robbed, one being shot in the leg when he showed fight.

But time was running out on the famous bandido. Governor Newton Booth had commissioned a party of manhunters under Alameda County Sheriff Harry Morse to track down the outlaws. Besides various county rewards, the state now offered $8,000 for Vasquez alive, and $6,000 for him dead.

After several other robberies, Vasquez separated from his men. He hid out in the cabin of an old camel driver named Greek George Caralambo, near Los Angeles, but was betrayed by the family of a niece whom he had seduced and made pregnant. Informed of the bandit's hiding place, Los Angeles Sheriff William Rowland dis-

patched a posse and, in a brief fight in which the noted outlaw was wounded

■ The house of Greek George, where Vasquez was captured. *California State Library.*

221

slightly by a shotgun blast, Vasquez was captured on May 13, 1874. The news was heralded around the state, and, in Los Angeles, large crowds gathered to see the most feared bandit since Joaquin Murrieta.

A local newspaper editor visited Vasquez in his cell, conducting one of the first interviews with the captured bandido:

> Los Angeles, May 15—Through the politeness of Sheriff Rowland, J. M. Bassett, editor of the *Herald* of this city, was today permitted to visit Vasquez and held a long conversation with him. Vasquez is still weak from loss of blood, and quite sore from his wounds. In appearance he is anything but the ferocious red-handed brigand his reputation has given him. He is a man of about medium stature, with a well-knit, wiry figure. He does not weigh over 140 or 150 pounds…. His general demeanor is that of a quiet, inoffensive man, and but for his calm, steady eye, which stamps him as a man of great determination and firmness, no one would take him for the terrible Tiburcio Vasquez.

When considered to be out of danger from his wounds, the bandit leader, in custody of Undersheriff Albert Johnson and several other officers, was put aboard the steamer *Senator*. Early on the morn-

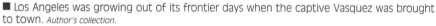

■ Los Angeles was growing out of its frontier days when the captive Vasquez was brought to town. *Author's collection.*

222

One of a group of photographs made of Vasquez in San Francisco. *California State Library.*

ing of May 27, 1874, the steamer arrived at the San Francisco wharf.

At the city prison, Vasquez was besieged by crowds of reporters and city residents clamoring to see the famous outlaw. The exasperated police chief, Theodore Cockrill, was said to have actually considered placing a group of Vasquez impersonators in other cells to enable the crowds to move through more quickly.

One of the visitors, a mining entrepreneur from the Mojave Desert country, asked for an interview at the window of Vasquez' cell door. It was Mortimer Belshaw, who had been robbed by the bandit at the Coyote Holes station. Belshaw asked for his watch back, stating he would be glad to pay for its return. The bandit was pleased at the remembrance of those halcyon days, but said he didn't have the watch, but that Chavez might have it. In a later conversation, Belshaw told a reporter "he knew that Vasquez was the man who did the shooting at the Coyote Holes affair. Mr. Belshaw's opinion of him, based on personal observation, is that he is 'a miserable, lying dog, but withal as courageous as a lion when fairly aroused.'"

Taken to San Jose, Vasquez was housed in the Santa Clara County jail and scheduled for trial on January 5, 1875.

■ Mortimer Belshaw, the big mine owner of Cerro Gordo, who visited Vasquez in his cell. *Author's collection.*

The trial was held in the Third District Court of Judge David Belden. Despite a valiant defense by Vasquez' three attorneys, the bandit chieftain was convicted and sentenced to hang on March 19. An appeal was unsuccessful. Through it all, Vasquez retained his composure, signing proclamations imploring children to follow the teaching of their parents and not to follow in his tragic footsteps. After assessing the satin lining of the casket he was to be buried in, the condemned man commented, "I can sleep here forever very well!"

Standing on the gallows, Vasquez displayed no emotion while

223

the sheriff adjusted the noose. "Pronto!" he said, just before the trapdoor dropped and his world turned black.

In October 1877, several successive inhabitants of Vasquez' old San Jose jail cell had to be removed due to some strange incidents. Two prisoners, named Bernal and Madden, insisted on being moved to different cells after claiming to have been awakened in the middle of the night to the clanking of chains and a shadowy figure standing near their cot. "These are the facts," noted a local newspaper account, "from which one can draw his own conclusions."

■ The Tiburcio Vasquez grave site in the Santa Clara Catholic cemetery. *Author's collection.*

San Quentin State Prison Register, Governor's Reward Papers, California State Archives, Sacramento; Truman, Benjamin Cummings, *Life, Adventures and Capture of Tiburcio Vasquez: the great California bandit and murderer*; Greenwood, Robert, *The California Outlaw*; Reader, Phil, *"Charole," The Life of Branciforte Bandido Faustino Lorenzana*; *Monterey Sentinel*, October 6, 1855; *Santa Cruz Sentinel*, February 28, 1857, September 16, 1871; *Los Angeles Star*, July 25, 1857, March 16, 1874; *San Francisco Daily Alta California*, June 27, 1859; *San Francisco Daily Evening Bulletin*, August 19, 1871, November 25, 27, 28, 1873, March 17, May 15, 1874; *San Francisco Chronicle*, October 21, 1877; *San Jose Daily Patriot*, May 19, 1874; *Fresno Weekly Expositor*, March 5, 12, October 29, 1873, January 28, November 19, 1874.

Frank Williams

■ Frank Williams thought stage
robbery was an easy way to
make a living. Well, maybe, but
the work offered no
guarantees as to a long life.
Author's collection.

His identity was never really established. Although his prison record states he was from Illinois, no one knew that for sure, either. He appeared as mysteriously as many highwaymen disappeared and his ultimate, tragic fate insured that his secrets would be maintained. He called himself Frank Williams, and his California story began on a snowy stage road in Northern California:

"Hold up there!"

The stagecoach rattled to a stop just short of a shotgun-wielding bandit standing alongside the road. It was the evening of November 28, 1889, and the Shasta to Redding coach was just a half-mile from Middle Creek Station. It promised to be another bitterly cold night. Luke Dow, owner of the line, sat on the seat next to the driver.

"Throw down the box!"

When the express box was tossed down, the highwayman next demanded the registered mail pouch.

"There isn't any," responded Dow.

"There is, and you want to throw it down damn quick if you don't want to lose the top of your head."

Dow still protested as the outlaw moved his shotgun ominously in the direction of the stage owner. Dow shrugged and tossed down the box.

"You're fooling with Jack Bryant," responded the bandit, "and he knows his business. Now, get out your ax, and cut this box open."

"We're not carrying an ax," again stalled Dow. At this, the bandit was furious.

"You lie, damn you. Get it out here quick. Didn't I tell you I knew my business? All stages carry axes."

With a shrug, Dow jumped down with his ax and chopped the box open. The coach was then allowed to proceed on its way.

The next morning, Dow led two officers to the site of the robbery. The *Redding Republican Free Press* reported:

> ...Under Sheriff Reynolds, Constable Crume and L. Dow went out yesterday morning in search of the robber. The last

■ Williams was good at what he did and was caught only by the most serendipitous circumstances. A posed photograph made in the early 1900s. *John Boessenecker collection.*

named returned, having found the shotgun, a roll of white blankets enclosed in a shawl strap, some tobacco, etc. lying on a rock near Salt Creek, a half-mile from the scene of the robbery. The articles were found exposed to view, and

from appearances the fellow may have been on the spot a few moments before. It was learned also that he had dinner in Shasta, and that the Bystle boys had seen him on the road. A good description was secured. The shotgun is of the same pattern as those used by Wells Fargo's messengers....

The bandit struck again on December 2, some 250 miles south in Mariposa County. Stopping the Merced to Mariposa stage near the village of Hornitos, the highwayman pointed his pistol at the driver and ordered him to throw out the mail pouch and express box. When the loot dissatisfied him, the bandit found a small safe in the coach, which he also managed to open. Quickly finishing his work, the robber motioned for the vehicle to move on.

On December 12, the Forest Hill stage was stopped in Placer County, but only one registered letter was reported stolen.

On December 15, another stage was stopped north of Nevada City. Five packages of registered mail were obtained, but the bandit failed to break open the express box. One hundred and forty-eight dollars were taken from two passengers. Only a pistol had been used in the holdups since the Redding robbery. Feeling the need for some rest and recreation in San Francisco, the robber made his way west to the Bay city.

■ The old San Francisco City Hall that housed various courts and the city's police department. Williams was snared here. *California State Library.*

227

The holdups had put all lawmen in the region on the alert. Tom Ryan, a plainclothes bailiff in San Francisco Police Court No. 3, took advantage of a recess to get out of the stuffy courtroom. While walking along Kearny Street, he noticed a man standing near the corner of Jackson. The officer immediately noticed the diamond ring on the little finger of the fellow's left hand.

Ryan was a good officer and had recently discussed the spate of California stage robberies with Detective Captain Isaiah W. Lees. A member of the police force since 1853, Lees was well aware that the robberies had generated reward offers totaling over $6,000—a formidable sum in those days. Some blankets, a rubber coat, and a sawed-off shotgun had been found after the Redding coach had been held up. Indications were they had been purchased in San Francisco so the items had been forwarded to Lees. A check of local pawn shops produced not only proof of purchase, but descriptions of the buyer that tallied with the stage driver's recollections.

■ The legendary Captain Isaiah Lees was as quick to sniff out a reward offer as he was a clue. *Author's collection.*

Several victims of the stage robberies had also remembered the bandit wearing a diamond ring on the little finger of his left hand. As Ryan stared at the man, he began recalling the fugitive's description: about twenty-five years old, five-foot-seven inches in height, with a blond mustache bearing traces of having been dyed black, and wearing ready-made country clothes. Ryan was dumbfounded. This man fit that description perfectly!

"Nice weather after the rain, ain't it," Ryan commented.

As the two men made small talk, Ryan acted like a tourist, saying he had been sightseeing, but was wondering what to do next.

"I struck something today," said the officer, "that was very amusing, though. I drifted up into one of these here police courts where they were trying a fellow for putting another fellow's eye out in a fight about a girl. Juiciest case I ever heard—fine looking woman, too."

The stranger thought he would tag along when Ryan returned to court, and the men walked back to the Old City Hall. Inside, Ryan told him to hold his seat while he ran an errand. He rushed over to the Washington Street pawnshop of Sol Lichenstein, where the stage robber's blankets had been purchased. Lichenstein agreed to accompany him back to court.

Inside the courtroom, Lichenstein took a look and nodded at Ryan. "Dots the man," he said as he left.

Police Court No. 3 was in the Old City Hall, which for many years had also been doing duty as police headquarters. The excited bailiff quickly appraised Captain Lees of the situation. Returning to court, Ryan and Lees eased into seats on either side of the suspect. Both men sized up the stranger to make sure he wasn't armed, then seized him.

In the detective's office, a large, roll-top desk was in one corner, while Lees' collection of mug books, criminal histories, and statistical tomes lined the walls.

As Lees began questioning the suspect, Ryan came in with Lichenstein, who again identified the prisoner as the man who had bought the blankets recovered by Wells, Fargo.

"That's so," admitted Williams, "I did buy blankets of you."

Next, a gunshop owner named Clabrough came in and identified Williams as the man to whom he had sold a sawed-off shotgun. He had described the prisoner perfectly. At the time of purchase, Williams had instructed Clabrough how to load the shells and when one of the shells was opened, it was found to be just as described.

"That's all true," blurted out Williams. "I bought the gun for eighteen dollars on speculation, and sold it in Sacramento for fifteen dollars. But you haven't proved I'm a stage robber, yet."

Lees, a master at interrogation, usually got his way, but the suspect was very careful. When confronted with evidence, Williams owned up to it, but continued to deny being a stage robber. On December 21, the prisoner was locked up, and Lees set out to find where the suspect was staying.

Williams apparently had arrived in town about December 17

and stopped at the Russ House under the name of J. W. Moore. He left a valise at the hotel, then the second night stopped at the Saint George House on Kearny Street, where another valise was left. On the evening of the nineteenth, Williams went over to Billy Scott's boarding house on California Street, a known opium hangout, where he entered and began preparing his pipe.

Purely by chance, an operative of Curtin's Detective Agency knocked on the door of Scott's house shortly after Williams' admittance. The detective had traced a dog, for which a one hundred-dollar reward was being offered, to the boarding house and to the very room in which Williams and several others were enjoying their pipes. Knocking on the door, he was refused admittance, but flashed his badge and forced his way in. Williams saw the badge and dropped his dope paraphernalia as he leaped through a window.

The detective was not sure just what had happened, but obviously the escaping man was a fugitive of some kind. The next day, the detective had recruited one of the dope users to point out the

■ Loading a stage in the days of Frank Williams. A hostler holds the lead team, while the passengers begin climbing aboard. *California State Library.*

suspect on the street, but before he could act, Williams was snatched up by Ryan and Captain Lees.

Lees quickly located the valises Williams had left at the two hotels. Both were treasure troves of evidence: hair coloring and shotgun shells, which proved to be the exact load he had puchased from Clabrough's shop. There was also a Colt .45 revolver and a plug of tobacco of the same brand found with his coat and blankets. A check and account book from a Helena, Montana, bank seemed puzzling, until Captain Lees put the dates of withdrawals and deposits together with the dates of a string of stage robberies in the area. The net was quickly closing.

The officers and postal officials felt they could clearly identify four Northern California robberies, as well as four others in the Gold Rush country, as the work of Williams. Several stage drivers in the north had described Williams as the robber and had noticed the bandit's "stocky" build. Williams, however, was noticeably slender. When a store clerk recalled that Williams had deliberately purchased an oversized coat, it was theorized that he had wrapped the blankets around his body, under his coat, to give himself a bulkier-appearing physique.

Williams was turned over to a deputy U.S. marshal and housed in the San Francisco County jail. With Lees' aid, several postal inspectors began building their case.

On January 14, three men came down from Placer County to identify the prisoner. On the night before the December 12 robbery, a man answering Williams' description stopped at Jim Dodds' house, where he was put up for the night. The next morning, Dodds walked a distance up the road with him. S. M. Bradley met the man on the road a short time later.

Williams and a group of fellow jail inmates were lined up in a room at the jail, and both men immediately identified Williams as the man they had met.

"I have never had the pleasure of making the acquaintance of either of you gentlemen," Williams said, "and you'll excuse me for failing to remember the circumstances that you mention."

Frank Powell, the driver of the Forest Hill stage, was brought in next to confront Williams. Again, the bandit feigned ignorance of any meeting.

The trial began in United States District Court on April 12. The many witnesses' testimony left little doubt as to the bandit's identity. Other evidence was merely frosting on the cake.

Convicted on three counts of stage robbery, on May 2, 1890, Williams was sentenced to life imprisonment at Folsom State Prison. The *San Francisco Chronicle* commented:

> Williams received the sentence unmoved, and soon afterward glided from the room in company with Marshal Long, who took him to Folsom on the first train.

■ George Contant as he appeared when he entered Folsom.
Troy Tuggle.

Before leaving, Williams gave his attorney, Carroll Cook, a letter to be mailed to a brother in New Mexico. The letter stated Williams was leaving soon for South America and might never return. If no word came from him, he was to be considered dead.

At Folsom State Prison, Williams was given his striped uniform, processed, and identified as convict No. 2212. He said he was from Illinois and gave his age as twenty-six, with no occupation.

Opened in July of 1880, Folsom was conceived and constructed as a maximum security facility. There were then no walls around the prison, but buildings, and the American River, formed a barrier on several sides. For the open areas, deadlines were established and carefully monitored by guard towers. A granite quarry provided work and material for all the structures.

Two cellblocks consisted of 328 cells, each seven by nine feet, with nine-foot ceilings. They were designed for two occupants, but were fre-

■ Two facing rows of cells at Folsom, doors open and ready for inspection. This was Frank Williams' new home.
Author's collection.

quently overcrowded, housing four or more convicts. Iron frames held straw-filled mattresses and several blankets. Two buckets provided toilet and drinking facilities. Ventilation and head-counting was accomplished through a ten- by three-inch opening in the cell's iron door.

■ William Fredericks, the man who brought the weapons to Folsom. He was later hanged for killing a bank clerk during a robbery.
Author's collection.

Folsom inmates were employed at various tasks. Besides quarrying granite, a dam and canal were being constructed, farming projects were in operation, and there was always the day-to-day maintenance. A powerhouse was being built to harness power at the dam, and in the winter of 1891, electric lights were installed throughout the prison.

As a "lifer," Frank Williams couldn't count on obtaining credits or time off for good behavior. Folsom was tough and as the years dragged by, few escape attempts were made.

In November 1892, a celebrity of sorts was ushered through Folsom's iron gates. His name was George Contant and he was a train robber whose partners—his brother John and one Chris Evans— were still at large. Contant had taken the surname of a stepfather,

■ The Folsom quarry where the big break took place. Williams, Contant, and the others climbed a steep trail on the bluff to the right, then fought their losing battle at the top.
California State Library.

while brother John had retained their deceased father's name of Sontag. George had participated in several train robberies in the Midwest. A recent holdup at Collis, California, with his brother and Evans had resulted in his Folsom sentence. In the prison pecking order, train robbers were at the top of the heap, and he was pointed out on the prison grounds as a celebrity would be on the outside.

"After I had arrived here," recalled Contant later, "I formed the acquaintance of Frank Williams serving a life sentence. I made a few inquiries about him and satisfied myself he was a man I could confide in, and I know he wanted his liberty about as bad as I did. We talked this matter up. He told me he could get a fellow to bring the guns provided I could get them."

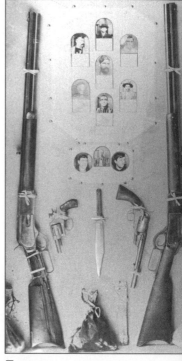

■ For many years the weapons used during the break were displayed in the Folsom prison office. *California State Library.*

Smuggling several letters to the Evans family in Visalia, Contant set his plan in motion. Evans' daughter Eva, who was engaged to George's brother, agreed to help with the escape plot. After killing three officers in several gunfights, Evans and Sontag were the most wanted train robbers in the country. But George was in prison now, and time had also run out on his erstwhile partners, who were shot up and captured in early June 1893.

Williams had talked convict William Fredericks into participating in the escape plot. When Fredericks was paroled on May 26, 1893, he lost no time in making his way south to Visalia, where Eva Evans told him where he could secure the needed weapons. That night, the ex-convict broke into the back room of a saloon and obtained two Winchester rifles, three pistols and a knife. Bundling the weapons up in his bedroll, he returned to Folsom, where he secreted them in some rocks in the prison quarry. Somehow, Fredericks got word to Frank Williams where the guns were hidden, and the convicts made their final plans.

"Williams," George Contant would later write, "who from the first took charge of our plans, told me where the guns were. He made all arrangements attendant upon the intended delivery, with the same cool calculation as a railroad official would in preparing reports for some change in plans or policies of the affairs of the company."

On the afternoon of June 28, 1893, Williams and Contant made final preparations for their desperate plan. Others involved were Anthony Dalton, a burly burglar, and stage robber "Buckshot" Smith. Just as eager were murderer Charles Abbott and another burglar named Hiram Wilson. All worked in the prison quarry.

Contant and the others first seized guard Frank Briarre, hoping to use him as a shield to get past the guard posts and into the brush and trees. Making their way out of the quarry by a steep, rocky path, the escape was foiled when Briarre jumped off the trail, dragging Smith back into the quarry with him.

With their cover gone, Contant and Williams both went down under the withering fire of the guards. The convicts all scrambled into a pile of rocks, where they began shooting at a nearby outpost. By the time Warden Charles Aull arrived on the scene, several of the escapees had been shot. Quickly assuming command, Aull ordered all the guards and officials present to begin firing their Winchesters in concerted volleys. Bullets

■ Contant and his pals had little chance against the blistering fire of the Gatling guns. Guards George Eveland (left) and P. J. Cochrane pose next to their deadly weapon atop one of the towers that surveyed the prison area.
Folsom History Museum.

235

ricocheting off boulders and the rock chips flying through the air turned the convicts' makeshift rock fort into a death trap. Finally a hat was seen waving from the besieged rock hideout. It was over.

A smoky haze had settled over the area as the guards and officials cautiously walked toward the clump of rocks. Warden Aull kept his rifle handy as he and his men approached Contant and Charles Abbott. Both had crawled from their hiding place badly wounded and splattered with blood.

Warden Aull looked into the group of rocks and boulders that had partially sheltered the convicts. Dalton, Williams, and Wilson were piled on top of each other, all dead. Their bodies were terribly torn up by bullets. Two other convicts were wounded by the guards' fire, but neither seriously. The only man of the group to escape unscathed was Buckshot Smith who had tumbled down the hill with Guard Briarre. Both had been out of range of the guard's deadly fire.

Later in Captain Richard Murphy's office, the three dead convicts were laid out in a row. Witnesses agreed it was a "horrid" sight:

> Dalton was shot in the shoulders and heart, and when turned over his back was fairly riddled with bullets.
>
> Wilson had only a few shots. Williams' stomach was filled with bullets and torn and riddled so badly that his bowels were cut to pieces and their contents covered his body. He must have received a full charge from the Gatling gun....

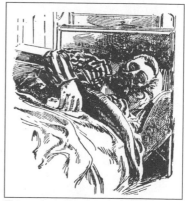

■ George Contant lying wounded in the prison hospital. *Contemporary newspaper sketch in author's collection.*

Actually, one account stated that Williams had concealed a sack of cartridges in his shirt that had exploded when struck by a guard's bullet. This had caused the terrible damage. Mercifully, the sack of bullets had probably been hit after he was dead on the ground.

A photograph, found in Williams' pocket that day, eventually found its way to the desk of Captain Lees. Lees couldn't give any meaning to the image that showed a young woman of nineteen or twenty holding the bridle of a beautiful saddle horse. The old captain studied the daguerreotype carefully. The figure smiling back at him closely resembled Williams himself. Perhaps it was the dead outlaw's twin sister. Or, perhaps it was Williams dressed like a woman.

What was the secret of Williams' hidden past? The old lawman instinctively knew that he probably would never know.

Warner, Opie L., *A Pardoned Lifer: Life of George Sontag, etc.*; San Quentin State Prison Register; California State Archives, Sacramento; *Placer Herald*, September 7, 28, 1889; *Fresno Daily Evening Expositor*, December 23, 1889; *Nevada City Daily Transcript*, December 17, 18, 22, 24, 1889; *San Francisco Examiner*, December 21, 22, 1889, April 18, 1890; *San Francisco Chronicle*, December 21, 24, 1889, January 15, April 19, 1890; *San Francisco Daily Alta California*, April 20, 23, May 3, 1890; *San Francisco Daily Evening Bulletin*, December 21, 1889; *Redding Republican Free Press*, November 30, December 14, 1889; *Mariposa Gazette*, May 3, 1890; *San Joaquin Valley Argus*, December 7, 1889.

BIBLIOGRAPHY

A partial list of authorities consulted

BOOKS

As Prescribed by Law, A Treatise on Folsom Prison. (no author given) Represa, California: The Represa, Press, 1940.

Banning, Capt. William, and Banning, George Hugh, *Six Horses.* New York, London: The Century Co., 1930.

Beers, George. *Vasquez, or the Hunted Bandits of the San Joaquin.* New York: Robert DeWitt Co., 1875.

Berry, M.D. John J. (Ed.). *Life of David Belden.* New York and Toronto, Canada: Belden Bros.,1891.

Block, Eugene B. *Great Stagecoach Robbers of the West.* Garden City, N.Y.: Doubleday & Company, Inc.,1962.

Boessenecker, John. *Badge and Buckshot.* Norman and London: University of Oklahoma Press, 1988.

_____. *Lawman: The Life andTimes of Harry Morse, 1835 —1912.* Norman: University of Oklahoma Press, 1998.

_____, and Dugan, Mark. *The Grey Fox: The True Story of Bill Miner, Last of the Old-Time Bandits.* Norman and London: University of Oklahoma Press, 1992.

Boggs, Mae Helen (Bacon). *My Playhouse was a Concord Coach.* Oakland: Howell-North press, 1942.

Borthwick, J. D. *Three Years in California.* Oakland: biobooks, 1948.

Boyd, William Harland. *Stagecoach Heyday in the San Joaquin Valley, 1853 - 1876.* Bakersfield: Kern County Historical Society, Pioneer Publishing Company, 1983.

Campbell, Marguerite, and Staff. *Mariposa Gazette 1854 - 1979.* Mariposa: Mariposa Gazette, 1979.

Collins, William, and Levene, Bruce. *Black Bart, The True Story of the West's Most Famous Stagecoach Robber.* Mendocino: Pacific Transcriptions, 1992.

Dajani, Laika. *Black Bart, Elusive Highwayman- Poet.* Manhattan, Ks.: Sunflower University Press, 1996.

Dillon, Richard. *Wells Fargo Detective: A Biography of James B. Hume. New York:* Coward-McCann, 1969.

Ford, Tirey L. *California State Prisons, their History, Development and Management.* San Francisco: The Star Press, 1910.

Giles, Rosena A. *Shasta County, California.* Oakland: Biobooks, 1949.

Goodwin, C. C. *As I remember Them.* Salt Lake: Salt Lake Commercial Club, 1913.

Greenwood, Robert. *The California Outlaw.* Los Gatos: The Talisman Press, 1960.

Harlow, Alvin F. *Old Waybills.* New York, London: D. Appleton-Century Company, 1934.

Hoeper, George. *Black Bart, Boulevardier Bandit.* Fresno: Word Dancer Press,1995

Holliday, J. S. *The World Rushed In.* New York: Simon & Schuster, 1981.

Lamott, Kenneth. *Chronicles of San Quentin.* New York: David McKay Company, Inc., 1961.

Lowrie, Donald. *My Life in Prison.* New York and London: Mitchell Kennerley, 1912.

Moody, Ralph. *Stagecoach West.* New York: Thomas Y. Crowell Co. 1967.

Nadeau, Remi. *The Silver Seekers.* Santa Barbara: Crest Publishers, 1999.

Nichols, Nancy Ann. *San Quentin: Inside the Walls.* San Quentin: San Quentin Museum Press, 1991.

Northrup, Marie E. *Spanish-Mexican Families of Early California: 1769-1850*, Vols. 1 and II, New Orleans: Polyanthos, 1976.

Outland, Charles F. *Stagecoaching on El Camino Real.* Glendale: The Arthur H. Clark Company, 1973.

Reader, Phil. *"Charole," The Life of Branciforte Bandido Faustino Lorenzana.* Santa Cruz: Cliffside Publishing, (no date).

Report of Jas. B. Hume and Jno. Thacker, Special Officers, Wells, Fargo & Co's Express, Covering a Period of Fourteen Years, giving losses by Train Robbers, Stage Robbers and Burglaries, etc. San Francisco: H.S. Crocker & Co., 1885.

Rogers, Justus H. *Colusa County.* Orland, California: 1891.

Sawyer, Eugene T. *The Life and Career of Tiburcio Vasquez, the California Stage Robber.* Oakland: Biobooks,1944.

Secrest, William B. *Lawmen & Desperadoes.* Spokane, Washington: The Arthur H. Clark Company, 1994.

_____. *California Desperadoes.* Clovis: Word Dancer Press, 2000

Truman, Benjamin Cummings. *Life, Adventures and Capture of Tiburcio Vasquez; the Great California Bandit and Murderer.* Los Angeles: The Los Angeles Star, 1874.

Warner, Opie L. *A Pardoned Lifer, Life of George Sontag.* San Bernardino: The Index Print, 1909.

Wilson, Neill C. *Treasure Express: Epic Days of the Wells Fargo.* New York: The Macmillan Company, 1938

Zanjani, Sally. *Jack Longstreet, Last of the Desert Frontiersmen.* Athens, Ohio: Swallow Press/Ohio University Press, 1988.

PERIODICALS & JOURNALS

Ashcroft, Lionel. "San Quentin Prison, Its Early History and Origins." *Marin County Historical Society,* Spring, 1993.

Banning, George Hugh. "Stage Wheels Over the Padres Trail." *Westways,* July 1934.

Edwards, Harold L. "The Story of John Keener and William Dowdle." *Los Tulares,* Quarterly Bulletin of the Tulare County Historical Society, September, 1991.

_____. "The Disappearance of Dick Fellows." *Historic Kern.* Quarterly Bulletin of the Kern County Historical Society. March, 1994.

_____. "A Footnote in Tulare County History," *Los Tulares.* Quarterly Bulletin of the Tulare County Historical Society, September, 1995.

Chegwyn, Michael. "Showdown with Shotguns: The Capture of Buck English." *True West,* November, 1997.

Humpal, Mark. "The Concord Coach and Me." *Yankee magazine.* July, 1982.

Jones, J. R. "Handlers of the Sixes."*Sunset,* December, 1928.

O'Dell, Roy P. "Milton Sharp, Scourge of Wells Fargo." *National Association for Outlaw and Lawmen History, Inc.,* July-September, / October-December, 1999.

Ramey, Earl. "The Beginnings of Marysville." Part III, *California Historical Society Quarterly.* March, 1936.

(No author given). "Saint or Sinner: Interesting Tales of a Trinity Badman," *Yearbook.* Trinity County Historical Society, 1963 - 1965.

Secrest, William B. "The Return of Chavez." *True West.* January - February, 1978.

Stott, Kenholm. "Fifty Years of Stagecoaching in Southern California." *Brand Book Number One.* San Diego California Corral of the Westerners.

Truman, Major Ben C. "Knights of the Lash," *Overland Monthly.* March, April, 1898.

Ward, Henry. "Stagecoach Days in California: Reminiscences of H. C. Ward." *California Historical Society Quarterly.* September, 1934.

Winther, Oscar O. "Stagecoach Scenes in Northern California." *Pacific Historical Review,* Vol. III, 1934.

UNPUBLISHED MATERIALS

Daggett Scrapbooks, Vol. 3. California Section, California State Library, Sacramento.

John Boessenecker Collections, photographs and data, including Detective Edward Byram's San Francisco Police Record Books and Journals, 1876 - 1908.

Special Collections, Henry Madden Library, CSUF Fresno, including Schutt Collection; Lee Rice Typescript.

Snyder, Andrew. "True Story of the Vasquez Murders at Tres Pinos." Collection of Edna Zyl Modie.

Shasta County Historical Society Archives.

Trinity County Historical Society Archives.

GOVERNMENT DOCUMENTS

California State Assembly. "Report of Committee Relative to the Condition and/ Management of the State Prison." In: Assembly Journal appendix, Document Number 26, 1855 session. Sacramento: B.R. Redding, State Printer, 1856.

California State Legislature. "Annual Report of State Prison Director for the Year 1859." In: Legislative Journals appendix, 1860 session. State Printer, Sacramento, California.

California State Legislature. "Report of the Directors of the California State Prison." July 1, 1871. In: Legislative Journal appendix, 1872 session. Sacramento: State Printing Office, 1872.

California State Legislature. "Report on the State Prison by the Joint Committee of the Senate and Assembly." 1872. In: Legislative Journal appendix, 1872 session. Sacramento: State Printing Office, 1872.

California Death Certificate Index, 1905 -. California Section, California State Library, Sacramento, California.

California Supreme Court Reports. People v. Vasquez, 49 Cal. 560 (Jan. 1875).

_____People v. Myers et al., 70 Cal. 582 (Aug. 1886).

_____ People v. Milton Shepardson, 49 Cal. 629 (April, 1875).

Compendium of the Codes and Statutes relating to State Prisons and Prisoners, etc., January 1st, 1884 (includes a list of prisoners at Folsom), Sacramento: State Printing Office, 1884.

Fresno County Superior Court Archives, Justice Court and Trial Records, Fresno, California.

Governor's Pardon Files. California State Archives, Sacramento, California.

Governor's Reward Papers. California State Archives, Sacramento, California.

"List of Convicts on Register of State Prison at San Quentin." Marin County, California, Sacramento, J.D. Young, Supt. State Printing, 1889.

Medical and Pension Records of John D. Gundlack, Military Reference Branch, National Archives.

Oregon State Archives, Salem, Oregon.

Police mug books. Sacramento City Archives, Sacramento, California.

_____. San Francisco Police Department, San Francisco, California.

"Register and Descriptive List of Convicts under Sentence of Imprisonment in the State Prison of California." San Quentin, California State Archives, Sacramento, California (Individual convicts).

NEWSPAPERS

Auburn Placer Herald

Bakersfield Kern County Weekly Courier

Bakersfield Kern County Weekly Gazette

Bakersfield Southern Californian

Butte Weekly Record

California Police Gazette (San Francisco)

Calaveras Weekly Citizen

Calaveras Prospect

Folsom Weekly Telegraph

Fresno Bee

Fresno Morning Republican

Fresno Weekly Expositor

Fresno Weekly Republican

Gilroy Advocate

Grass Valley Daily Union

Indianapolis News (Indiana)

Los Angeles Daily News

Los Angeles Star

Los Angeles Times

Mariposa Free Press

Mariposa Gazette

Mariposa Mail

Merced San Joaquin Valley Argus

Monterey Californian

Monterey Sentinel

Marysville Daily Herald

Marysville Daily Appeal

Mendocino Beacon

Mendocino Dispatch Democrat

Milledgeville Weekly News

Napa Register

Nevada Democrat (Nevada County, Ca)

Nevada City Daily Transcript

New York Sun

Oroville Weekly UnionRecord

Oroville Weekly Mercury

Portland Oregonian

Placer Herald

Placerville Mountain Democrat

Redding epublican Free Press

Reading Independent

Redding Searchlight

Sacramento Daily Bee

Sacramento Daily Union

Sacramento Record

Sacramento Record-Union,

Sacramento Daily Bee

Salinas Index

San Andreas Independent

San Francisco Daily Evening Bulletin

San Francisco Chronicle

San Francisco Daily Alta California

San Francisco Evening Post

San Francisco Examiner

San Francisco Herald

San Francisco Morning Call

Stockton Daily Evening Herald

Stockton San Joaquin Republican

San Jose Daily Patriot

San Jose Herald

San Jose Mercury

San Luis Obispo Morning Tribune

Santa Cruz Sentinel

Santa Cruz Pacific Sentinel

Shasta Courier

Sonora Union Democrat

Stockton Evening Mail

Stockton Independent

Visalia Weekly Delta

Weekly Colusa Sun

Yreka Journal

Yreka Union

Yuma Sentinel

Index

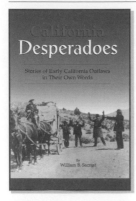

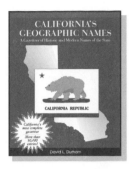

CALIFORNIA'S GEOGRAPHIC NAMES

A Gazetteer of Historic and Modern Names of the State
Compiled by David L. Durham

"The quantity and value of the information included in this work are simply staggering...a boon to historians, genealogists and outdoor folk of all kinds."
— Robert C. Berlo,
Secretary of the California Map Society

"I am impressed! California's Geographic Names *is the new standard."*
— Robert J. Chandler, Wells Fargo Historian

$195.
Hardcover • 1,680 pages • 8½" x 11"
Bibliography • Index • ISBN 1-884995-14-4

The definitive gazetteer of California.

BOULEVARDIER BANDIT BLACK BART

The Saga of California's Most Mysterious Stagecoach Robber and the Men Who Sought to Capture Him
By George Hoeper

"...immense value and a fine read."
— *True West Magazine*
"Enticing"
—*Library Journal*

$9.95
Historic Photos • Maps • Bibliography • Index
5½" x 8½" • 168 pages • ISBN 1-884995-05-5

REMEMBERING CESAR

The Legacy of Cesar Chavez
Introduction by Paul Chavez

Compiled by Ann McGregor
Edited by Cindy Wathen
Photographs by George Elfie Ballis

"...[Remembering Cesar] reminds us of who he really was and what he really did over a lifetime of struggle....evokes Chavez both as historic figure and as shimmering symbol."
—Jonathan Kirsch,
Los Angeles Times

$25.00
Hardcover • 10" x 9" • 112 pages
ISBN 1-884956-11-4

The first book to receive the endorsement of the Cesar E. Chavez Foundation.

Available from bookstores, on-line bookstores or by calling 1-800-497-4909

ABOUT THE AUTHOR

Born in Fresno, California, in March of 1930, William B. Secrest grew up in the great San Joaquin Valley. After high school he joined the Marine Corps where he served in a guard detachment and in a rifle company in the early years of the Korean War. Returning to college, he obtained a BA in education, but for many years he served as an art director for a Fresno advertising firm.

Secrest has been interested in history since his youth and early began comparing Western films to what really happened in the West. A hobby at first, this avocation quickly developed into correspondence with noted writers and more serious research. Not satisfied in a collaboration with friend and Western writer Ray Thorp, Secrest began researching and writing his own articles in the early 1960s.

Although at first he wrote on many general Western subjects, some years ago Secrest realized how his home state has consistently been neglected in the Western genre and concentrated almost exclusively on early California subjects. He has produced hundreds of articles for such publications as *Westways*, *Montana*, *True West*, and the *American West*, while publishing seven monographs on early California themes. His book *I Buried Hickok* (Early West Publishing Co.) appeared in 1980, followed by *Lawmen & Desperadoes* (The Arthur H. Clark Co.) in 1994, *Dangerous Trails* (Barbed Wire Press) in 1995, and *California Desperadoes* (Word Dancer Press) in 2000. A biography of noted San Francisco police detective Isaiah Lees has been accepted for publication. Future projects include a biography of Harry Love, the leader of the rangers who tracked down Joaquin Murrieta and *When the Great Spirit Died*, a history of the California Indian wars.